Learn Italian

A Comprehensive Guide to Learning Italian for Beginners, Including Grammar and 2500 Popular Phrases

Contents

Part 1: Italian

Learn Italian for Beginners: A Simple Guide that Will Help You on Your Language Learning Journey

Introduction

The fourth most studied language in the world, according to the General Assembly of the Italian Language in the World, is, in fact, Italian.

It is surprising to discover that the language of a very small Mediterranean peninsula can compete with much more widespread ones. With over two million scholars each year, Italian exceeds French, despite the spread of this latter language in Africa and North America.

Why? There are many reasons behind the decision to learn Italian: from having Italian relatives to wanting to travel to one of the most beautiful countries in the world. However, there is no need to make hypotheses—if you are reading this introduction, you have been led here by your desire to learn this language.

The purpose of this book is to present itself as the best solution for those approaching Italian for the first time. This is not a booklet with a handful of sentences already built or a two-thousand-page manual on how to become a Neo-Latin linguist.

What the next few pages lay out is the groundwork for proper communication in Italian. You will see the construction of sentences, the use of accents, and then the most common expressions of this idiom.

Italian is a musical language, beautiful to hear and speak, but very difficult to master. This is why you will take small steps, moving forward only once a concept is fully understood.

You will start with the pronouns, singular and plural, and discover the first differences that run between English and Italian.

At this point, the book will focus on verbs, to explain and analyze all the elements that are part of a sentence, before discovering the most common sentences used in Italian.

This way, the language you will learn will be the one used every day, which will allow you to move freely around the Italian streets and get to know the uses and customs of Italian.

You will see how to present yourself, friends, and family, talk about school and work, enjoy art and food, and get to the most common questions that every aspiring Italian speaker asks.

This manual will cover everything you need to know to take your first steps in Italy. For this reason, much of the book is dedicated to the Italian culture. This is because it is essential to understand the people behind a language in order to love it even more and fully understand it. Knowing the culture will allow you to develop more conversational Italian, as well as having all the information you need if you ever decide to travel to Italy.

The book is divided into three major sections.

The first section is dedicated to Italian grammar, which is necessary to understand how to construct and understand a sentence.

The second section is dedicated to traveling in Italy, including information and essential phrases. This section is not only meant for those who want to visit this country, but also for those who want to know all the most common phrases to be exchanged with people who do not know each other.

Finally, the third section proposes an in-depth study dedicated to those who are thinking of moving to Italy, an overview of Italian culture, further education on the Italian people, and more everyday phrases.

Based on this, you might regard this book as a training course in which to learn Italian from every point of view, to fully understand it and speed up your learning process.

So, without further ado, let's start by talking about the construction of the sentence.

Pronouns... single, plural, formal, and informal.

The grammatical aspect is the most technical and tedious to deal with when learning a new language. Despite this, you need to understand the functioning of Italian sentences.

Once you understand the behavior of the two main elements of each sentence, the pronoun and the verb, you can move among the common phrases of this language.

Speaking of pronouns, right from the start, you will begin to notice the profound differences between English and Italian. For this reason, take your time and read the first chapter carefully.

Before moving on to the analysis of every type of pronoun, it is necessary to take a small step back to understand the sentences that are later used as examples.

Pronunciation

Pronunciation is usually a more advanced topic while learning a different language, especially in a guide based on learning the most common sentences that help to be an active part of an Italian conversation.

For this reason, the pronunciation is often proposed at the final phase of a guide, but this book teaches it in the early chapters to allow you to improve much more.

If pronunciation was delegated to the last part of the book, readers could have some difficulties not only with reading the sentences in the guide, but they also might not be able to correct their potential pronunciation mistakes.

Thus, all the technical parts are within the early chapters, so you can understand both Italian sentence structure and how sentences and words are pronounced.

You will find that repeating words while proceeding will improve your pronunciation by the end of the guide.

It is also encouraged that you be patient and begin your journey into the Italian language by starting with the single letters.

Despite the rules, always remember that the phonetics in Italian is much simpler than you think. This is because Italian words are almost always read as they are written. For this reason, once you learn the basic rules of various letters' pronunciation, you will discover that learning to pronounce words is suitable for all. Moreover, once you learn the first words, others will follow the same examples, creating an exponentially faster improvement process.

The Vowels

Let's start with the vowels since the consonants have a similar pronunciation to the English ones (with few exceptions). The Italian vowels are five:

A   E   I   O   U

Below is the pronunciation of each vowel:

A

The **A**'s pronunciation is the same as the U in the English word "**Cut**". Luckily, the pronunciation remains the same, so once you have practiced the form, you can repeat it on every word that includes it.

E

E shows itself in different forms. Mainly the Italian **E** has two sounds based on the accent mark (visible or not) on it, which tends to be confused, even by Italians based on their regional background.

This different explanation is important as with a different accent mark on it, the whole meaning of the word could change. For example:

Pèsca – Peach

Pésca – To fish

This is a subtle nuance you will learn with time and experience, mostly because the accent marks in the examples are not visible in the written language. These are shown only when the accent marks fall on the last letter of the word.

So, how is the letter **E** pronounced?

The open E, as for "Pèsca", is pronounced similarly to the E of the English word "rest". While the closed E of "Pésca" (to fish) is similar to the E of the English word "appointment".

As previously mentioned, there is no way of knowing when to use the open or closed E—unless you have experience with the language. You may find the E with an accent mark, but only when it is the only one or at the end of a word.

For example:

Lui **è** bello – He is handsome

Perché l'ho detto io – Because I said so.

In these cases, remember that "è" is pronounced as "rest" and "é" is pronounced as "appointment".

I

I is one of the vowels that sound different from the English language. The pronunciation of I in Italian is similar to the **Y** in English, like in the word "baby" or even the double **EE** as in the word "meet".

O

O has two distinct pronunciations based on the hidden accent, so much that in many Italian regions, they are used incorrectly.

The pronunciation of **O** is similar to the English word "dog", but it can also sound closed, such as the English word "post".

U

U is similar to the double **OO** in English, like for the word "doom" or even the same **U** in the word "loud".

By knowing the pronunciation of the vowels, you can pronounce most Italian words correctly. There are some special cases concerning the consonants, which you will see in the next section of this chapter.

Consonants

Most of the Italian consonants, as mentioned, have a pronunciation similar to the English ones, which will be convenient when learning this language.

However, there are exceptions.

C

In Italian, **C** has two different pronunciations: one is soft, and the other is hard, with both based on the letter that follows.

If the vowel **I** or **E** follows the letter C, then it will have a soft sound, similar to the English word "chilly". If instead it is followed by any other letter, **C** will have a hard sound, similar to the English word "cat".

Note: if the letter C is followed by the letter **H** and then by an **I** and **E**, it will still sound hard, such as in the English word "cat".

For example:

Ciao (Hi) – soft sound

Chiesa (Church) – hard sound

G

G follows the same rules as **C**: it has a soft sound in the presence of the letter **I** or **E** (similar to the English word "June") and a hard sound with other letters (similar to the English word "Gift").

If an **L** follows the **G** and then an **I** or **E**, it will have a very particular sound, almost non-existent in the English language. The closest word to that could be "million" with the double **LL**, but the sound is still slightly different.

Remember: there are irregular words that maintain a hard pronunciation (as in the English word "Glimpse"), even in the presence of these vowels, such as "Glicemia" (Glycemia)—although these are very rare.

Another very common combination of the letter G is the one created with the consonant N. GN has a particular sound that can also be found in the Spanish ñ. This construction is found in words like:

Signore – Mister

H

H is mute and used to make other consonants hard (**C** or **G,** as you have seen before) or is not pronounced at all.

Example: the word "hotel", in Italian, is pronounced as if the H was not present.

Q

Q is not used so much in the Italian language, although it is part of important words, such as "acqua" (water). Usually, it is also accompanied by the letter **C**, for all those words that descend from the word "acqua", such as:

Acquitrino – Marsh

Acquario – Aquarium

However, it can be found even as a single letter in words like:

Quadro – Painting

Fortunately, in both cases, this letter's pronunciation remains the same, which is very similar to the English letter **K**, with a hard pronunciation, such as the letter **C**.

S

The **SC** couple can have a soft or hard sound too. It follows the same rules as **C**, and the soft sound occurs only if it is followed by an **I** or **E**. In this case, it has a pronunciation similar to the English **SH** (shoe). Some examples:

Pro**sci**utto – Ham

Scelta – Choice

While, in any other case, they have a hard sound, like the English word "task", here are some examples:

Mo**sca** – Fly

Scarpa – Shoe

As in the case of the **C**, if an **H** and the vowels follow the **SC**, the sound still remains hard:

Schiena – Back

Furthermore, the letter **S** is one of those consonants that has a double sound in the Italian language. It can come closer to the letter **Z** sound, as in the English word "zebra", or even have a much sweeter sound, like the letter **S** of the English word "still".

The following are some examples of words that contain the **S** and how its sound may change from word to word:

Casa (*House*) – Hard sound, **Z**

Borsa (*Bag*) – Soft sound, **S**

Studiare (*To study*) – Soft sound, **S**

Rosa (*Rose*) – Hard sound, **Z**

How to know when one sound should be used rather than another? Unfortunately, even in this case, as in other phases of this manual, only experience can help you, and the more you speak the language, the more you will realize when to use a certain pronunciation.

Overall, the letter **S** is often pronounced with the soft sound of "still", but there is a large number of words in Italian in which the pronunciation has a much harder sound.

Z

Z is also pronounced differently based on its position within a word.

When **Z** is at the beginning of a word, it acquires a hard, buzzing-like sound, like the one of the letter **S** but even more distinct. You can see it in words like:

Zucchero (Sugar)

Zaino (Backpack)

However, it can also have a softer sound, just like the English **TS** that can be found in words like "cats":

Grazie (Thank You)

Ozio (Laziness)

Despite the rule that **Z** at the beginning of a word has a hard sound and the one inside the word has a soft sound, in reality, it changes a lot from individual to individual. Some people say *Zucchero* and *Zaino* both with a soft **Z** and vice versa, so there is no need to pay too much attention to this detail.

Double Consonants

In Italian, it is not so rare to find double letters. Actually, this happens almost all the time, to the point that if you wanted to translate this sentence that you are reading right now into Italian, you would find at least a dozen of them.

But how should you behave with this peculiarity of the Italian language?

Do not worry—it is not the case to be concerned about! A double letter simply indicates that the sound of the original consonant must be accentuated. Whether it has a soft or hard sound, it is enough to accentuate its presence by saying it for a slightly longer period than the usual pronunciation.

And with this, you have completed most of this language's peculiarities. As you can see, there are differences in pronunciation, but they are not so emphasized.

In addition, many consonants are missing from the list: so how do the rules work for them? They have not been added simply because they work in the same way as the English language.

Consonants such as **B, D, F, L, M,** and so on have the same English language pronunciation, which certainly makes it easy to learn the Italian pronunciation.

To sum up:

- **A** is pronounced as the **U** from the English word "**cut**".

- **E** is pronounced like the **E** from the English word "**rest**" or as the **E** of the English word "**appointment**".

- The **I** is pronounced like the **Y** from the English word "**baby**" or as the double **EE** from the word "**meet**".

- The **O** is pronounced like the **O** of the English word "**dog**".

- **U** is pronounced as the **U** from the English word "**loud**" or as the double **OO** of the word "**doom**".

- The **C** and the **G** can have a soft or hard sound. The soft sound is like the English words "**chilly**" and "**June**", while the hard sound is similar to the English words "**cat**" and "**gift**".

- If **GL** is followed by **I** or **E** (apart from rare exceptions), the sound will be soft and similar to the English word "**million**".

- **G** makes another sound thanks to the combinations of **N**. In this case, it will create a sound very similar to the Spanish letter **ñ**.

- **Q** is always pronounced as **K**, with a very hard sound.

- **SC** follows the same rules as **C**. In front of an **I** or **E** it has a soft sound like "**shoe**"; otherwise, it has a hard sound like for "**task**".

- The **S** can also have a hard or soft sound, depending on the word in which it is found. The soft sound is similar to the **S** in the English word "**still**", while the hard sound comes close to **Z**, in words like "**zebra**".

- **Z** can have a harder sound (especially if found at the beginning of a sentence) or a softer sound (if found within the sentence instead); in the latter, it is similar to the English's **TS** sound ("**cats**").

- When you come across double consonants, such as **CC**, **LL**, **MM**, and so on, it simply means that the sound of the mentioned consonant must be emphasized. You can do this by making it sound slightly longer than usual.

As mentioned at the beginning of the section, pronunciation is a delicate subject to be improved, and it takes a long time before reaching a level where you won't be recognized as an outsider while speaking the Italian language.

This brief guide will help you to deal with Italian words more confidently and invite you to read the words in the next pages aloud, by yourself, while trying to follow the advice given in this chapter.

In what other ways can you improve your Italian pronunciation? You can follow a rule applied to every language: try to sing the Italian songs you like, watch Italian movies in the original language, and try to pronounce as much as possible those words you may find difficult.

The most complicated step that you will have to face regarding Italian pronunciation is the soft sounds. For this reason, this aspect is highlighted several times, mostly because in other languages (like English) hard sounds are more common.

Especially for certain consonants, it is natural to associate a hard sound to letters like **G** and **C**, when very often they actually have an altered soft sound.

Thus, please pay attention to this aspect so that you won't find any problems with these letters.

And remember: the way to correct pronunciation is a long but enjoyable path because it is full of small yet motivational goals.

Dictionary

It is not possible to write an entire Italian dictionary that fits into this book. However, the purpose of this manual is not to provide a too detailed understanding of the Italian language, but rather, to be a handbook for learning how to speak Italian quickly.

Thus, a chapter is dedicated to the words that are used more in the given examples and that you will often use in your sentences—to learn them quickly.

The words have been divided according to the context, and, for this reason, the chapter is not made so that you have to learn all the words listed below in a single session. This is a reference at your disposal so that at any time while reading this book or practicing a conversation, you can return to these pages and find the word you are looking for.

Family / Famiglia

Cognato/a	–	Brother/Sister-in-law
Famiglia	–	Family
Figlio/a	–	Son/Daughter
Fratello	–	Brother
Genero/a	–	Son/Daughter-in-law
Madre	–	Mother
Nonno/a	–	Grandfather/Grandmother
Padre	–	Father
Sorella	–	Sister
Suocero/a	–	Father/Mother-in-law
Zio/a	–	Uncle/Aunt

Nipote   –   Nephew/Niece

Parente–   Relative

Note: With this last word, it is usually called a "false friend". What is it all about?

This is a word that's very similar to another in Italian but has a different meaning. In this case, the situation becomes more complicated since both of these words fall within the family context.

The word "Parente" in Italian looks much "Parent" in English, but the meaning is different:

Parente–   Relative

Genitore   –   Parent

Having made this necessary clarification, here are the words concerning the family sphere:

Marito   –   Husband

Moglie   –   Wife

Cugino   –   Cousin

School / Scuola

Asilo   –   Kindergarten

Classe   –   Class

Compagno   –   Classmate

Compito in classe   –   Class assignment

Compito a casa   –   Homework

Penna   –   Pen

Matita   –   Pencil

Maestro   –   Teacher (primary school)

Quaderno   –   Exercise book

Professore	–	Professor
Zaino	–	Backpack
Ricreazione	–	Recess
Scuola Elementare	–	Primary school
Scuola Media	–	Middle school
Scuola Superiore	–	High school
Libro	–	Book
Calcolatrice	–	Calculator
Orologio	–	Clock
Gomma	–	Eraser

This last word is particular, as its direct translation is "Rubber". In fact, the word "Gum" indicates both the instrument used to delete and the material itself.

Colla	–	Glue
Mappa	–	Map
Righello	–	Ruler
Forbici	–	Scissors

Work / Lavoro

Assunto	–	Hired
Collega	–	Colleague
Computer	–	Computer
Licenziato	–	Fired
Orario di lavoro	–	Working time
Pausa Pranzo	–	Lunch break
Scrivania	–	Desk

Stipendio	–	Salary
Straordinari	–	Overtime
Turno	–	Work shift

Food / Cibo – Beverage / Bevande

Acqua	–	Water
Acqua frizzante	–	Sparkling water
Ananas	–	Pineapple
Aglio	–	Onion
Basilico	–	Basil
Birra	–	Beer
Carne	–	Meat
Formaggio	–	Cheese
Lasagna	–	Lasagna
Latte	–	Milk
Melanzana	–	Eggplant
Pane	–	Bread
Pasta	–	Pasta
Peperone	–	Pepper (peperone, not pepperoni)
Pesce	–	Fish
Pizza	–	Pizza
Prosciutto	–	Ham
Salame	–	Salami
Spaghetti	–	Spaghetti
Succo di frutta	–	Fruit juice
Tonno	–	Tuna

Uovo	–	Egg
Vino	–	Wine

[Note: Coca Cola and Fanta are called as their brand. Soda is a different drink in Italy]

Time and Weather – Tempo (same meaning)

Secondo	–	Second
Minuto	–	Minute
Ora	–	Hour
Giorno	–	Day
Settimana	–	Week
Mese	–	Month
Anno	–	Year
Sole	–	Sun
Pioggia	–	Rain
Nebbia	–	Fog
Nuvoloso	–	Cloudy
Neve	–	Snow

[Note: You will see the days of the week and months of the year in the dedicated section, as included in the manual is a slight in-depth analysis that you should find interesting.]

Prepositions

Di	–	Of
A	–	To
Da	–	From
In	–	In

Con	–	With
Su	–	Up
Per	–	Through
Tra	–	Between
Fra	–	Between

These prepositions are not useful words like the ones seen so far, but they are very present in the various Italian sentences, and, for this reason, are on this list.

Similar to these words, there are other terms usually used in the construction of sentences, such as:

Davanti	–	In front
Dietro	–	Behind
Dopo	–	After
Fuori	–	Out of
Lontano	–	Far
Mediante	–	With (just like "con")
Prima	–	Before
Sopra	–	On
Sotto	–	Under

Within this chapter, you saw what is called a "false friend"—a term that may seem to have one meaning, but instead, means something else.

Since these terms are insidious, the main false friends that are created between Italian and English will now be listed.

False Friends

Before reviewing the list below, this is how the table works. On the left of the table is the English term you are familiar with, and at its right, is the correct Italian translation of the term. On the right of the table is the Italian term similar to the English word but with a different meaning, which is reported on the far right.

To give an example:

"To annoy" is translated into Italian with "Infastidire", while the Italian verb "Annoiare" is translated into English with "To bore".

It seems clear that these two terms have a very different meaning, but despite this, many people confuse the two terms, even in professional translations that then reach the small and big screen.

It is not essential to know all of these words, but if you have any doubts, you can find the answers in this list.

English word	Translation in Italian	*Italian False Friend*	Meaning of the false friend
Convenience	Comodità	*Convenienza*	Profit
Corpse	Cadavere	*Corpo*	Body
Definitely	Certamente	*Definitivamente*	Ultimately
Delusion	Illusione	*Delusione*	Disappointment
Disgrace	Vergogna	*Disgrazia*	Misfortune
Disposable	Usa e getta	*Disponibile*	Available
Editor	Redattore	*Editore*	Publisher
Actual	Effettivo	*Attuale*	Present
Actually	In realtà	*Attualmente*	Currently
Addiction	Dipendenza	*Addizione*	Sum
To annoy	Infastidire	*Annoiare*	To bore
To attack	Assalire	*Attaccare*	Stick
Educated	Colto	*Educato*	Polite

Education	Istruzione	*Educazione*	Upbringing
Entitled	Avente diritto a	*Intitolato*	Titled
Estate	Proprietà	*Estate*	Summer
Eventually	Alla fine	*Eventualmente*	Possibly
Factory	Fabbrica	*Fattoria*	Farm
Familiar	Ben conosciuto	*Familiare*	Related to family
Flipper	Pinna	*Flipper*	Pinball machine
Front	Facciata	*La fronte*	Forehead
Furniture	Mobili	*Fornitura*	Supply
Gracious	Clemente	*Grazioso*	Pretty
Gymnasium	Palestra	*Ginnasio*	High school
Inhabited	Abitato	*Inabitato*	Uninhabited
Injury	Ferita, lesione	*Ingiuria*	Insult
Large	Grande	*Largo*	Wide
Lecture	Conferenza	*Lettura*	Reading
Library	Biblioteca	*Libreria*	Bookshop
To license	Dare una licenza	*Licenziare*	To fire
Lunatic	Pazzo	*Lunatico*	Moody
Cave	Caverna, grotta	*Cava*	Quarry
Code	Codice	*Coda*	Tail
Cold	Freddo	*Caldo*	Hot
Commodity	Merce, prodotto	*Comodità*	Comfort
To con	Imbrogliare	*Con*	With

Luxury	Lusso	*Lussuria*	Lust
Magazine	Rivista	*Magazzino*	Warehouse
To magnify	Ingrandire	*Magnificare*	To praise
Mansion	Villa	*Mansione*	Duty
Mess	Confusione	*Messa*	Mass
Misery	Sofferenza	*Miseria*	Poverty
To attend	Assistere	*Attendere*	To wait
Attitude	Atteggiamento	*Attitudine*	Aptitude
Audience	Pubblico	*Udienza*	Hearing
To avert	Allontanare	*Avvertire*	To warn
Barracks	Caserma	*Baracca*	Shack, hut
Morbid	Morboso	*Morbido*	Soft, tender
To nominate	Proporre per una candidatura	*Nominare*	To name
Basket	Cesto	*Basket*	Basketball
Box	Scatola	*Box*	Garage
Brave	Coraggioso	*Bravo*	Good, clever
Camera	Macchina fotografica	*Camera*	Room
Camping	Il campeggiare	*Camping*	Campsite
Notice	Avviso	*Notizia*	News
Novel	Romanzo	*Novella*	Short story
To occur	Accadere	*Occorrere*	To need
Ostrich	Struzzo	*Ostrica*	Oyster
Parent	Genitore	*Parente*	Relative
Patent	Brevetto	*Patente*	Driver's license
Pavement	Marciapiede	*Pavimento*	Floor
Petrol	Benzina	*Petrolio*	Oil, petroleum
Prepared	Disposto a	*Preparato*	Trained
Preservative	Conservante	*Preservativo*	Condom
Presumption	Supposizione	*Presunzione*	Conceit
To pretend	Fingere, simulare	*Pretendere*	To claim, assume
To process	Elaborare	*Processare*	To put on trial
Proper	Appropriato	*Proprio*	One's own
Puzzle	Problema, enigma	*Puzzle*	Jigsaw puzzle
Rape	Stupro	*Rapa*	Turnip
Rate	Velocità, tasso	*Rate*	Instalments
To realize	Rendersi conto	*Realizzare*	Fulfil, carry out
Record	Disco	*Ricordo*	Memory
Concurrence	Coincidenza	*Concorrenza*	Competition
Confidence	Fiducia	*Confidenza*	Intimacy

Conservatory	Serra	*Conservatorio (di musica)*	School of music
Consistent	Coerente	*Consistente*	Substantial, large
To control	Dominare	*Controllare*	To check
Relevant	Pertinente	*Rilevante*	Remarkable
To retain	Conservare	*Ritenere*	To think, to believe
To retire	Andare in pensione	*Ritirare*	To withdraw
Romance	Storia d'amore	*Romanzo*	Novel
Rotten	Marcio	*Rotto*	Broken
Rumor	Pettegolezzo, diceria	*Rumore*	Noise
Sane	Equilibrato	*Sano*	Healthy
Scholar	Studioso	*Scolaro*	Pupil
Sensible	Sensato	*Sensibile*	Sensitive
Slip	Sottoveste	*Slip*	Briefs, knickers
Spot	Foruncolo, puntino	*Spot*	Advert, commercial
Candid	Schietto, sincero	*Candido*	Snow white
Canteen	Mensa, borraccia	*Cantina*	Cellar, wine shop
Case	Scatoletta	*Case*	Houses
Casual	Informale	*Casuale*	Chance

The Rule of the 5 W

As in the English language, in Italian, there are five interrogative particles, which are good to recognize in a sentence. The name "Rule of 5 W" arose from a journalistic guideline to answer the reader's questions, but the same principle will be explained here regarding how these particles work and translate into Italian.

So, let's start in alphabetical order.

What?

The literal translation of "What" is "Cosa", which is the most generic word that exists in the Italian language. Since "Cosa" can also be translated with "Thing", it is clear that it is widely used within the language.

This interrogative particle is used to gain information on a thing, plant or animal, but not a person.

Let's try to see it in a certain context and within an interrogative sentence:

"Cosa vuoi per cena?"

"What do you want for dinner?"

The purpose of this word is very similar to the English "What" and is also used to ask for clarifications if something is not clear.

Example:

P: "I hate you!" – "Io ti odio!"

A: "**What**?!" – "**Cosa**?!"

P: "You heard me!" – "Mi hai sentito!"

The only time when confusion might arise is when the "Cosa" is used as a translation of "Thing" since it is a double meaning.

So, even though the literal translation of "What" is "Cosa", sometimes it can also be translated as "Che".

Here is an example:

"What did you do yesterday?"

*"**Cosa** hai fatto ieri?"*

*"**Che** hai fatto ieri?"*

In both cases, the sentence has perfect sense. The "Che" is mainly used when you would ask information about a specific non-human thing. For example, when you would like to know what breed a dog is or a certain kind of plant:

"What breed is that dog?"

*"Di **che** razza è quel cane?"*

When?

"When" is used to identify a period of time, and in Italian, is translated as "Quando". This particle is then used in the sentences regarding a question or making a statement about a specific moment in time.

Here are some examples:

"When will we go to the sea?"

"Quando andremo al mare?"

In this case, luckily, there is no risk of confusing this word with another that has the same meaning (as in the "What" case).

Where?

"Where" is translated into "Dove" in Italian. This particle is found in sentences expressing a question or a statement about a specific place.

Here are some examples:

"Where do you live?"

"Dove abiti?"

"Where do we go to eat?"

"Dove andiamo a mangiare?"

Of course, just as in the previous cases, "Dove" can also be used in affirmative sentences:

"Here's where I live: in Rome."

"Ecco dove vivo: a Roma."

"That is the country where I was born."

"Quello è il Paese dove sono nato."

Unlike the word "What", this word has only one meaning, just as the word "When".

Who?

"Who" can be translated "Chi" in Italian. This particle is used to ask questions and information regarding a person.

A good example is:

"Who are you?"

"Chi sei tu?"

Why?

This is the most particular particle to remember. Unlike in English, where there are two words with the same meaning to be used in an interrogative or affirmative context (why and because), in Italian, you are faced with a single word: "Perché".

Here are some examples:

"Why did you call me?"

"Perché mi hai chiamato?"

"Because I need you."

"Perché ho bisogno di te."

As you can see, the same word is used in both Italian sentences.

Note: the last letter of the word "Perché" has an accent mark. This means, as explained in the chapter dedicated to pronunciation, that the final "e" must be pronounced strongly, like in the word "appointment".

Although it is possible to use the same word in both affirmative and negative sentences, some alternatives exist in Italian that can be used instead of that (but only in affirmative sentences).

Words like "Poiché" benefit from the same translation:

"I came because I needed you."

"Sono venuto poiché avevo bisogno di te."

Thus, ends your lesson on interrogative particles. As you can see, it is simply a matter of remembering what term the translation corresponds to. This way, you will immediately have an advantage in understanding a question and replying accordingly.

To sum up:

- "What" is translated into "Cosa" or "Che".
- "Where" is translated into "Dove".
- "When" is translated into "Quando".
- "Who" is translated into "Chi".
- "Why" is translated into "Perché" or "Poiché", but the latter only when the sentence is affirmative.

Ringraziare e Scusarsi (Being Thankful and Sorry)

As a fundamental part of many conversations (as you will see later in the section about asking directions), it is time to dedicate yourself to learning how to apologize or thank a person in Italian.

Although they may sound trivial, the words "thank you", "excuse me" and "I'm sorry" are part of everyday life.

You will start by studying this and learning, step by step, the language differences in Italian. For example, you will see how "excuse me" and "I'm sorry" are translated with the same word.

Let's start with "how to express gratitude" while learning one of the best-known Italian words right after "Ciao".

Grazie (Thank you)

This is a translation that will help you the most because "Thank you" is "Grazie" in Italian, a word perfect for any circumstance and whomever you are talking to.

As you will see in the coming chapters, the way of speaking, as well as the pronouns used, tend to change according to the situation (whether formal or informal). However, this doesn't occur with "Grazie".

As already stated, "Grazie" is really common in daily spoken Italian.

Sometimes, "Grazie" is combined with a pronoun, but only while responding to another person's gratitude. However, it is much easier to understand it with an example.

Here is a scenario to explain the concept:

Luca invites Marco to eat pasta at his house. Being grateful, Marco gives some eggs to Luca.

M: "Grazie per la pasta."

M: "Thank you for the pasta."

L: "**Grazie a te** per le uova."

L: "Thank you for the eggs."

As you can see, in the first sentence, "Grazie" is not combined by any pronoun and is followed by the reason for the gratitude.

In the second sentence, as a reply, Luca is being thankful to Marco for bringing him eggs.

Although "Grazie" can be used in every circumstance, there are specific cases in which you should express respect towards an important person, like a professor or employer.

Here, it is possible to use the word "La ringrazio" or "Grazie a Lei". "La ringrazio" can be used as gratitude opposed to "Grazie a te" (in this case "Lei" is used instead of "Te" since it is a rule in the formal Italian language).

Curiously, there is another formal, although extremely archaic, word of expressing gratitude: "Obbligato" (Obliged), which is very similar to the Portuguese word "Obrigado".

There are also other words to express gratitude. A more formal word, yet less used than others, is "Essere grato" (to be grateful), which is a verb that follows the conjugation of the verb Essere (a verb you will see later on).

Let's now move on and see how to apologize in Italian. You will also see in how many ways you can say "Scusa".

Scusa (Sorry)

One of the most complicated aspects of learning a language is when you have to face a word with multiple meanings, and "Scusa" is one of those. Let's analyze this word to help you use it correctly in a future conversation.

1) The most common translation is:

"Scusa" – "Sorry"

As in English, the Italian "Scusa" is used to apologize to others. However, unfortunately, if "Sorry" is translated into "Scusa", you cannot say the same for "I am sorry".

In this particular case, the most common translation is instead:

"Mi dispiace" – I'm sorry

What is the main difference? "Scusa" indicates an apology for something that was done/your fault; "Mi dispiace", however, can also be used when you have nothing to do with the problem you are facing.

Some examples are:

"Scusa per averti rotto la penna." – "Sorry for breaking your pen."

"Mi dispiace per la morte di tuo padre." – "I'm sorry for your father's death."

The difference is clear, but "Mi dispiace" can further be used for apologizing for what you have actually done:

"Mi dispiace per averti rotto la penna." – "Sorry for breaking your pen."

As you can see, the English translation has not changed at all; the difference lies in the original meaning of the word and not in its usual meaning. By saying "Scusa", you are asking forgiveness for the problem that occurred.

The complete sentence construction would actually be: "Scusami"—that means "Scusa me".

Saying "Mi dispiace" instead informs the other person that you are sorry for what happened to them.

These are just shades of the Italian language, but they are important to learn since it is always convenient to know when and how to apologize to others.

So, this is the real meaning of "Mi dispiace".

2) As mentioned before, "scusa" can have other meanings as well. It can be translated into "Excuse". In this particular case, it means a "Giustificazione" (justification), as in this example:

Marco: "Io sono stato malato; qual è la tua scusa?"

Marco: "I was sick; what's your excuse?"

To sum up:

> • "Thank you" is translated into "Grazie", which can be used in every context and with any person. Despite this, to show respect to a person you do not know or toward an older person, you should use the word "La ringrazio" while using the pronoun "Lei".

> • "I'm sorry" can be translated into "Mi dispiace". It is used to demonstrate sorrow for a certain event external to you. Saying "Scusa" instead asks for forgiveness for something you did.

> • The word "Scusa" has many other translations, such as "Excuse".

The Construction of the Sentence

Despite the differences between English and Italian, the sentence structure is very similar.

Let's start by looking at a simple sentence:

John *eats* <u>a</u> **sandwich**

John *mangia* <u>un</u> **panino**

The number of words, in this case, is the same, and it is easy to understand which English word corresponds to the Italian one.

In learning Italian, the luck is that it uses the same alphabet as English. The two languages have also influenced each other in the past and continue to do so today.

There are Anglo-Saxon words that have been contaminated by the Latin: think of "Tooth" and "Dentist". The translation of "Dentist" in Italian is "Dentista"—very similar.

Despite this, it will be necessary to develop a vocabulary to understand the different sentences—however, one thing at a time. First, you need to understand how to construct a sentence and then learn all the words.

The biggest difference in the construction of the sentence that runs between the English and the Italian is the interrogative form. While in English, the subject and the verb change position in formulating a question, in Italian, this does not happen.

Here is the phrase:

Is she married? **She is** married.

In Italian, it becomes:

Lei è sposata? **Lei è** sposata.

As you can see, the subject remains in the same position even in the interrogative form.

This is an important aspect since you are looking at the same sentence's structure. And it is the base of all the Italian grammar, so naturally, you may experience difficulties in switching between English and Italian.

Always remember: Italian sentences follow a specific order:

Subject – Verb – Article – Object + Any other elements

Even if there may be differences in this regard, made by a simple personal taste (it is possible to move the elements within the sentence while maintaining their meaning, even at the disadvantage of the sentence's fluency), this rule applies to most Italian sentences.

Here are some examples:

Carl eats an apple – Carl mangia una mela

Carl – subject – *Carl*

Mangia – the singular third person of the verb to "Mangiare" (to eat) – *Eats*

Una – feminine article – *An*

Mela – object – *Apple*

As you can see, both sentences have the same structure and the same number of words (obviously, this is not always the case, but the differences are not as marked as you could imagine). Everything changes with any interrogative form. Even the most basic question:

Hi, John, how are you?

Becomes:

Ciao, John, come stai?

Let's analyze this sentence:

Ciao – greeting – *Hi*

John – proper noun – *John*

Come – adverb – *How*

Stai – The second-person singular of the verb to "Stare" (to stay) – Are

Many differences emerge from a single sentence. The first is that, in Italian, the verb "Stare" (to stay) is used instead of the verb "Essere" (to be). In this particular case, it is a person's health and indicates that person's condition.

The second big difference is that, in Italian, the pronoun "Tu" has disappeared, as it has been overlooked. However, you will focus more on this topic in another section.

Had it not been overlooked, the position of the word "Tu" would have been:

Ciao, John, tu come stai?

As you can see, while in English the pronoun "you" has been placed at the end of the sentence, in Italian, it remains at the beginning of the sentence.

It is a difficult difference to master, but it is important to remember it to speak fluent Italian.

The Neutral Gender

You can further see the big difference between English and Italian on the list of the various pronouns:

I	Io
You	Tu
He/She/It	Lui/Lei
We	Noi
You	Voi
They	Loro (or Essi)

As you can see, in Italian, the equivalent of the pronoun "it" is not present. In fact, the neutral gender does not exist, and every word is either male or female.

Even inanimate objects have a gender. Here are some examples:

The chair – La sedia (female)

The book – Il libro (male)

Unfortunately, there is no precise rule that establishes when the male form should be used or when you should opt for the female one. Only experience can help you in this sense.

The Other Genders

As you will see in the following chapters, the gender of a word plays a crucial role for the article used with it (read the dedicated chapter on articles). So how is it possible to understand the genre of a word at first sight?

As with other examples, experience still plays an important role, but it is possible thanks to a small trick to understanding it in 90 percent of cases.

Usually, if words are ending with the vowel A, they are feminine, while those ending with the vowel O are masculine. Of course, this is not true in all cases, but it is good to make an initial selection of words.

Then there are words ending with other vowels. How do they work? Usually, there are names ending in –E, and although part of them are masculine, this is not always true. Some examples are:

Il prete (male) – The priest

Il mese (male) – The month

La rete (female) – The web

La pelle (female) – The skin

So, as mentioned before, it is only experience that can save you from any potential error. It is also necessary to pay even more attention, as there are words that may appear to be of a certain gender but turn out to be another.

For example:

La moto (female) – The motorcycle

As you can see, the word ends with the vowel O but is still a feminine word. Why? Because, in this case, it is the short version. The complete word would be "Motocicletta", which is feminine and keeps the same gender even in the short version.

Of course, some words end with a consonant, but their number is low compared to others, and for this reason, it is enough to remember their specific gender. Also, many of these have foreign and/or Latin origins, such as:

Il gol – *Male*

Il bar – *Male*

Lo sport – *Male*

L'email – *Female*

Il gas – *Male*

Speaking of masculine and feminine gender, another aspect to take into consideration is that while there are words that belong to one gender, there are many others that can belong to both of them, such as:

Amico – *Friend (male)*

Amica – *Friend (female)*

As you can see, the words that refer to a person or animal, overall support both genders because a person or animal can show themselves belonging to a certain sexual gender.

Is it enough to change the letter O with an A, then? Usually, yes, but let's see some examples:

Maestro – *Teacher (male)*

Maestra – *Teacher (female)*

Ladro – *Thief (male)*

Ladra – *Thief (female)*

Poliziotto – *Police officer (male)*

Poliziotta – *Police officer (female)*

But it is not always like this because not every word ends with the letter O or A. Let's think about, for instance, words that refer to people but end with an E:

Dottore – *Medic (male)*

Dottoressa – *Medic (female)*

Leone – *Lion*

Leonessa – *Lioness*

Principe – *Prince*

Principessa – *Princess*

As you can see from the examples above, in most of these cases, there is a change from -E to -ESSA. This rule has its exceptions, though, as there are names that end in –O, but in feminine words still become -ESSA:

Soldato – *Soldier (male)*

Soldatessa – Soldier (female)

In addition, there is a whole series of irregular names that have a real and separated form from these rules, such as:

Attore – *Actor*

Attrice – *Actress*

It is hard to remember all of these differences, except with experience, but usually, the names work as seen above.

Note: although the names that often end with E are considered masculine, it is good to remember that most of the feminine singular names that end with A, obtain an E in their plural.

Let's look at some examples:

Donna (woman)   Donne (women)

Borsa (bag)   Borse (bags)

Gatta (female cat)   Gatte (cats)

It is quite simple to distinguish one word from the singular masculine and one from the feminine in the plural. So, with a little attention, you should have no problem.

However, this aspect was worth underlining to avoid any potential mistake made in good faith.

The Pronoun "You"

Another fundamental difference that runs between English and Italian is the translation of the pronoun "You".

While in English, "You" can refer both to one or more people, in Italian, there are two distinct words. "Tu" is the singular pronoun and "Voi" is the plural form.

Let's look at some examples:

You are John

Tu sei John

You are John and Michael

Voi siete John e Michael

This difference is easy to master because it is sufficient to remember which pronoun should be used in front of one or more people.

The Pronoun "Lei"

In the list of the pronouns seen above, "Lei" is the literal translation of "She". Unfortunately, this is not always the case, as "lei" also assumes a different meaning based on the context.

In English, whether you are addressing a friend or an employer, the pronoun "You" is always used. In Italian, the situation is quite different.

While the translation "Tu" can be used in informal environments, when you talk to people you don't know or who have a position above yours (teachers, employers, seniors), you must use the pronoun "Lei" instead of "Tu".

Since this concept is a bit complicated, here are some examples:

Talking to a friend: "**Tu** sei John?" (Are you John?)

Talking to a stranger: "**Lei** è John?" (Are you John?)

Even if the meaning of the sentence in English has not changed, another pronoun is used in Italian. The literal English translation of the second sentence would be "Is she John?", which, of course, makes no sense.

Although this is a difficult aspect to master, it is also very important because it's the best way to convey courtesy in a formal environment.

Sometimes people use the pronoun "Voi" (plural You) or "Loro" (They) instead of "Lei" in communicating in an extremely formal way. Don't worry though: this is an archaic construction, and it is only used in specific regions of Southern Italy.

This, however, should not make you think that this aspect is not important: giving the "Tu" to a person you are not familiar with can be offensive and bad manners—based on the person you are talking to.

As you will soon see, most of the Italian personal pronouns can be left out from the sentences without changing their meanings.

Just in case you address a person with "Lei", this pronoun is almost always highlighted and not left out, to maintain the formalities between two people interacting with each other.

The Implied Pronoun

So far, you have seen three major differences, but unfortunately, the differences in the use of pronouns do not end here.

Let's now talk about the implicit pronouns.

While in English the pronoun or subject of a sentence is always specified, in Italian, it is often eliminated from the sentence as it is not necessary.

Example:

I am hungry.

(**Io**) ho fame.

You can see the pronoun in the Italian sentence between parenthesis because it is often omitted in the spoken language. In fact, the sentence without a pronoun, "Ho fame", makes perfect sense as it is.

Don't worry though: using the pronoun within the sentence is not wrong. You can also translate it with "Io ho fame", and the sentence will be correct anyway.

With time and experience, you will learn when it is possible to cut the pronoun from the sentence without losing its meaning.

This difference is mentioned just so that you are not confused when the pronoun is not specified in a sentence.

Of course, any pronoun you saw earlier can be left out from an Italian sentence. Actually, it is more common not saying the initial pronoun since it could sound too forced in the sentences.

Let's see some examples of sentences used in everyday life where the pronouns have been omitted:

- *Mi passi il sale?* – Can you pass me the salt?

This is a very common sentence, and, as you can see, it does not contain any first pronouns. It is also an interrogative form, so it is worth analyzing it to show once again the differences between Italian and English.

(Tu) – Second singular person, pronoun removed – *You*

Mi – First singular person (you will better see this pronoun in the next section) – *Me*

Passi – Second singular person verb to "Passare" (to pass) – *Pass*

Il – Male article– *The*

Sale – *Salt*

Once again, you can see that while in English the subject comes after the verb, in Italian, it is found (if not omitted) at the beginning of the sentence.

The second singular person "Tu" is almost always left out, like "Io" because it is easy to understand that if you are talking about yourself or talking straight to your interlocutor, it is not necessary to repeat the pronoun. The same can be said for "Noi" and "Voi", the plural version of the first and second person, even if the omission is much less marked in this case.

Curiously, the pronoun can be said in two particular cases:

- When an alternative is proposed to a previous statement.

To see this, imagine a chat between Marco and Luca, who are discussing where to go with their friend for the holidays:

Marco: "(Noi) Vorremmo andare in montagna, quest'anno…"

Marco: "We would like to go to the mountains this year…"

Luca: "Noi vogliamo andare al mare."

Luca: "We want to go to the sea."

As you can see, in Marco's sentences, the "Noi" (We) pronoun is not specified, while in Luca's response, he is using the pronoun to highlight that his group has a different will.

Here's another example:

Antonio: "Ho già mangiato oggi."

Antonio: "I already ate today."

Andrea: "Io ho ancora fame."

Andrea: "I'm still hungry."

This example follows the rule stated before as well.

- When the rest of the sentence is implied.

In this case, the pronoun becomes essential as the whole sentence is left out. Often this form is connected to the previous one, as it can be shown as a response to a previous statement.

Here's an example:

Marco: "Andiamo in montagna?"

Marco: "Let's go to the mountains?"

Luca: "Io no."

Luca: "Not me."

In this case, the personal pronoun has been specified because if Luca would have replied with only "No," it could have mean blocking the whole group rather than expressing a personal choice.

These are, however, extremely particular cases, so it is generally possible to identify the implied pronoun by checking the verb within the sentence. Since each person has their own conjugation of the verb (as you will see in the chapter dedicated to this element of the sentence), it is easy to identify the subject of a sentence even if it is not specified.

The Object Pronoun

What has been analyzed so far has only been the personal pronoun as a subject. Another great aspect to take into consideration, regarding sentence construction, is the personal pronoun as an object.

You know the English equivalent, but how does the Italian behave in this sense?

Me	Me/Mi
You	Te/Ti
Him	Lo/Gli
Her	La/Le
Us	Noi/Ci
You	Voi/Vi
Them	Loro/li

The neutral is not reported because it does not exist in Italian—it simply follows the rules of Him/Her.

As you can see from this brief outline, all personal pronouns as objects have a double form in Italian.

This is because the sentence can always be formulated in two different ways and, in particular, there is what is commonly called "integration of the pronoun". This means that sometimes the pronoun can be integrated into the verb.

Don't worry: here are some examples to help you understand:

I know **him**.

(Io) **lo** conosco.

This is the basic case. As you can see, the subject is again in brackets because it can be eliminated and the object pronoun "him" becomes "lo".

I talk to **him**.

Gli parlo io.

In this case, the object pronoun is still "him", but in Italian, it becomes "Gli" due to the construction "to him".

I sent **him** a letter

Gli ho mandato una lettera

In this case, the pronoun "Gli" is used because the sentence can also be formulated as "I sent a letter to him".

Understanding how this type of pronoun works is simpler than one would think, as everyone behaves the same way.

Note: the use of Lo/Gli and La/Le is often mistaken by native Italians, just as "Your" and "You're" is often mistaken by native English speakers.

Let's look at a more complicated case:

Could you bring **me** a glass of water?

Mi puoi portare un bicchiere d'acqua?

As mentioned earlier, the object pronoun can be integrated within the same verb. Thus, the initial "Mi" of the sentence moves to the end of the verb:

Puoi portar**mi** un bicchiere d'acqua?

However, even in this case, it is a nuance of the more advanced language that you can get with experience. For the moment, just keep in mind the different pronoun objects that can be used in Italian.

The Adjective and the Possessive Pronoun

Although there are many different types of pronouns, the purpose of this book is to be as direct and simple as possible. For this reason, this section talks about another aspect of fundamental importance in the construction of sentences: possessive adjectives, which are different according to the subject in question:

My	Mio/a
Your	Tuo/a
His	Suo
Her	Sua
Its	Suo/a
Our	Nostro/a
Your	Vostro/a
Their	Loro

There are many things to say about these adjectives, so let's go in order.

Starting from the first, you immediately notice that the equivalents of "My", "Our" and "Your" have a double form. "My" can become "Mio" or "Mia" based on the gender of the object in question.

As mentioned earlier, every word in Italian is either male or female, and the gender of the word also influences the personal adjective.

Here's a direct example:

That is **my** house.

Quella è la **mia** casa.

In this case, the adjective "mia" is used because "casa" is a female word. If it were a male word, it would have been:

He is **my** brother.

Lui è **mio** fratello.

Of course, when talking about inanimate objects, it could be more difficult to understand this difference, as it is necessary to adapt the neutral English to the Italian gender. In fact, the direct translation of "His" and "Her" is simply "Suo" and "Sua".

Remember also that "Your", in Italian, changes based on whether the subject is a single person or more people. In the first case, it will be "Tuo", and in the second, it will be "Vostro".

Imagine a waiter showing customers to a table:

(One person)

This is **your** table.

Questo è il **tuo** tavolo.

(Two people)

This is **your** table.

Questo è il **vostro** tavolo.

Fortunately, the situation is not complicated by talking about possessive pronouns, as they are generally equal to adjectives:

Mine	Mio/a
Yours	Tuo/a
His	Suo
Hers	Sua
Ours	Nostro/a
Yours	Vostro/a
Theirs	Loro

As you can see, nothing changes, but be careful: the article generally anticipates the possessive pronoun.

Example:

This bag is **mine.**

Questa borsa è *la* **mia.**

To sum up:

- In Italian, there is no neutral gender; every word is female or male.

- The pronoun "You" is translated as "Tu" when referred to a single person and as "Voi" when referred to more than one person.

- In formal environments, "You" behaves as if it were the pronoun "She".

- Very often the pronoun is implied in Italian sentences.

- In Italian, the object pronoun can be integrated into verbs.

- In Italian, the possessive adjective and the possessive pronoun are equal, but the second is preceded by an article.

- In Italian, usually, the names ending with -O are masculine while the ones ending with -A are feminine. Names ending with -E belong to both categories.

- Some names can be both masculine and feminine, depending on the person or animal's gender that they belong to. In this case, usually, the masculine name ending with -O will end with an -A if feminine and masculine names ending with -E will end with -ESSA if feminine.

This is probably one of the more difficult chapters of the book, but it is also one of the most important, and, no matter how heavy it is to deal with, it is essential to understand the most common phrases in Italian.

How Verbs Are Conjugated

The second essential part for understanding an Italian sentence is the verb. In this sense, there is good news and bad news. The good news is that most verbs are conjugated in the same way, so if you manage to learn one, you will understand them all.

Unfortunately, though, many irregular verbs have their own behavior, but this will be discussed later.

Let's start with the two fundamental verbs in each language: "to be" and "to have".

"To be", present:

I am	Io sono
You are	Tu sei
He is	Lui è
She is	Lei è
We are	Noi siamo
You are	Voi siete
They are	Loro sono

"To have", present:

I have	Io ho
You have	Tu hai
He has	Lui ha
She has	Lei ha
We have	Noi abbiamo
You have	Voi avete
They have	Loro hanno

As you can see, while in English, the form of the verb changes just twice in all conjugations, every person in Italian has a different verbal form.

There is no other way to learn these verbs except by using your memory. For this reason, you will have to arm yourself with patience and dedicate some time to this section.

-are, -ere & -ire

Before analyzing the various verbal forms in the Italian language, it is good to take a step back and identify verb types that can be encountered. Basically, the infinitive forms of Italian verbs can end in three different ways: -are, -ere or -ire.

Here are some examples taken from the most used verbs in Italian:

-ARE:

Mangiare (*to eat*)

Camminare (*to walk*)

Studiare (*to study*)

Lavorare (*to work*)

Parlare (*to talk*)

-ERE:

Bere (*to drink*)

Sedere (*to sit*)

Scegliere (*to choose*)

Cadere (*to fall*)

Chiedere (*to ask*)

-IRE:

Dire (*to say*)

Capire (*to understand*)

Partire (*to leave*)

Why is it so important to highlight this aspect? Because depending on the infinitive's type, you will find a different conjugation of the various persons.

For this reason, in the next paragraphs, a practical example of each one of these terminations is offered, for each verbal time that will be analyzed, to better understand the difference between the various verb forms.

The Present

Except for irregular verbs, most verbal forms behave the same way.

Take, for example, the present of the verb "Mangiare" (to eat):

I eat	Io mang**io**
You eat	Tu mang**i**
He eats	Lui mang**ia**
She eats	Lei mang**ia**
We eat	Noi mang**iamo**
You eat	Voi mang**iate**
They eat	Loro mang**iano**

As seen above, the last letters of each verb were highlighted because it is how a verb is conjugated. The root "mangi" is the same as the infinitive "**mangi**are". At this point, the same letters are always added.

Let's take another verb and see how it behaves. This is the case, for example, for the verb "Camminare" (to walk):

I walk   Io cammin**o** (cammin + o)

You walk   Tu cammin**i** (cammin + i)

He walks   Lui cammin**a** (cammin + a)

She walks   Lei cammin**a** (cammin + a)

We walk   Noi cammin**iamo** (cammin + iamo)

You walk   Voi cammin**ate** (cammin + ate)

They walk   Loro cammin**ano** (cammin + ano)

By learning how the verb conjugates for different pronouns, you can use almost all the verbs. That said, sometimes there may be small differences in the vowels.

Here's another example, the verb "Dormire" (to sleep):

I sleep   Io dorm**o**

You sleep   Tu dorm**i**

He sleeps   Lui dorm**e** (dorm + e)

She sleeps   Lei dorm**e** (dorm + e)

We sleep   Noi dorm**iamo**

You sleep   Voi dorm**ite** (dorm + ite)

They sleep   Loro dorm**ono**

Let's see the most common verbs that follow the traditional conjugation:

Mangiare (to eat)

Presentare (to introduce)

Imparare (to learn)

Lavorare (to work)

Studiare (to study)

Vivere (to live)

Dormire (to sleep)

Pagare (to pay)

How do you conjugate verbs? Simple: first, you need to identify the root. To do this, it is usually sufficient to remove the final part -are / -ere / -ire to the verb at the infinitive:

Mangi-are

Present-are

Impar-are

Lavor-are

Dorm-ire

Sed-ere (to sit)

At this point, add the final letters seen earlier. Let's say you want to use the phrase "He eats":

Take the root of "to eat": mangi-

Add the vowel relative to the third-person singular: -a

And here is the sentence: "Lui mangia".

Once this is established, you are going to complete the section dedicated to the present with the third conjugation, -ERE, of which you have not seen an example in this part yet.

To do this, you will use the verb "Bere: (to drink):

Io bev**o**   I drink

Tu bev**i**	You drink
Lui bev**e**	He drinks
Lei bev**e**	She drinks
Noi bev**iamo**	We drink
Voi bev**ete**	You drink
Loro bev**ono**	They drink

As you can see, there are not many differences between the verbs that end with -IRE, -ERE or –ARE—if not with some vowels within the various conjugations.

Irregular Verbs

The rules you have seen before are valid in most cases, and in this next section, you will use the regular verbal forms for the examples.

Keep in mind that there are the irregular verbs. One of the most used verbs is "Andare" (to go), which behaves quite uniquely in the conjugation:

I go	Io vado
You go	Tu vai
He goes	Lui va
She goes	Lei va
We go	Noi and**iamo**
You go	Voi and**ate**
They go	Loro vanno

As you can see, the verb turns out to be irregular because its root changes during the conjugation. Only the first and the second plural person keeps the same root as the infinitive.

From this point of view, even the verbs "Essere" and "Avere" can be considered irregular because their root changes during their conjugation, but since they are the main verbs of each language, it is normal that they have their own separate rule.

The Past

You will study all the tenses: most of them are essential for normal communication and are related to an advanced study of Italian.

The two tenses that you will be dealing with in this manual are the past and the future, as they are the most used in common Italian.

Speaking of the past, there are two forms: the past "Imperfetto", which indicates a continuous action in the past, and the "Remoto" past, which indicates a finished action far in the past.

A third form of the past is the "Passato Prossimo", and that is what you will see now because it is the most used and easiest to learn.

Present Perfect

Let's look at the verb "Mangiare" (to eat) as an example:

I ate	Io ho mangiato
You ate	Tu hai mangiato
He/She ate	Lui/Lei ha mangiato
We ate	Noi abbiamo mangiato
You ate	Voi avete mangiato
They ate	Loro hanno mangiato

How does the construction of this tense work? Simply take the present of the verb "to have" or "to be" (every verb requires one in particular) and add the past participle of the verb itself:

Io (first-person singular)

ho (first-person singular of the verb "to have")

mangiato (past participle)

Getting the past participle is very simple: just take the root mentioned before (mangia-) and add -**to**.

Here are some examples:

Dormire (to sleep) – **Dormi**to

Camminare (to walk) – **Cammina**to

Studiare (to study) – **Studia**to

In this regard, it is good to remember that there are verbs that work in a particular way in this case as well. As, for example, the verb "Leggere" (to read): the present perfect of this verb is "Letto", a verbal form in which it loses the consonant GG.

Which present should be used between "to be" and "to have"?

"To have" is used with:

- Transitive verbs: I read a book – Io **ho** letto un libro

- Verbs of movement, like walking.

 On the other hand, "to be" is used with transitive verbs.

After having seen a conjugation's example of -ARE, this time, you will see an example of the conjugation in –ERE. Since you already saw above that the present perfect of the verb to read is "Leggere", let's use just this verbal form:

Io ho letto	I read
Tu hai letto	You read
Lui ha letto	He read
Lei ha letto	She read
Noi abbiamo letto	We read
Voi avete letto	You read
Loro hanno letto	They read

As you can see, the present perfect is one of the easiest verbal forms to learn after learning the present, as it always uses the present of "avere" or "essere", followed by the participle.

For the conjugation -IRE and the last example, you are going to use a verb that requires the verb "essere" in its construction, "Partire":

Io sono partito	I left
Tu sei partito	You left
Lui è partito	He left
Lei è partita	She left
Noi siamo partiti	We left
Voi siete partiti	You left
Loro sono partiti	They left

Things get a little more complicated when it comes to talking about the Imperfect.

Imperfect

The imperfect is a verbal form that expresses a continuous action in the past. While the present perfect identifies something recently accomplished, the imperfect is the ideal if you want to indicate extended action for a certain period in the past.

How is this verbal form created? In most cases, it is enough to take the present and add -AV (if -ARE), -EV (if -ERE) or -IV (if -IRE) between the root and its conclusion.

A practical example is with the verb "Mangiare" (to eat). In the present:

Io mangio	I eat
Tu mangi	You eat
Lui mangia	He eats
Lei mangia	She eats

Noi mangi**amo**	We eat
Voi mangi**ate**	You eat
Loro mangi**ano**	They eat

In the example seen above, the root of the verb is underlined, and its final part is in bold. Let's now see how the imperfect is formulated. To do this, italics have highlighted the added part:

Io mangi*av*o	I ate
Tu mangi*av*i	You ate
Lui mangi*av*a	He ate
Lei mangi*av*a	She ate
Noi mangi*av*amo	We ate
Voi mangi*av*ate	You ate
Loro mangi*av*ano	They ate

As you can see, it is quite simple to express the imperfect once you understand the present. As usual, let's look at an example with the conjugation with –ERE. In this case, "Read" (t*o read*):

Io leggevo	I read
Tu leggevi	You read
Lui leggeva	He read
Lei leggeva	She read
Noi leggevamo	We read
Voi leggevate	You read
Loro leggevano	They read

So, therefore, let's see an example of the third conjugation, the one ending with -IRE. In this case, "Capire" (to understand):

Io capivo	I understood

Tu capivi	You understood
Lui capiva	He understood
Lei capiva	She understood
Noi capivamo	We understood
Voi capivate	You understood
Loro capivano	They understood

While the rule of the "present" + av/iv/ev is often used, it is not always correct. For example, the present of "capire" (to understand) is:

Io capisco	I understand

While the past is:

Io capivo	I understood

As you can see, the word has changed from the present to the past, losing the consonants "sc".

Always remember: the imperfect states an ongoing action that happened in the past.

Let's now see the last type of past that you will study in this guide: the Simple Past.

Simple Past

The Simple Past can easily be considered the opposite of the Imperfect. While, as you have seen before, the Imperfect indicates an ongoing action in the past, the Simple Past indicates an accomplished action that took place a long time ago.

So, you cannot use it to talk about the movie you saw last week or even three months ago: the Simple Past period concerns years and its use is less highlighted compared to the ones you have learned so far, but nonetheless, is as important as them.

The Simple Past turns out to be more complicated than the two alternatives that came first, so take all the time you need to understand it.

In fact, this verbal form has its own conjugation, which cannot be traced back to the addition of letters as in the previous cases. Let's look at it using the first conjugation in -ARE, always with the verb "to eat" (*to eat*):

Io mang**iai**   I ate

Tu mang**iasti**   You ate

Lui mang**iò**   He ate

Lei mang**iò**   She ate

Noi mang**iammo**   We ate

Voi mang**iaste**   You ate

Loro mang**iarono**   They ate

As you can see, the Simple Past presents itself in a completely original form compared to the other verbal forms, and for this reason, it must be remembered.

For the sake of completeness, let's once again see the other two conjugations, with the verb "Leggere" (*to read)* and the verb "Dormire" (*to sleep):*

Io lessi   I read

Tu leggesti   You read

Lui lesse   He read

Lei lesse   She read

Noi leggemmo We read

Voi leggeste   You read

Loro lessero   They read

As you can see in this case, the word's root changes, losing the two GG, just as it happened with the participle, which in this case is replaced by two SS.

Io dormii	I slept
Tu dormisti	You slept
Lui dormì	He slept
Lei dormì	She slept
Noi dormimmo	We slept
Voi dormiste	You slept
Essi dormirono	They slept

Unfortunately, there are not many other tips as it is, in reality, a more mnemonic exercise. Remember, however, that by knowing the Present Perfect and the Imperfect, you will still find yourself with an excellent ability to describe the past.

So, take your time and study the Simple Past with all the patience you need.

Of course, there are many other articulate verbal forms to describe the past, but as previously mentioned, these lessons provide something different than a usual grammar book.

In this guide, lessons are given on the sentence's construction and the elements that compose it, in order to help you better understand most of the common Italian sentences.

Now it is time to see what the future holds for you because, in the next section, you are going to learn about the future dedicated verbs.

The Future

The future is another commonly used verbal form and is the first that uses the much-known Italian accents. Let's see a classical conjugation of this verb:

I will eat	Io mang**erò**
You will eat	Tu mang**erai**
He will eat	Lui mang**erà**
She will eat	Lei mang**erà**
We will eat	Noi mang**eremo**
You will eat	Voi mang**erete**
They will eat	Loro mang**eranno**

Although it may seem complicated to look at, it is simpler than one might think because, once you learn the terminations of the various conjugations, they will be the same for almost all verbs:

I will study	Io studi**erò**
You will study	Tu studi**erai**
He/She will study	Lui/Lei studi**erà**
We will study	Noi studi**eremo**
You will study	Voi studi**erete**
They will study	Loro studi**eranno**

Let's see how the conjugation's verb with -ERE works while using the verb "Cadere" (*to fall*):

Io cadrò	I will fall
Tu cadrai	You will fall
Lui cadrà	He will fall
Lei cadrà	She will fall
Noi cadremo	We will fall
Voi cadrete	You will fall
Loro cadranno	They will fall

As you can see, the verb works in the same way even in this particular case. So, let's see the third conjugation with -IRE using the verb "Pulire" (*to clean*):

Io pulirò	I will clean
Tu pulirai	You will clean
Lui pulirà	He will clean
Lei pulirà	She will clean
Noi puliremo	We will clean
Voi pulirete	You will clean
Loro puliranno	They will clean

Even if the Italian forms are much more complicated than the English ones, as they change shape with each person, once you understand these verbal forms, you can communicate naturally with a native speaker.

Despite you having dealt with two heavy topics one after the other, the personal pronouns and the verbs, it was essential to talk about these two elements of the sentence right away so that they could be used in common phrases in the following chapters.

Don't worry: just one final step and you will be able to move on to a much lighter topic—talking about articles and numbers in Italian culture and language.

To sum up:

- The majority of Italian verbs follow three conjugations; in other words, they can end in three different ways in their infinitive form.

- These conclusions are -ARE, -ERE and –IRE, and they are influenced by verbs conjugated in the various persons.

- Besides these, there are irregular verbs that do not follow a specific rule, but instead, have their own conjugation. Verbs such as "Essere" (to be), "Avere" (to have) and "Andare" (to go) are exceptional cases in which not only the various conjugations' final part changes but also the root itself.

• There are many verbal forms in Italian, even more than in other languages. There are many past verbs like the Simple Past, the Present Perfect, the Imperfect, and so on. Even the Italians themselves find it difficult to master all of them—that is why it's highly recommended that you start by learning the Present, Past, and Simple Future.

• The Present Perfect is made by taking the verb "to be" or "to have's" present and adding the same present perfect of the verbal form.

• Imperfect is (usually) obtained by adding the suffix -av between the verb's root and its present conclusion.

• The Future and Simple Past both have their own conjugation, which is necessary to learn without any shortcuts.

Altri Modi Verbali (Other Verb Tenses)

The two verbs in this chapter are not the easiest to learn, but luckily, there is good news:

> 1. The verbs are part of the advanced grammar. For this reason, they are not essential during a basic conversation, so you can take all the time you need to learn them.

> 2. The verbs work similarly in both English and Italian, so it will not be as difficult to understand them once the initial difficulties have been overcome.

If the verbs do not fit into a basic conversation, why is it necessary to study them? It is important to know the verbal forms because they compose the hypothetical phrase.

Since, in daily life, you may impose conditions, formulate hypotheses, and talk about the consequences of your actions, you need to know the appropriate verbs to do so.

You will deal with these two verbal forms separately before joining them in the hypothetical phrase, so you'll advance step by step and use a large number of examples to learn the verbs better.

Let's start with the "Congiuntivo" (Subjunctive).

Congiuntivo (Subjunctive)

The subjunctive is every Italian student's nightmare, so much that many Italian speakers are still not able to use this verb correctly and confuse it with the "Condizionale" (Conditional), which is discussed later.

However, this should not worry you: learning to use this verb is not that difficult, just follow some tricks to understand when and where it should be used.

The best use of the subjunctive is in a hypothetical phrase. For this reason, you will use this construction to learn how to use it.

Basically, the subjunctive is a verbal way used in the presence of a "Se" (If) or a "Che" (that).

However, before seeing it within a sentence, let's try to combine it with the various persons.

-ARE verb, "Mangiare" (to eat):

Io mang**i**	I eat
Tu mang**i**	You eat
Lui mang**i**	He eats
Lei mang**i**	She eats
Noi mang**iamo**	We eat
Voi mang**iate**	You eat
Loro mang**ino**	They eat

From this conjugation, it is easy to understand why it is so difficult for Italian people to learn this verb. On the other hand, it is easy to mistake it as the present. Let's make a comparison between them:

Presente Indicativo	Presente Congiuntivo
Io mangi	Io mangio
Tu mangi	**Tu mangi**

Lui mangi	Lui mangia
Lei mangi	Lei mangia
Noi mangiamo	**Noi mangiamo**
Voi mangiate	**Voi mangiate**
Loro mangino	Loro mangiano

As you can see, out of seven persons, three have the same conjugation, and the others just differ in less or one more letter.

The second thing that can be noticed in the translation is that, in English, the subjunctive is not used but replaced by the verb corresponding to the indicative.

It is complex, but combining a verb in -ERE and one in -IRE can help you understand the Italian grammar a little more.

Let's look at the verb "Cadere" (to fall):

Io cada**l** fall

Tu cada	You fall
Lui cada	He falls
Lei cada	She falls
Noi cadiamo	We fall
Voi cadiate	You fall
Loro cadano	They fall

As you can see, although it is a bit more complicated, due to the lack of this verb in English, the two verbs work in the same way.

So, let's try a verb that ends in -IRE, like "Nutrire" (to feed):

Io nutra	I feed
Tu nutra	You feed
Lui nutra	He feeds

Lei nutra	She feeds
Noi nutriamo	We feed
Voi nutriate	You feed
Loro nutrano	They feed

The conjugation is very similar in all three cases. What you have seen so far is the present subjunctive. Let's now look at the imperfect subjunctive tense, which is essential to construct your hypothetical phrase.

The English equivalent is the indicative past:

Io nutrissi	I fed
Tu nutrissi	You fed
Lui nutrisse	He fed
Lei nutrisse	She fed
Noi nutrissimo	We fed
Voi nutriste	You fed
Loro nutrissero	They fed

So, here is the difficulty of the verb: as you can see, present and past are quite different from each other. Luckily, once you have learned these two tenses, you will have practically mastered the subjunctive.

Now it is time to look at the Italian conditional and then build your hypothetical phrases.

Il Condizionale (The Conditional)

The conditional is the counterpart of the subjunctive in a hypothetical phrase. It is used to express an action depending on certain conditions.

Unlike the subjunctive, there is a corresponding form in English, and it is the one obtained using "Would".

Let's look at some examples trying to combine the verb "Mangiare" (to eat):

Io mangerei	I would eat
Tu mangeresti	You would eat
Lui mangerebbe	He would eat
Lei mangerebbe	She would eat
Noi mangeremmo	We would eat
Voi mangereste	You would eat
Loro mangerebbero	They would eat

Since an English counterpart of this verb exists, it is easy to understand how it works in Italian.

For example:

Io mangerei la pasta	I would eat the pasta

This is a sentence in which the conditional has been used correctly. What happens if you add a second sentence with the subjunctive?

Il Periodo Ipotetico (The Hypothetical Sentence)

The hypothetical sentence is presented in different forms, and all of them include two sentences: one assumes that an action is taken and the other one requires a condition to be respected. For example:

Mangio la pasta **se** tu la cuoci.	I eat pasta **if** you cook it.

The key behind this hypothetical sentence is the conjunction "If" (Se). Let's see how to correctly formulate this sentence using the subjunctive and the conditional.

The conditional must be used in the sentence that expresses an action under condition:

Mangerei la pasta se…	I would eat pasta if…

The subjunctive is used in the sentence that sets the condition:

...se tu la cuocessi.   ...if you cooked it.

Combining these two sentences, you get:

Mangerei la pasta se tu la cuocessi   I would eat pasta if you
cooked it.

Obviously, the sentence can be expressed as the opposite:

Se tu cuocessi la pasta, Io la mangerei   If you cooked the pasta,
I would eat it

It is unlikely that you will understand these perfectly in just a few sentences, but it was necessary to introduce them so that you can recognize them during your conversations in Italian. With time and practice, you will find yourself using both forms naturally.

To sum up:

- In addition to the indicative, there are two more verbal modes, such as the subjunctive and the conditional.
- The Italian subjunctive does not have a corresponding verbal mode in English, so it is translated using the indicative.
- The subjunctive is often used with the presence of conjunctions like "Che" and "Se" (that and if).
- The Italian conditional corresponds to the English use of "would".
- While expressing a hypothetical sentence, the conditional is often used in one sentence and the subjunctive in another.

Articles

Speaking of sentence construction, the other topic to be discussed is the use of the articles in Italian.

Compared to pronouns and verbs, this field is much easier to understand, but nonetheless, it is necessary to pay attention.

The two main articles are the literal translation of the English ones. As in English, you can find "**a/an**" and "**the**", while in Italian, you find "**un**" e "**il**".

Unfortunately, as you have seen up until now, Italian words tend to change according to the masculine or feminine gender, and the same happens for articles. The article will always have the same gender as their words.

The

Let's start with the determiner article "**the**". In which way is it translated in Italian?

It will be translated as "**IL**" when the following word is masculine:

Il ragazzo.

The boy.

If a feminine word follows the article, it will become "**LA**" instead:

La mamma.

The mother.

Both articles have a plural version, of course. In the masculine's case, it would be "**I**":

I ragazzi.

The boys.

The feminine article becomes "**LE**":

Le mamme.

The *mothers.*

Quite easy to remember, right? But the explanations are not finished yet because there are two more special cases.

There is another determiner masculine article that has been used with only certain words, "**LO**":

Lo pneumatico.

The *tire.*

In this particular case, it will only help you with experience and a dictionary, so remember not to be too harsh on yourself since many native-speaking Italians make mistakes and use "**IL**" rather than "**LO**".

So, there is no way of knowing when to use "LO" instead of "IL"? Actually, yes, but it is extremely technical. This article is mainly used with words that start with certain consonants.

What are these?

The masculine words starting with an S and followed by another consonant:

Lo squalo – *The shark*

Lo scontro – *The clash*

Lo spagnolo – *The Spanish*

The masculine words starting with an X, but they are very rare in Italian:

Lo xeno – *The xenon*

Lo xilofono - *The xylophone*

The masculine words starting with Y, but they are also very rare in Italian:

Lo yogurt – *The yogurt*

Masculine words starting with the letter Z, such as:

Lo zabaione – *The eggnog*

Constructed words starting with PS, PN, or GN:

Lo psicologo – *The psychologist*

Lo pneumatico – *The tire*

Lo gnomo – *The gnome*

The plural of "**LO**" become "**GLI**", which follows the same rules listed above.

Another aspect to keep an eye on while talking about determiner articles is that sometimes the feminine article can be replaced by an apostrophe. Not "**LA**", but **L'**. This happens only when the word that follows an article starts with a vowel.

For example:

L'amica. [La amica]

The *friend (female).*

Even "**LO**" can benefit from this, while still following the same rule:

L'orto. [Lo orto]

The *vegetable garden.*

When to Use the Definite Article

Now that you have seen different types of definite articles, it is time to learn which cases they should be used in.

1. The first case talks about a specific person. The literal translation of the sentence would be:

Mr. Rossi

è:

Il signor Rossi

The article has been placed before the translation of the word "Mister" since you are talking about a specific person and not a generic "Mister Rossi" you do not know personally.

2. It is the same if you are talking about a lawyer, doctor, or any other professional.

Dr. Bianchi

Il dottor Bianchi

3. The same can be said for continents, nations, and territorial zones (such as islands, mountains, etc.). Here are some examples:

Italy (country)

L'Italia

Europe (continent)

L'Europa

White Mountain (mountain)

Il Monte Bianco

Elba (island)

L'Elba

Toscana (region)

La Toscana

4. The definite article can be used while talking about sports as well:

Football

Il calcio

Basketball

La Pallacanestro

5. Or while talking about languages and the time:

It's three o'clock.

*Sono **le** tre.*

English

L'inglese

6. And even while talking about materials, such as:

Gold

L'oro

Cotton

Il cotone

Overall, this is how definite articles work.

A/an

The indefinite article follows more or less the same rules. It starts with a "Un" (a) if followed by a masculine word:

Un cavallo.

A horse.

Then, you use "**Una**" when the following word is feminine:

Una borsa.

A bag.

As for a determiner article, even in this case, you have a second form for the masculine one, which is "**Uno**" and it is used with the same words as "Lo".

Uno squalo.

A shark.

While for a feminine article, in this case, you can have a last letter's elision if there are feminine words. So not "Una" but rather **Un'**.

Un'amica.

A friend (female).

On the contrary, of the determiner article, the masculine "Un" will never get an apostrophe. So, if a word starts with a vowel, the article will simply remain "Un":

Un albero.

A tree.

Let's now see the plural versions. In this case, since "**Uno**" also indicates the first number "**One**", on a plural, it is used as an article that states a higher number, just like you would use the English word "**Some**".

Masculine word "**Dei**":

Un gatto.

A cat.

Dei gatti.

Some cats.

Feminine word "**Delle**":

Delle bambole.

Some dolls.

"**Degli**" for the plural form of "**Uno**":

Degli squali.

Some sharks.

Because of the indefinite article's nature, it also means "One" as a number. The plural version of "Uno" can be replaced with other indefinite adjectives, such as "Alcuni", "Taluni" and "Certi", which can be all translated into the English word: "Some".

To sum up:

- The determiner article "**The**" will be translated in different ways based on the following word's gender (the masculine **Il/Lo** and the feminine **La/L'**) or its number (the plural masculine **I/Gli** and feminine **Le/L'**).

- The indefinite article "**A/an**" will be translated the same, always based on the word's gender (masculine **Un/Uno** and feminine **Una/Un'**) or based on their numbers (masculine **Dei/Degli** and feminine **Delle**).

- The masculine determiner article LO occurs in certain cases only; for example, when the masculine word starts with an X, Z, Y, PS, PN, or GN and the letter S plus another consonant.

- The determiner article is used in some other cases, like: for specific persons, countries, regions, territorial areas, materials, sports, time, and languages.

- The plural form of the indefinite article UN/UNA can be replaced even by indefinite adjectives like "Alcuni", "Taluni" and "Certi". All of them can be translated into "Some".

Numbers

Numbers are almost as important as the alphabet, and they are usually one of the first elements that are explained in each language. And Italian is no exception.

Fortunately, the differences between Italian and English are not many since numbers behave the same way in both languages. They are unique from one to ten, follow a precise rule from eleven to twenty, and then follow a second rule for the rest of the numbers.

Let's start with numbers one to ten:

One	Uno
Two	Due
Three	Tre
Four	Quattro
Five	Cinque
Six	Sei
Seven	Sette
Eight	Otto
Nine	Nove
Ten	Dieci

The numbers of the second decade, up to twenty, in English, follow the rule of -teen. In Italian, there is a similar rule, that of the -dici:

Eleven	Un**dici**
Twelve	Do**dici**
Thir**teen**	Tre**dici**
Four**teen**	Quattor**dici**

Fif**teen**	Quin**dici**
Six**teen**	Se**dici**
Seven**teen**	**Dici**assette
Eigh**teen**	**Dici**otto
Nine**teen**	**Dici**annove
Twenty	Venti

As you can see from this example, from the eleventh to the sixteenth number, the word is made up of the root's number (the first ten) plus the suffix -dici that indicates the tens.

This rule reverses in the last three numbers before reaching the twenty, with the -dici that has been placed at the beginning of the word.

From twenty-one onwards, the numbers are easily understood as they use the root of the ten, just like in English, and the number:

Twenty-one	Ventuno
Twenty-two	**Venti**due
Twenty-three	**Venti**tré
Twenty-four	**Venti**quattro
Twenty-five	**Venti**cinque

etc...

The first twenty-four numbers are generally the most important because they are the ones that are normally used to define the time of day. By the same principle, to scan minutes and seconds, it is also necessary to know the numbers up to sixty.

Let's now see the tens up to one hundred:

0	Zero	*Zero*
10	Dieci	*Ten*

20	Venti	*Twenty*
30	Trenta	*Thirty*
40	Quaranta	*Forty*
50	Cinquanta	*Fifty*
60	Sessanta	*Sixty*
70	Settanta	*Seventy*
80	Ottanta	*Eighty*
90	Novanta	*Ninety*
100	Cento	*One hundred*

Learning these terms looks more difficult than it is. Except for the first three, from thirty onwards, all the words are made of the base number plus the suffix -ENTA/ANTA.

Curiously, in the Italian tradition, this term also has symbolic value—since the moment a person turns thirty years old, it is usually said as "si entra negli –enta" (*We are in the -enta*), while the moment someone turns forty years old, it is common to say "si entra negli –anta" (*We are in the -anta*).

From 100 onwards, the numbers are extremely easy to remember because they simply take "cento" and add the whole number. Here are some examples:

100	+	6	=	106
Cento	+	*Sei*	=	*Centosei*
100	+	35	=	135
Cento	+ *Trentacinque*		=	*Centotrentacinque*

For the other hundreds, it is simpler to enter the corresponding number before the word "cento":

900 **Nove**cento

400 **Quattro**cento

This is up to a thousand. In Italian, the word thousand is written as "Mille" and works exactly like the numbers seen so far.

The only difference between the "Mille" and the "Cento" is that, to formulate the next thousands, it is necessary to put the corresponding number first and then change "Mille" into "Mila":

100	200
Cento	***Due****cento*
1000	2000
Mille	***Due****mila*

The Hour in Italian

When learning a foreign language, being able to ask and communicate the time is one of the first aspects taught, given its great use in everyday life.

Speaking of the hour in Italian, first of all, it is good to remember that Italians use a system of hours different from the "a.m. and p.m." one.

The hours start at 00:00, commonly called "Mezzanotte" (Midnight) and end at 23:59 p.m. (11:59 p.m.); twenty-four hours without being divided between morning and afternoon, using normal numbers. Only noon and midnight have different names.

Here are some examples:

Midnight	Mezzanotte
One a.m.	l'una
Two a.m.	le due
Three a.m.	le tre
Four a.m.	le quattro
Five a.m.	le cinque
Six a.m.	le sei

Seven a.m.	le sette
Eight a.m.	le otto
Nine a.m.	le nove
Ten a.m.	le dieci
Eleven a.m.	le undici
Twelve p.m.	Mezzogiorno

(noon)

As you can see, time is always accompanied by an article in Italian. So, the English sentence:

It's **three** o'clock.

Becomes:

Sono le **tre**.

After noon, the hours take on a double meaning. On the one hand, you see the system based on twenty-four hours:

One p.m.	le tredici
Two p.m.	le quattordici
Three p.m.	le quindici
Four p.m.	le sedici
Five p.m.	le diciassette
Six p.m.	le diciotto
Seven p.m.	le diciannove
Eight p.m.	le venti
Nine p.m.	le ventuno
Ten p.m.	le ventidue
Eleven p.m.	le ventitré

Despite this, in spoken Italian, wide use is made of a division similar to the English one. In this case, the afternoon hours return to be under twelve:

Onep.m.	l'una
Two p.m.	le due
Three p.m.	le tre
Four p.m.	le quattro
Five p.m.	le cinque
Six p.m.	le sei
Seven p.m.	le sette
Eight p.m.	le otto
Nine p.m.	le nove
Ten p.m.	le dieci
Eleven p.m.	le undici

This way of talking about time is very similar to English. For this reason, it is preferable for those approaching Italian from this language. A conversation can, therefore, be:

What time is it?	Che ore sono?
It's three o'clock.	Sono le tre.

And this conversation is fine whether it is three in the morning or the afternoon. But be careful: if the context is missing, it will be necessary to specify the time of day to which that hour refers.

While the hours based on the 24-hour cycle are precise, if you divide the day into two twelve-hour bands, you will have twice the two, three, four and so on.

Since there is no a.m./p.m. formula in Italian, you will have to accompany the time with the time of day:

I woke up at **three a.m.** – Mi sono svegliato alle tre **di notte**

The sentences to be used are, therefore:

Di notte (night)

Di mattina (morning)

Di pomeriggio (afternoon)

Di sera (evening)

As you may have noticed from the previous examples, another difference runs between Italian and English when it comes to time. While in English, the neutral pronoun "it" is always used, in Italian, it is generally replaced with the third person plural.

If it were "They", therefore, you must use the verb: "sono".

The Italian equivalent of "It is", "è", is used only for midnight, noon, and the first hour "l'una".

Half an Hour and a Quarter

So far, precise hours have been discussed, but, of course, you cannot ignore the minutes. It is extremely simple to say the time in Italian, as it is enough to report the hour and minutes using the numbers:

03:21   Sono le **tre e ventuno.**

To these are obviously added the idioms for the quarter of an hour and half an hour.

Here are some direct examples:

It's **a quarter** past three.

Sono le tre e **un quarto.**

It's **a quarter** to three.

Sono le tre meno **un quarto.**

It's **half** past three.

Sono le tre e **mezzo.**

As these are common forms, don't worry too much about it as, in Italy, it is very common to simply say the time using the numbers for the minutes.

Ordinal Numbers

In the previous sections, the cardinal numbers were discussed because they are the most used in the Italian language. Let's now take a look at the ordinal numbers.

In this regard, you will be happy to discover that the functioning of ordinal numbers in Italian is very simple: except for the first ten that are, of course, unique, all others follow the same rule.

First – Primo

Second – Secondo

Third – Terzo

Fourth – Quarto

Fifth – Quinto

Sixth – Sesto

Seventh – Settimo

Eighth – Ottavo

Ninth – Nono

Tenth – Decimo

To obtain most of the other Italian ordinal numbers, it is sufficient to insert "-esimo" at the end of the cardinal number.

Some examples:

Ventuno – Ventun**esimo** (21st)

Trentacinque – Trentacinqu**esimo** (35th)

Diciassette – Diciassett**esimo** (17th)

Unlike the English ordinal numbers, however, the Italian ones are used very rarely.

While ordinal numbers are used in English calendars, cardinal numbers are used in Italian ones.

Here's how the date looks:

The **fifteenth** of December

Il **quindici** dicembre.

Curiously, only the first day of the month is called "Primo" (First), while for all others the normal numbers are used (sometimes the last day of the month is called "Ultimo" (Last)).

For this reason, you will very rarely use ordinal numbers, but it is still good to know them.

One of the few cases in which these numbers are used is when talk about children, to explain which one was born before or after.

In these cases, a word consisting of the ordinal number and the word "genito" (born) is used:

Primogenito

Secondogenito

"Primogenito" therefore literally means "Firstborn".

Money in Italy

Speaking of numbers in Italy, a small paragraph relating to money in this country is included. It is especially useful for those who come from a country that has a different currency than the Euro, such as England (pound) or the United States (dollar).

In fact, as just mentioned, Italy does not have its own currency but uses the single European currency: The Euro.

The currency's value varies continuously over time and during history. It is usually found somewhere between the US dollar and the British pound regarding its purchasing power.

While traveling in Italy, you could find yourself using this currency with cents and banknotes.

The cents are made of eight types, although the use of three of these is starting to be reduced more and more throughout the country.

They are:

1 centesimo (0,01)

2 centesimi (0,02)

5 centesimi (0,05)

10 centesimi (0,10)

20 centesimi (0,20)

50 centesimi (0,50)

1 euro (1,00)

2 euro (2,00)

On the other hand, the banknotes are divided into seven different denominations:

5 euro (5,00)

10 euro (10,00)

20 euro (20,00)

50 euro (50,00)

100 euro (100,00)

200 euro (200,00)

500 euro (500,00)

It is good to know that before implementing the Euro, the old national currency was called "Lira". Its value was clearly inflated, to the point that, at the time of the change, with €500 you could get 1 Million Lire.

This is why, since Italy implemented the Euro, many people are said to be unhappy about this decision that, according to them, has doubled the costs and halved the revenues.

The Lira, although not used anymore, still plays a huge role in contemporary Italian culture, as many people still remember it with nostalgia and expressions that are still in the daily spoken language.

It is not so uncommon to hear Italian people complaining about their economic situations with the expression:

"Non ho una lira." – "*I don't have a lira.*"

Before moving on to the final part of this chapter, let's try to insert the various types of numbers into a simulated conversation. This way, you can review how these words are used and learn through conversations in Italian:

A: "Buongiorno, vorrei due biglietti per il treno per Firenze."

A: "Good morning, I would like two tickets for the train to Florence."

B: "Ecco a lei; le conviene sbrigarsi: il treno arriva tra cinque minuti.

B: *"Here you are; you should hurry: the train arrives in five minutes."*

A: "Grazie, quanto le devo?"

A: "Thank you, how much do I owe you?"

B: "Sono quindici euro e trenta centesimi."   B: *"It's fifteen euros and thirty cents."*

A: "Accidenti! Non ho una lira! Posso pagare con la carta di credito?"

A: "Damn! I don't have a lira! Can I pay with a credit card?"

B: "Certo, non è il primo cliente con questo problema oggi…"

   B: *"Of course, you are not the first customer with this problem today…"*

A: "Grazie. Arrivederci!"   A: *"Thank you. Goodbye!"*

B: "Arrivederci!"   B: *"Goodbye!"*

Let's try to see what is interesting in this dialogue. First of all, numbers are widely used. It starts with the customer asking for two tickets to go to Florence. Then it turns out that the train would arrive in five minutes, and costs fifteen euros and thirty cents.

In the end, you also know the way to say "I don't have a lira," so you can see how much is used in spoken Italian.

Finally, an ordinal number was used: the seller said that the customer is not the "primo" (first) to pay with the card.

The conversation you just followed represents a normal exchange between two people. It is easy to understand how knowing the numbers in a given language is important, as they are your key to understanding time, paying, and much more.

To sum up:

   - Numbers from 0 to 10 have names to learn.

   - Numbers from 11 to 19 gain the suffix (or the prefix) -dici that specify the obtained ten.

   - From number 20 onwards, you need to add the minor number next to the ten.

   - The number 100 is indicated with the word "Cento". To indicate all subsequent hundreds, simply enter the corresponding number first (example: **Due**cento).

   - The number 1,000 is indicated with the word "Mille". In this case, to indicate all the next thousands, it is necessary to insert the corresponding number before and change "Mille" into "Mila" (Es. **Tre**mila).

- Italy uses a time system based on twenty-four hours, but the twelve-hour division is also accepted. For the latter, it is necessary to specify what moment of the day it refers to, stating whether it is morning, afternoon, evening, or night.

- The ordinal numbers are used, usually, to indicate an order of arrival, that is why their use is limited compared to cardinal numbers.

- The Italian currency is the Euro, although there is still some nostalgia towards the old currency (the Lira) that keeps occurring in daily spoken expressions.

Giorni, Mesi e Anni (Days, Months and Years)

The days of the week and months of the year are a necessary field to know when it comes to learning Italian. Moreover, luckily, the months' names are very similar to each other—having the same origin in both English and Italian.

In the next section, you will start from the months and then examine the days of the week—since they have different names compared to the English ones.

I mesi dell'anno (The months of the year)

The calendar used in both English-speaking countries and Italy is the same:

Gennaio	January
Febbraio	February
Marzo	March
Aprile	April
Maggio	May
Giugno	June
Luglio	July
Agosto	August
Settembre	September
Ottobre	October
Novembre	November
Dicembre	December

As you can see, there are small differences in the phonetics of both languages, but they still remain extremely intuitive.

For example, even before translating the list into English, you would have no trouble recognizing which month was "Settembre".

Unfortunately, for the days of the week, it is not so easy.

I giorni della settimana (The days of the week)

The days of the week are taken from celestial bodies and the deities of the country where the language was developed.

While, in Italian, you could find names taken from the Latin deities, in English, the names come directly from Norse gods.

Let's see all of them with their origins:

Lunedì (Luna)	Monday (Moon)
Martedì (Marte)	Tuesday (Tyr)
Mercoledì (Mercurio)	Wednesday (Woden)
Giovedì (Giove)	Thursday (Thor)
Venerdì (Venere)	Friday (Frigg)
Sabato (Saturno)	Saturday (Saturn)
Domenica	Sunday (Sun)

Domenica had the same meaning as in English. In the past, Domenica was called, in Latin, *dies solis*, the day of the sun. With Christianity's influence, it then became *die domini*, the day of the Lord.

Also, here are some day-related words:

Oggi	Today
Ieri	Yesterday
Domani	Tomorrow
Dopodomani	The day after tomorrow
Settimana	Week
Fine settimana	Weekend

| Mese | Month |
| Anno | Year |

Greetings

As with every language, the Italian greetings play a fundamental role in your interactions with every Italian person you meet. A correct greeting is your best calling card, and the first step that will decide the direction your conversation will take.

This section of the guide is extremely mnemonic, as it is simply a matter of remembering what greeting should be used in a certain context. For this reason, it is recommended to face it with patience and read the examples provided several times.

Let's start with the most used greetings, "Buongiorno" and "Buonasera". The more generic "Greetings", which, in Italian, is translated as "Salve", is not so commonly used and is often considered outdated in a more natural conversation. For this reason, it is quite easy to understand how to start a conversation based on the time of the day.

Buongiorno, buon pomeriggio, and buonasera.

Learning how to use these greetings is the best way to interact correctly with any person, both in informal and formal environments. "Buongiorno" (Good morning) is used in almost every context, but overall greetings change throughout the day.

"Buongiorno" (Good morning) is used from the early hours of the day to noon;

"Buon pomeriggio" (Good evening) is used from one in the afternoon to five/six in the afternoon; "Buonasera" (Good evening) is used from six in the afternoon onwards; and

"Buonanotte" (Good night) is mostly used to greet someone before going to bed.

A piece of trivia: The word "Buongiorno" has also become famous in the world thanks to the not very natural interpretation of the actor Brad Pitt in the movie *Inglourious Basterds*. The actor greets the Nazi character Hans Landa with "Buongiorno," but he actually used the wrong term—he should have used "Buonasera" since the whole scene is set during the evening.

Now, let's take a look at some greeting examples using the three terms listed above:

Buongiorno, posso avere un caffè?

Good morning, can I have some coffee?

Buon pomeriggio, abbiamo appena finito di pranzare.

Good afternoon, we have just finished lunch.

Buonasera, vorrei un biglietto per Bastardi senza Gloria.

Good evening, I would like a ticket for Inglourious Basterds.

Buonanotte; a domani!

Good night; *see you tomorrow!*

As you can see, these types of greetings are perfect for every context, like with a bartender you just met at the bar or with a friend at the cinema. Even in the workplace and with people with different or higher roles, these kinds of greetings still remain appropriate.

The same cannot be said for one of the most famous greetings in the world: "Ciao", as you will see later.

It is important to notice that the greetings related to the time of the day just talked about can only be used at the beginning of a conversation. Greet a person who is about to leave using "Buongiorno" is incorrect; instead, it is possible to use a similar form that expresses a wish.

In this case, two options are available:

Buona giornata!

Have a nice day!

and

Buona serata!

Have a nice evening!

It is quite easy to understand which of the two terms should be used based on the time of day.

Lastly, although "Buongiorno" is not used at the end of a conversation, it is often used as the only greeting in meeting a person passing through. If you want to briefly greet a person (like on the street, in the office or at school), a simple "Buongiorno", maybe also combined with a smile, is the best and fastest way to convey your greeting.

Ciao and Salve

"Ciao" is one of the most popular Italian greetings, although often used differently than its original meaning.

While greetings like "Buongiorno" and "Buonasera" are only used at the beginning of a conversation, "Ciao" can be used freely, both at the beginning and end of a conversation. "Ciao" remains the same regardless of the time of day, making it the easiest Italian greeting to learn and use.

Despite this, "Ciao" is an informal greeting and can only be used with people you have certain confidence with; otherwise, you risk being disrespectful to others.

A "Ciao" variant already seen is "Salve". It is a more effective and correct greeting that can be used in more formal environments—although it is still recommended to use the greetings above and those related to the times of the day as well.

Let's see a couple of examples with "Ciao" and "Salve":

Ciao, come stai?

Hi, how are you?

Salve, sono qui per un colloquio di lavoro.

Hello, I'm here for a job interview.

Remember: "Hello" cannot be used with people you do not know or whom you are not close enough to allow such an informal greeting.

How to end a conversation

Although this topic has already been examined, there are other ways to end a conversation.

At the end of an informal discussion, "**Ciao**" can be used safely to greet a friend/acquaintance who is leaving. Greeting a person with only "Ciao", however, could turn out to be incomplete if not accompanied by a construction like:

Ciao, alla prossima!

Goodbye, see you soon!

Ciao, ci vediamo presto!

Goodbye, see you soon!

Overall, you can just use "Ciao" as a greeting, but adding a sentence that expresses the wish to see the other person again is a really polite way to end a conversation.

Of course, even in this case, you are talking about informal environments: a friend or acquaintance can both be greeted in this way, but not a stranger or employer. For the latter, a greeting based on the time of the day, like "Buona giornata", turns out to be the best and most polite option.

A very well-known greeting for ending a conversation is also "**Arrivederci**" (See you later), which is slightly less informal than "Ciao" and is the same as "**Ciao**, ci vediamo presto".

Its use is therefore limited only to all those people you know you will meet again. It can, however, also be used in formal environments, as it is more than right to greet a professor or work colleague you will meet again in the future.

If "Arrivederci" can only be used with people you know you will meet again, there is a greeting that is destined for those people you will never meet again: "Addio", a greeting that is rarely used— mostly because of its seriousness that implies you will never meet the person in question again.

"Addio" is especially used for paying respects to a dead person, which means it is the last *ever* greeting towards a person—that is why it is also uncommon in daily Italian language.

Phone greetings

Speaking of greetings at the beginning and end of conversations, you should not ignore telephone calls, an omnipresent element in everyday life. So, how do Italians start and end a phone call?

Luckily, in this case, it is easy to understand how to answer the phone correctly: usually, an Italian who receives a phone call will answer by saying: "**Pronto?**" Its literal translation from Italian to English would be like "Ready?" but it does not make sense as it has no real meaning in Italian either.

The Italian "Pronto?" means, more or less, "Who is it?", and the complete construction is often made of just the sentence: "Hello, who is it?"

While those who receive the call will start the conversation with "Pronto?", the caller will instead interact as if they are both standing in front of each other—so by normally greeting with "Buongiorno/Buona sera/Ciao..." and, of course, telling them who they are.

Even the greetings at the end are the same as a normal conversation, so let's see an example of a typical Italian phone call. In the call, **A** (Andrea), a boy, is calling his girlfriend, **L** (Ljuba), to invite her out to dinner.

A little trivia: Unlike other countries, in Italy, "Andrea" is a mostly male name.

L: "Pronto?"

L: "Hello?"

A: "Ciao, Ljuba, come stai?"

A: "Hi, Ljuba, how are you?"

L: "Andrea! Tutto bene, tu?"

L: "Andrea! All good, how about you?"

A: "Bene. Ti va di andare a mangiare una pizza stasera?"

A: "I'm fine. Do you want to go eat a pizza tonight?

L: "Volentieri! A dopo!"

L: "Gladly! See you later!"

A: "A dopo. Ciao!"

A: "See you later. Bye!"

L: "Ciao!"

L: "Bye!"

In the conversation, you can see several aspects being highlighted during this chapter. The phone call started with a "Pronto?" said by Ljuba, who received the phone call.

After the formalities, "Ciao" was used both at the beginning and end of the conversation, as it allowed in an informal conversation.

Below is a more formal telephone conversation in which you will see the appropriate greetings and way of speaking in this particular circumstance.

The conversation is between **P** (Professor), who calls **S** (Student) on the telephone to communicate their final exam grade:

S: "Pronto?"

S: "Hello?"

P: "Buongiorno, signor Rossi, sono il professor Bianchi."

P: "Good morning, Mr. Rossi, I'm Professor Bianchi."

S: "Buongiorno, professore!"

S: "Good morning, professor!"

P: "La chiamo per comunicarle il risultato dell'esame di matematica. Ha preso 30!"

P: "I called to tell you the result of the math exam. You got 30!"

S: "Grazie, professore! È un'ottima notizia!"

S: "Thank you, professor! It's great news!"

P: "Ottimo lavoro; buona giornata."

P: "Well done; good day."

S: "Grazie; buona giornata a lei!"

S: "Thank you; good day to you too!"

This conversation is slightly more difficult than the others, but let's analyze it step by step. First of all, you can see that the call starts in the same way: "Pronto" is not informal or formal, as it is often not possible to know who is calling.

In this case, no "Ciao" is used as in the previous phone call because a formal conversation has been established between the two since the professor's introduction. You, therefore, find greetings like "Buongiorno" and "Buona giornata", as seen earlier.

It is important to notice that a formal environment, as already seen in the previous chapters, requires the third female person "Lei" instead of the second person "Tu". Always remember this sentence construction, as it is typically Italian and does not exist in English.

A little trivia: If your country has a different grading system, you may not understand what "You got 30!" means. In the Italian university system, the grades range from 0 to 30, where 18 is sufficient, and 30 is the highest grade that can be obtained.

Greetings in E-mails and Mail

Although it is rare to write a letter nowadays, it can still happen. While it is not so rare to write e-mails anymore, this is the most used and common way to communicate in formal environments, such as school or work—hence why it is important to know how to behave during the beginning and end of greetings.

Let's start with a simple example: an informal e-mail. You want to write an email to an Italian friend and show them how fluent you are with their mother language.

How should you start the e-mail?

"Ciao" is the correct way to start an e-message since it is addressed to a friend, such as:

Ciao, Marco,

Come stai? È tanto tempo che non ci sentiamo, così ho deciso di scriverti un'email.

[...]

Hi, Marco,

How are you? It's been so long since our last chat, so I decided to write you an email.

[...]

Another way to start an informal e-mail is by using "**Caro/a**", which is similar to the English word "Dear":

Caro, Marco,

Come stai? Ho saputo che hai iniziato un nuovo lavoro; sono felice per te!

[...]

Dear, Marco,

How are you? I have heard that you have started a new job; I am happy for you!

[...]

Of course, the whole discussion changes if you need to write a more formal email, say addressed to a professor or employer. In addition to the e-mail mode and the use of "Lei", as seen recently, even the initial and final greetings are different from an e-mail exchange between two friends.

The best way to start a formal email is to use the right terms to show others respect. For this reason, the word "**Esimio/a**" (distinguished) or "**Spettabile**" (esteemed) are often used, followed by the recipient's name.

To make it clearer, let's look at two examples. In the first one, you will use an email between a student and a professor, while the second will be between a worker and an employer:

Spettabile Professor Bianchi,

Le scrivo per chiederle maggiori informazioni sull'orario della prossima lezione.

Cordialmente,

Andrea Rossi

Esteemed Professor Bianchi,

I am writing to ask you for more information on the timetable for the next lesson.

With regard,

Andrea Rossi

As you can see, just like in any other language, there is an initial formal construction—in this case, "Dear", and a final one to end the email.

In Italian, the most used closures are:

• Cordialmente (Sincerely) – which expresses cordiality and is aimed at concluding the letter with good manners.

• Distinti saluti (Best regards) – in addition to cordiality, it also transmits a kind of detachment and respect towards the other.

As seen in the previous example, the Italian third female person is always mandatory in this case too:

Le *scrivo per chiederle maggiori informazioni [...]*

As stated before and to make it clearer, let's look at an example in a working environment:

Esimio Dottor Favilli,

Con la presente le comunico la mia adesione al seminario di questo fine settimana.

Distinti saluti,

Andrea Rossi

Distinguished Dr. Favilli,

I hereby inform you of my adhesion to this weekend's seminar.

With best regards,

Andrea Rossi

Final Greetings

Here are a couple of common greetings used in daily Italian language and conversations:

Ci vediamo domani – See you tomorrow

Piacere di conoscerti – Nice to meet you

Ci vediamo presto – See you soon

Alla prossima – Until next time

To sum up:

- There are two kinds of greetings. The first one is based on the time of the day and is used in both formal and informal environments (**Buongiorno, Buon pomeriggio,** and **Buona sera**). The second one (**Ciao**) is only used in informal environments but is still not influenced by the time of the day.

- An informal and similar word like "**Ciao**" is "**Salve**"—less used than the first one but still correct in spoken Italian.

- "**Ciao**" can be used both at the beginning and the end of a conversation. "**Salve**" can be only used at the beginning, as like "**Buongiorno**", "**Buon pomeriggio**", and "**Buona sera**".

- To end a conversation with the latter, it is common to use a form of a wish, such as: "**Buona giornata/serata**".

- "**Arrivederci**" is a greeting that can only be used while ending a conversation, and only if it is expected that you will meet the person again.

- "**Addio**" is a greeting used at the end of a conversation and only to people you are sure not to meet again.

- An Italian answering the phone will always say "**Pronto?**", so the rules regarding greetings will follow the same rules as an eye to eye conversation.

- There are several ways to start an e-mail. If it is informal, it's possible to use "**Ciao**" and "**Caro/a**" followed by the recipient's name.

- If the e-mail is a formal one, the names will be "**Spettabile**", "**Esimio**", and "**Gentile**".

- The closure greetings in both letters and e-mails are, usually, "**Cordialmente**" or "**Distinti saluti**".

Frasi Comuni In Italiano (Basic Italian sentences)

Before going too deep into the Italian language, in order to be able to speak about your life, school, and work, let's summarize what you have seen so far. In this chapter, a series of basic Italian sentences are listed that will come in handy.

In this particular case, you will see sentences composed (usually) of one to five words that are included in the basic Italian.

Let's get started with:

Thank you – Grazie

You have already seen how it is possible to express gratitude in Italian and how to apologize. In this chapter, in addition to refreshing your memory on words you have already learned, you will also take a look at more complex constructions. As an example, while "Grazie" expresses gratitude, you may feel so grateful that a simple "Grazie" is not enough.

In English, you would use "Thank you very much", but in Italian?

Thank you very much – Grazie mille

The literal translation of this expression is "Thanks one thousand," which, like many other literally translated sentences, does not make any sense.

"Grazie mille" is the shortened version of "Grazie mille volte", so that would be translated into "Thank you one thousand times."

Some other guides dedicated to learning Italian show an alternative translation, "Grazie tante".

Although the translation is correct, this sentence is often used sarcastically, and for this reason, it is far from a true grateful feeling.

"Grazie mille" is used much more widely in daily spoken Italian.

You're welcome – Prego

For responding to "Grazie", Italian uses the expression "Prego" (literally "I pray") just as "You're welcome" is used in English.

The word "Prego", however, is also used in another context: when you hold the door for someone, or while handing out an object to someone, you can still say, "Prego."

Please – Per favore

"Per favore", just like its English counterpart, is an expression used for asking a courtesy from someone you are talking to. Its literal meaning would be something like "Do me a favor", but, of course, it is simply a common construction in spoken Italian.

There is a variation to this answer: "Per piacere", which has the same meaning (even if it is used, usually, in more informal environments)

Yes – Sì

The definitive positive answer.

No – No

This is probably one of the easiest words to remember, but keep in mind how the letter O is pronounced in Italian rather than in English.

Excuse me?/Pardon me? – Mi scusi?

A cordial expression for asking permission. There is a more informal version used when, for example, you need to walk through a crowded place. In this case, it is said: "Permesso."

I'm sorry – Mi dispiace

The most used word for expressing sorrow. This sentence has already been explained in the dedicated chapter, and that is why it is not going to be examined in depth now. However, it is worth adding that if you are going to show grief over the death of a person to someone, then you must use the word "Condoglianze" (My condolences).

I don't understand – Non capisco

Usually, this sentence is compared to the previous one in order to say sorry for not understanding a certain thing.

I don't speak Italian – Non parlo italiano

A very useful sentence to use at the beginning of your journey through learning Italian. Another good and useful alternative to this is: "Sto imparando l'italiano" (I am learning Italian).

I don't speak Italian very well – Non parlo molto bene l'italiano

As you can see, the Italian language is mostly anticipated by the article. The article can be added in the previous sentence, but only in the case that it can be eliminated to make it shorter.

If this confuses you, always use the article.

Do you speak English? – Parla Inglese?

The third-person singular (Lei parla) is used because it is a sentence often used while talking to a stranger (perhaps for asking directions). If, instead, you are asking it to a friend or family member, you can use the second person: "Parli Inglese?"

Speak slowly, please – Parli piano, per favore

Even in this case, you can apply the same rule as before.

Repeat, please – Ripeta, per favore

The sentence is correct and is the best to use if you have not mastered the language yet. However, it lacks courtesy, so it would be better to put the sentence this way:

Mi scusi, può ripetere? – Excuse me, could you repeat, please?

What's your name? – Come ti chiami?

You already saw both the verb and the names.

How are you? – Come stai?

This is the most basic sentence to ask about someone's health. If you want to ask how life is going or just as a courtesy to someone, you can use the sentence: "Come va?" instead.

In addition to these basic sentences, there are a variety of idioms and proverbs typical of the Italian language that you might not understand if you have not heard them before. For this reason, in the last chapters of the book, this specific topic will be of focus, offering you the third and also the last point of in-depth analysis of Italian words right after the vocabulary and this one dedicated to basic sentences.

About Me

After seeing the most common use of many Italian expressions, it is time to start talking about you. The ability to introduce yourself and make yourself known is essential in every language: people want to know who you are before opening themselves up to you.

This chapter will focus on personal information and how it is possible to talk about yourself and ask others something.

The Name

Naturally, you will have to introduce yourself once you arrive in Italy. In Italian, there are two ways of saying one's name.

The first is the most literal but least smooth way to do it and is also the easiest to use for an English speaker since it is the direct translation of the English construction.

In English, you would present yourself as:

"My name is Paolo."

This sentence makes perfect sense in Italian as well, and it is expressed by:

"Il mio nome è Paolo."

Let's analyze each word of the sentence:

Il (as you saw in the first chapters, the article is essential in Italian)

Mio (first-person possessive pronoun, the equivalent of "my")

Nome (noun, direct translation of "name")

È (the verb essere – "to be", third-person singular and translation of "is")

Paolo (name)

Clear, right? Actually, this is a very technical construction, and you will hardly hear an Italian saying their name in this way. Usually, only three words are used in Italian:

"Mi chiamo Paolo."

The direct translation of this sentence would be: "I call myself Paolo", but it doesn't make any sense.

Let's reanalyze the sentence:

Mi (third-person singular, a reflexive pronoun, and the direct translation of "myself")

Chiamo (verb, first-person singular of verb "chiamare" – "to call")

Paolo (name)

The first construction you have read is also correct, but a shorter version and construction often replace it:

"Sono Paolo."

In this case, there are only two words:

Io (implied subject, typical in Italy as seen earlier – "I")

Sono (the verb "to be", first-person singular – "am")

Paolo (name)

The last name doesn't usually follow any specific rules, and it is introduced with the name while it's hardly used in a conversation. Curiously, based on different Italy's regions, the last name can replace the name during a conversation, and the article precedes it.

Example:

Paolo Bianchi

Usual case – "Lui è **Paolo**" (using the name)

Regional case – "Lui è **il Bianchi**" (using the last name)

Do not worry too much about this variation, though, because it is really informal and restricted to certain Italian regions.

However, while introducing yourself, you must remember another word: "Piacere". This word is the short version of "Piacere di conoscerti" (Nice to meet you) and is always used during the first meeting between two people.

When this pronoun is used, the sentence could be shortened even more to using only the name.

Instead of:

"Sono Paolo."

You will get:

"Piacere, Paolo."

Let's look at a more focused example to understand better what is explained above.

Example of Paolo and Luca who are talking while meeting for the first time:

Paolo: "Ciao, io sono Paolo."

Paolo: "Hi, I'm Paolo."

Luca: "Ciao, Paolo, io sono Luca."

Luca: "Hi, Paolo, I'm Luca."

The same interactions while using "Piacere di conoscerti":

Paolo: "Ciao, io sono Paolo."

Paolo: "Hi, I'm Paolo."

Luca: "Piacere di conoscerti, Luca."

Luca: "Nice to meet you, Luca."

However, as stated before, the sentence "Piacere di conoscerti" is shortened to "Piacere" most of the time:

Paolo: "Ciao, io sono Paolo."

Paolo: "Hi, I'm Paolo."

Luca: "Piacere, Luca."

Luca: "Nice ~~to meet you~~, Luca."

It is implied that during this conversation, both gave each other a handshake, which is a current gesture during first meetings in Italy.

The sentences to remember related to this context are:

- *"Come ti chiami?" – "What's your name?"*
- *"Qual è il tuo cognome?" – "What's your last name?"*

I'm From...

Another common piece of information to provide while introducing yourself is your home country, and

there are different ways to say this. One is the almost direct translation from English: "I am from..."; although there are some differences.

In Italian, the sentence used is:

"Sono di Roma."

Let's reexamine the sentence word by word:

Io *(implied subject – "I")*

Sono *(verb to be, first-person singular – "am")*

Di *(preposition, belonging complement – "of")*

Roma *(city)*

In the Italian sentence, the city where they are from is not specified, like in the English sentence; rather, it is specified as belonging to that city, as like they were part of it.

This is the most common form to find during an introduction. Between these, you find a similar sentence to the English one:

"Vengo da Roma." – I come from Rome (literal translation).

"Sono nato a Roma." – I was born in Rome.

Eventually, it is common to get a reply with an adjective after asking about the birthplace. So, instead of saying:

"Io sono di Roma." *– I am of Rome.*

They could say:

"Sono romano." *– I am Roman.*

While talking about your home country, another very common and useful word is the English translation of "mother tongue". As in English, the Italian word indicates being perfectly fluent in a certain language, so that means a literal translation.

The Italian word is "madrelingua" where "madre" means "mother" and "lingua" means "tongue". The only difference between Italian and English is that, in the first case, the words are combined, while in English, they are not.

I Live In...

You have seen the past explored; now, it is necessary to talk about the present, and then explain where your current home is. Before seeing the various sentences, it is worth highlighting that, in Italian, two words can indicate the act of "living somewhere".

The first one is the verb "to live", as is the same in English. The sentence is:

"I live in Rome."

And the literal translation is:

"Io vivo a Roma."

The literal English translation may be helpful in order to use the verb "to live" as it is perfectly acceptable in spoken Italian.

In Italian, however, you will often hear another term that has the same meaning: "Abitare".

While "Vivere" overall means "Being alive", and its meaning is used within the context of "Living in a place", "Abitare" only means "Living in one place". For this reason, it is a more precise term than "Vivere", but it is not necessarily the only correct way to use it.

That is why the sentence:

"I live in Rome."

Can be translated into:

"Io vivo a Roma."

And also as:

"Io abito a Roma."

And both options listed above are correct.

The sentence changes slightly if, instead of saying only the city, you will mention the state or the address where you are staying. Nonetheless, in both cases, you will not have to use the preposition "a" but the "in" preposition.

Here are some direct examples:

I live in Rome – Io vivo **a** Roma

I live in Italy – Io vivo **in** Italia

I live in Giovanni Gianni street, 43 – Io vivo **in** Via Giovanni Gianni, 43

This is a little difference that it is useful to remember in order to speak Italian correctly.

Pet

Another important aspect of many people's lives, other than being a great conversation topic, is pets. Many people have a dog or a cat, and how can you talk about them? First of all, it is worth knowing the different animals' names.

Here are some examples:

- Dog   –   Cane
- Cat   –   Gatto
- Mouse   –   Topo
- Snake   –   Serpente
- Hamster   –   Criceto
- Bunny   –   Coniglio
- Parrot   –   Pappagallo
- Ferret   –   Furetto
- Fish   –   Pesce
- Goldfish   –   Pesce rosso

A little trivia: "Goldfish" is translated as "Pesce rosso", which literally means "Red fish".

As previously mentioned, there is not a neutral gender in Italian, so that is why when you are talking about your pets, you will have to refer to them with their gender.

I'm Going Out Tonight

During previous chapters and sections, there were many examples of how to correctly behave in a working environment. However, it is also true that there is more to life than just work!

Let's look at some words that can be useful while talking about enjoyable events:

- Cinema – Cinema

The word is the same as in Italian, but the pronunciation is different. The first part, "Ci-", is pronounced like the "Ch-" in the English word "Cheetah".

- Restaurant   –   Ristorante
- Pizzeria   –   Pizzeria
- Bar   –   Bar
- Pub   –   Pub

As you can see, luckily, many Italian and English words have been influenced by each other—that is why they are the same or easy to remember.

When referring to nights out, the Italian verb for that is the same as the English language: "Uscire" (to go out), and in this case, it is quite easy to use too.

Curiously, the verb "Prendere" is also similar to the English "Pick up"—although the literal meaning is slightly different, the application is the same.

Let's see some sentences that use both verbs:

*Stasera **esci**? – Are you **going out** tonight?*

*Ti passo **a prendere** alle sei. – **I'll pick** you up at six.*

In the second sentence, it is important to notice two things. The first is the verbal form application in this sentence: even if you are talking about the future, and, in English, it uses "will" for the same purpose, in Italian, it can be used in a very natural way—in the present instead.

This, of course, is if you are talking about a very close present.

If you are talking about months instead:

Ti passerò a prendere il dieci gennaio. – I'll pick you up on January 10.

Another thing that could be noticed in the example is that, even though the verbal form is similar, the Italian verb "Prendere" is always combined with another verb like "Passare" (to pass) or "Venire" (to come).

If we recheck the sentence:

Ti passo a prendere alle sei.

And split it word for word:

Io (sentence implied subject – "I")

Ti (second-person singular pronoun – "You")

Passo (first-person singular of the verb "Passare" – "Pass")

A prendere (the infinitive verb "Prendere" – "to pick up")

Alle sei (time – "at six")

The sentence could be a little confusing because of the pronoun's position "Ti", but as you have already seen in the chapter about this sentence's part, the pronoun can be moved to many points of the sentence.

It can be moved next to the verb (but the sentence would be too complex):

*(Io) passo a prendere **te** alle sei. – I'll pass to pick you up at six.*

Although written like this, it is much similar to the English structure and is too forced/unnatural.

The most used version in spoken Italian is the one united with the verb itself:

*(Io) passo a prende**rti** alle sei.*

Let's see some useful sentences for planning a night out:

- Do you want to go out with me? – **Ti va di uscire con me?**
- Do you want to go to the cinema tonight? – **Vuoi andare al cinema stasera?**

Remember that in the informal environments, usually, you can reduce everything to just a few simple words. This subject cannot be explained too much in this guide because these shortcuts are based on how much you could be familiar with a person, but you can still say:

Pizza, stasera? – Pizza, tonight?

The sentence, without verbs and subjects, still makes sense in a familiar environment—that is why, as much as it is important to learn more words and be fluent in Italian, remember that *experience* is really helpful to overcome difficult times while learning the language.

The Birthday

This is a topic discussed often but shows differences between English and Italian.

The most important difference is the word used to point to the moment of birth, which is a very subtle difference:

I was born on 21 April 1992

Io sono nato il 21 Aprile 1992

The main difference between the two verbs, both English and Italian, is that the English one is used as a passive form. "I was born" states that, in that certain moment or even place, *I* have been born from my mother.

In Italian, however, the verb shows a more active form and states the birth itself as an action.

It is not so important when it comes to learning Italian, but still, it is an interesting curiosity worth knowing.

For this reason, the literal translation is almost used (as you can see from the number of words) from the English.

If you want to say just the birthday instead, it will be enough to say:

My birthday is April 21

Il mio compleanno è il 21 Aprile

There is still a little difference compared to English while saying your age.

In English, there are usually two different ways:

I'm twenty-seven

or

I'm twenty-seven years old.

In Italian, there is a word in the middle of the two. It is not enough to say only the number; it has to come with the word "anni" (years):

Io ho ventisette anni

It must be noticed that the verb "to have", in Italian, "Io ho" (I have) is used, while in English, the verb "to be", "I'm/ I am" is used.

The classic birthday song has the same origins, both in the English and Italian versions, so you are talking about a literal translation:

Happy birthday to you

Happy birthday to you

Happy birthday dear [NAME]

Happy birthday to you

«Tanti auguri a te

tanti auguri a te

tanti auguri a [NOME]

tanti auguri a te»

A little trivia: During a birthday, you may hear the sentence "Cento di questi giorni" (one hundred of these days). This sentence is a wish of long life and is very common among Italian traditions: wishing for hundreds of these days (birthdays), is wishing for many other hundreds of years of life to the guest of honor.

There is another word that is very common while talking about birthdays: the verb "Compiere" (to do), which is used to communicate the day of birth in an active form.

For example:

Oggi compio gli anni.

And its literal translation is:

Today I do my years.

Which does make sense.

The translation based on that meaning is:

Oggi è il mio compleanno.

It may be way more complicated to understand than other literal translations you have already seen, but you could hear this construction while talking to an Italian person.

Now, let's take a step back and look at a conversation that uses the information provided in this chapter:

A: **"Buongiorno. Sto cercando un libro per il mio compleanno."**

A: "Good morning. I'm looking for a book for my birthday."

B: **"Buongiorno. Vediamo se posso aiutarla. Come si chiama?"**

B: "Hello. Let's see if I can help you. What's the name?"

A: **"Si chiama... "Il Sentiero dei Nidi di Ragno", di Italo Calvino."**

A: "It's called ... *The Path of the Spider's Nest*, by Italo Calvino."

B: **"Intendevo lei: come si chiama?"**

B: "I meant you: what's your name?"

A: **"Mi scusi. Mi chiamo Antonio, e lei?"**

A: "Sorry. My name is Antonio, and you?"

B: **"Barbara... Vediamo di trovare questo libro..."**

B: "Barbara ... Let's find this book ..."

A: **"Grazie. Vengo da un paesino, e non sono abituato a queste librerie gigantesche!"**

A: "Thanks. I'm from a small town, and I'm not used to these gigantic bookstores!"

B: **"E come facevi a leggere?"**

B: "And how did you read?"

A: **"Avevo qualche libro, ma il mio coniglio se li è mangiati."**

A: "I had some books, but my rabbit ate them."

B: **"Davvero? Allora questo è un regalo per il suo coniglio!"**

B: "Really? Then this is a gift for your rabbit!"

A: **"No, oggi è il mio compleanno; il suo è ancora lontano!"**

A: "No, today is my birthday; his birthday is still far away!"

To sum up:

- Saying your name in Italian uses two different verbal forms, such as the verb "essere" (to be) and the verb "chiamare" (to call).
- Stating your home country also uses two different verbal forms: the verb "essere" (to be), which states belonging to a certain city or nation, and the verb "venire" (to come).
- Stating where you currently live uses the verb "vivere" (to live) or the more specific verb "abitare".
- Speaking about a very near future uses the present instead of the future.
- Speaking about birth uses the passive verb in English, while in Italian, it uses an active verbal form.

Leisure and Art

It is not possible not to talk about this topic as Italy offers so much in the way of art and entertainment. Life is not just made up of work and study—as important as these are. For this reason, you will now learn some typical phrases that can be used in this context.

Cinema and Television

One of the most common phrases about cinema is:

"Il mio film preferito è..." – "My favorite movie is..."

As you can see, the construction of the sentence is very similar, both in English and in Italian, so what is there to know about the world of cinema, as far as Italy is concerned?

• The theaters – Despite its profound theatrical history, the average Italian rarely goes to the theater to see shows, which is why many theaters are also used as cinemas. The term "Teatro" (theater), therefore, indicates the place where it is usually possible to watch live comedies and tragedies.

• Cinema – You have already seen in previous chapters how the word "Cinema" is pronounced. Speaking of cinema, you can also hear the word "Multisala" (Multiplex), which is a particular type of cinema in which different films are projected in different rooms at the same time.

When talking about films with an Italian person, it might surprise you to discover that doubling the films that come from abroad is a fundamental part of Italian culture.

Watching a film in the original language, in fact, is a custom that has caught on only in the last few years—thanks to the advent of the internet—, but despite this, many Italians watch movies only if they have been translated and dubbed in their language.

The Italian dubbing school is among the best in the world and is a source of pride for many enthusiasts in the sector. For this reason, the realization that an Italian has of a movie is fundamentally different from one of the spectators in the original country of that film—an aspect to take into consideration when you talk about movies.

Another question linked to the world of cinema is:

"Chi è il tuo attore preferito?" – "Who is your favorite actor?"

And a shared phrase:

"Era un film bellissimo; mi sono commosso/a" – "It was a great movie; I was moved."

Knowing that all the movies that are broadcast in Italy have been redubbed in Italian could upset you, but don't worry—there is good news in this regard.

Firstly, in doing so, you have at your disposal a huge number of films in Italian that you can use as material to improve your knowledge and pronunciation of the language. Almost all movies of big productions enjoy a masterful dubbing, so try searching for your favorite dubbed movie in Italian.

Secondly, if you are in Italy and wish to see a film in the original language, always remember that many multiplexes offer screenings in the original language.

Let's see how you can ask about it:

"Il film con Tom Hanks è in Inglese?" – "Is the movie with Tom Hanks in English?"

Often it will be enough to ask directly at the cinema box (or you can y search on the internet).

Other phrases that can be useful in this context:

"L'ho già visto" – "I've already seen it."

"È sottotitolato in Inglese?" – "Is it subtitled in English?"

"Ci sarà un intervallo?" – "Will there be an interval?

The final question can already be answered in this guide: most Italian cinemas have removed the interval from their projections, even if it is not a written rule.

Other words to know about this topic:

Film	–	Movie
Attore	–	Actor
Attrice	–	Actress
Regista	–	Movie director
Sceneggiatore	–	Screenwriter
Commedia	–	Comedy
Tragedia	–	Tragedy
Sottotitoli	–	Subtitles
La prima	–	Premiere

In this case, the Italian term literally means "The first" and refers to the first screening of the film in question.

Fila	–	Queue
Corto	–	Short film
Fine	–	The end

Trama –   Plot

To these words are also added all those that are inherent to the genre of the film, such as:

Azione	–	Action
Orrore/Paura	–	Horror
Guerra	–	War
Romantico/D'amore	–	Romantic/Love
Fantascienza	–	Science fiction

And many other words, even more specific about this world. Maybe you would like to express an opinion after seeing the movie.

First, is the standard phrase:

"Il film era…" – "The movie was…"

At this point, you can add what you thought of the movie while watching it. Here are some common terms:

Avvincente	–	Gripping
Veloce	–	Fast-moving
Noioso	–	Boring
Terribile	–	Awful
Pauroso	–	Scary
Triste	–	Sad
Brutto	–	Bad

But, of course, art is not limited to just the big screen. There are many other areas where you can practice your Italian.

La Musica / The Music

Music often gets to us on a personal level, as many people usually play a musical instrument. For this reason, it is possible to talk about this topic from different points of view.

From a listener's point of view, a common question is:

- **Ti piace la musica?** – Do you like music?

If you were asked this question, the answers you could give are:

- **Mi piace la musica.** – I like music.
- **Non mi piace la musica.** – I don't like music.

If the topic develops further, it is possible to go into more detail by asking what kind of music a person likes to listen to. Fortunately, at least concerning the musical genres born in countries beyond the Alps, the name remains the same.

Here are some direct examples to consolidate the concept:

Musica Pop   –   Pop Music

Musica Rock   –   Rock Music

Musica Metal –   Metal Music

And so on.

The two questions generally asked about music are:

-        **Chi è il tuo cantante preferito?** – Who's your favorite singer?
-        **Qual è la tua band preferita?** – What is your favorite band?

You will discover that Italians, while carrying a famous musical tradition, greatly appreciate foreign music, and, in this case, you don't have to worry about the songs being translated.

The field of music, in this sense, has remained untainted.

However, if your passion for music has led you to play a musical instrument, you may want to know what the various instruments are called:

Chitarra   –   Guitar

Pianoforte   –   Piano

Violino	–	Violin
Batteria	–	Drums
Flauto	–	Flute
Basso	–	Bass
Tromba	–	Trumpet

Curiously, while the names of some instruments remain similar both in English and in Italian (as in the case of the violin), there are other instruments whose name is very different from the English version.

An example is "Batteria" (drums) whose name literally indicates the electric battery used, for example, in machines.

La Pittura e La Scultura / Painting and Sculpture

Painting in Italy is a fundamental part of its past, thanks to the masterpieces born before, during, and after the Renaissance.

There is a reason why Italy is considered one of the countries of art par excellence, and painting and sculpture (of which will be discussed shortly) play a fundamental role in this artistic tradition.

Let's look at some useful phrases and terms to use in this context:

"Dove è il museo più vicino?" – "Where is the closest museum?"

"Mi piace quel pittore!" – "I like that painter!"

"Voglio andare a vedere quella mostra." – "I want to go see that exhibition."

Even more important is to know all the terms that can be used within these sentences. Here are the most common words when speaking of an artistic environment:

Il quadro	–	The painting
Il pittore	–	The painter
L'affresco	–	Fresco

Il pennello	–	Brush
La mostra	–	Exhibition
Il Rinascimento	–	The Renaissance
Il Medio Evo	–	Middle Ages
La scultura	–	Sculpture
La galleria	–	Gallery
Asta	–	Auction
Guida	–	Guide

Let's imagine you are at an exhibition. The questions that might be useful to know are:

"Posso scattare una fotografia al quadro?" – "Can I take a picture of the painting?"

This is a more than legitimate question to learn, as in many galleries, it is forbidden to take photographs of the works on display—even more so if the flash is used during photography, so it is important also to ask:

"Posso usare il flash?" – "Can I use the flash?"

Fortunately, as far as these small details are concerned, if you are visiting a museum or exhibition, it will always be specified on various signs.

To conclude this chapter, let's look at a conversation between two people with an artistic theme, where you will make extensive use of the sentences you have seen so far and the specific terms of this field:

A)   **"Che facciamo questa sera?"**
A) "What are we going to do tonight?"
B)   **"Non saprei. Hai qualche idea?"**
B) "I don't know. Do you have any ideas?"
A)   **"Potremmo andare al cinema. Stasera c'è quel nuovo film..."**

A) *"We could go to the cinema. Tonight there is that new movie…"*

B)   **"Quale? Quello con Will Smith come protagonista?"**

B) *"What? The one with Will Smith as the protagonist?"*

A)   **"No, il film animato scritto da Spielberg."**

A) *"No, the animated movie written by Spielberg."*

B)   **"Ah, no. L'ho già visto."**

B) *"Ah, no. I have already seen it."*

A)   **"Okay, che ne dici di andare ad ascoltareun gruppo musicale?"**

A) "Okay, how about going to listen to a band?"

B)   **"Quale gruppo?"**

B) "Which band?"

A)   **"Si chiamano Tenacious B. Li conosci?"**

A) "They are called Tenacious B. Do you know them?"

B)   **"Sì, ma non abbiamo i biglietti!"**

B) "Yes, but we don't have the tickets!"

A)   **"Hai ragione… Che ne dici di andare a vedere la mostra di Magritte allora?"**

A) "You're right… How about going to see Magritte's exhibition then?"

B)   **"Un'esibizione con i suoi quadri? Certo!"**

B) "An exhibition with his paintings? Sure!"

As you can see, it is quite simple to communicate in Italian about art: all you have to do is remember the correct words!

To sum up:

- In the Italian tradition, all foreign films (or at least those that reach Italian soil) are dubbed by overwriting the original language. Although it is, therefore, more difficult to watch a film in English in an Italian cinema, this also gives you a great opportunity to learn Italian by watching your favorite movies redubbed in the language.

Indicazioni (Directions)

While visiting Italy for the first time, it is important to know how to move around and ask for directions to visit places. To do this, it is good to know the typical expressions and how the road system works.

Unlike other countries in the world, the so-called neighborhoods in Italy are quite uncommon. Each city or town is divided into "Vie" (Streets) and "Piazze" (Town Squares), with a further subdivision for each building within it. Because of this, there are the "Numeri civici" (house numbers) to identify the various buildings in a certain city area.

In an Italian "via", usually, even numbers and odd numbers are placed on buildings in front of each other (so not on the same line) and in numerical order.

Here's an example: while entering "Via San Marco", you find on your left the street number 1, and on the right the street number 2. Continuing along the road, then, on the left, you see the numbers 3, 5, 7, 9, 11, 13... while on the right, you see the numbers 4, 6, 8, 10, 12, 14... and so on. Naturally, the order of the numbers can be increasing or decreasing, based on the direction from which you arrive.

Sometimes, these numbers may have a further division based on letters, so it is possible to find "numeri civici" like 1A, 1B, 1C and so on.

These numbers are also present in "Piazze" and the "Periferia" (suburbs area).

Before seeing some useful sentences to help you reach your destination, you have to learn how to ask information for reaching that destination. All the nouns in the vocabulary section have also been reported to let you check them quickly in the future.

Come Chiedere Informazioni? (How To Ask For Directions?)

If you want to arrive at a certain destination, you should ask directions correctly. In this section, you will also see some places of interest, but for now, let's start with the basic questions.

If you already know where to go, you should ask:

"Mi scusi. Sto cercando il Duomo, può aiutarmi?"

"Excuse me. I'm looking for the Duomo, can you help me?"

Let's analyze this sentence word by word:

Mi Scusi – It is easy to remember since it sounds like a reversed *Excuse me*. Remember always to use the third-person feminine with a person you do not know.

(Io) – Implied subject, *I*

Sto cercando – *am looking for*

Il Duomo – *The Duomo*

Può – *Can you*, in this case (Lei); it is also an implied subject

Aiutarmi – *Help me*, as you have already seen in the first chapters of the book, sometimes the particle "me" can be added to the verb.

This elision can be confusing for non-Italian speakers, but let's try to see how the sentence would be if the particle "me" weren't combined and with the presence of the subjects:

Mi scusi, Io sto cercando il Duomo. Lei può aiutarmi?

Excuse me, I'm looking for the Duomo. Can you help me?

In this case, the construction of the sentence is similar to English. Feel free to use this version if you find it easier to remember—it is correct even if it sounds a bit unnatural.

Let's see some other examples:

Sto cercando un ristorante. Può aiutarmi?

I'm looking for a restaurant. Can you help me?

Sto cercando un bagno. Può aiutarmi?

I'm looking for a bathroom. Can you help me?

Sto cercando la stazione. Può aiutarmi?

I'm looking for the train station. Can you help me?

After practicing asking for directions, you will have to learn the names of places you are interested in. Some places of interest are listed in the vocabulary within the first part of the book, but do not worry: now you will see some of the most common places in Italy with their description.

Punti di Interesse (Places of Interest)

- **Ospedale** – *Hospital*

This is, unfortunately, one of the most important places to reach, both while visiting Italy during holidays and while living in this country. The Italian healthcare system is public, although some additional costs may be applied in some cases.

The whole building is made of different medical divisions and the "Pronto Soccorso" (emergency room). In the Pronto soccorso, every patient is labeled with a different color code based on how severe their health conditions are.

- **Bar** – *Cafè*

The bar is the ideal destination for any refreshment break during your strolls through the Italian streets. In an Italian bar, it is possible, in general, to find sandwiches and desserts, as well as drinks and the famous Italian espresso.

This topic is discussed in more detail later, in the chapter dedicated to Italian food. Now you are going to talk more about the Bar itself.

Italian culture does not foresee the widespread presence of stores like Starbucks—although these are being born in the largest cities of the country, are often tainted by Italian tastes, and are so different from their American counterparts.

Italians are not used to coffee houses since people are more willing to drink coffee quickly rather than sit in a bar for several hours while working, for example. Anyway, they are rare and located in the largest cities.

There are two different kinds of bars usually more frequented during the evening:

The first one is the "Pub", which, as you can see, does not need an English translation since the meaning is the same. In a typical British pub, you can enjoy different types of alcoholic drinks (especially beers) with music in the background. These kind of pubs are for those who want a relaxing evening rather than dancing in a more crowded place like the Discoteca (Disco).

The second one is the "Paninoteca" (Sandwich place), and as the name suggests, it is a place where you can buy different kinds of sandwiches.

The Paninoteca is usually compared to fast food, although they distance themselves from true fast-food chains like McDonald's or Burger King for their more typical Italian food. However, fast-food chains, such as McDonald's, are very popular among Italian people, especially the youngsters, but their menu is completely different from other fast-food chains in order to meet Italian taste.

• **Ristorante** – *Restaurant*

Speaking of "Slow food", instead, the Ristorante (restaurant) is the most common and famous place to eat Italian food. In this kind of place, it is possible to sit and eat calmly. Actually, in Italy, there are not just Ristoranti but two other kinds of places to eat:

steria – The word "Osteria" (Tavern) meets its origin within the common people and dates back to ancient times—although today they have changed into a more modern type of osteria. What is the difference between a ristorante and an osteria? An osteria is more informal and specializes in regional Italian food rather than national dishes.

Trattoria – This word is usually confused with osteria, but they are completely different. The Trattoria is a place even more informal than the osteria, where the cuisine is more traditional, and it is not so uncommon to chitchat with the cook or waiters. According to many Italians, the Trattoria is usually the right place to find Italian cuisine at its true core. Also, the prices are much cheaper than the Ristorante and osteria.

- **Stazione** – *Train Station*

There is no need for a deep explanation about this place. It is, however, interesting to notice that in Italian, the word "Stazione" works perfectly on its own, without saying what kind of station it is, as in English.

Even if there are other kinds of Stazioni in the country, such as the subway or tram, they are only located in a few large cities, so they are not as common as the Stazione in Italy. So, saying Stazione is enough to find a train to take.

- **Albergo** – *Hotel*

Although the Italian translation is the one shown above, you don't have to worry too much about it: for finding a place to stay during your holiday in Italy, you will soon find many English words for such places.

Words like "Hotel", "Hostel" (sometimes translated into Ostello), and "B&B" are extremely common in Italy. Do not forget that since tourists around the world really appreciate Italy, it is not so surprising to find so many English words in this environment.

Il Sistema Metrico (Metric System)

A last useful tip: always remember that Italy uses the metric system. For this reason, it could happen that a passer-by, while responding to your directions' request, may indicate something in meters.

An example would be:

"Sto cercando un ristorante. Può aiutarmi?"

"I'm looking for a restaurant. Can you help me?"

"Ne può trovare uno a trecento metri in quella direzione!"

"You can find it three hundred meters in that direction!"

If you are visiting Italy for a few days, there is no need to learn the exact conversion between (for example) meters and yards, but knowing that one meter equals 1,09 yards may give you a picture of how much you should walk.

Continuing the previous example:

The passer-by said 300 meters, so how many yards are they? They are 328, so a little more than the ones said in meters.

Viaggiare in Italia (Travel in Italy)

If you plan to travel around Italy, it is good to know what options are available. There could be some differences compared to your home country that are useful to know to avoid stressful situations.

La Macchina (The Car)

The car remains one of the most used vehicles in the country, and almost every family owns at least one car. Cars are so popular because of a lack of widespread public transport, especially in peripheral areas. However, it is still possible to travel, even without owning a car.

As for cars, there is not much to know: car rental agencies are the best option for any tourist, and, most of the time, are located at the Aeroporto (airport).

In case you are coming from a country where there is the left-hand traffic practice (like, for example, the United Kingdom), be reminded that Italy is a right-hand traffic country. So be careful when driving!

The legal age for driving a car in Italy is eighteen years old, and for a motorcycle, the minimum driving age is fourteen years old.

The Italian translation for the English word "Car" is "Automobile". Usually, it is way more common to say the short version "Auto".

Another very common Italian word is "Macchina" that is literally translated into "Machine".

I Taxi (Taxi or Cab)

The use of taxis in Italy is quite uncommon compared to other countries in the world. If you come from a state where it is sufficient to reach out from the sidewalk to see the yellow car arrive, you may find yourself in trouble once you reach the Italian peninsula.

If you, for example, come from a country where it is enough to stick out your thumb on the street to call a taxi or cab, you too may find this quite difficult, if not impossible, once in Italy.

In Italy, taxis are considered a luxury due to their high prices. So, Italians use them very rarely for traveling. For this reason, it is not common to see them passing through the streets, as they do in other countries, such as New York, because they are usually waiting for potential customers at arrival places, such as a station or airport.

Gli Autobus (The Bus)

Opposed to taxis and their luxurious image, buses are among the most used public transport in Italy with their urban and extra-urban transport system. A ticket can be bought at one of the dealers or a vending machine, to then validate it once on the bus.

The Autobus tickets are usually sold in certain stores—most of the time in Tabaccheria (literally Tobacco Shop), Biglietteria (Ticket office) or a more uncommon ticket vending machine. You can also get your ticket from the Autobus driver, but in this case, you should have to have the exact amount of money in order to pay.

Inside the Autobus, there are several red buttons with the word "Stop" written on them to reserve your stop. The Autobus is the cheapest option to travel via; therefore, it means the vehicle may be slower or even more inefficient than other public transportation services (for example, most Italian autobuses do not have an air-conditioning system installed during summer). Autobus, however, are even used for traveling outside the city, covering long distances.

It is additionally good to remember that, in Italian, the Autobus is also called "Pullman" or more archaically: "Corriera".

I treni (Trains)

I Treni (trains) are one of the most used public transportation systems in Italy. However, they still lack many comforts, and it is not so uncommon to experience a delay, especially with regional trains that are not upgraded into newer models.

Train tickets must be bought at a ticket office or ticket vending machine at the station. The ticket must be validated before getting on the train; otherwise, you risk a penalty.

It is recommended to pay a higher price and take a non-regional Treno. As previously mentioned, due to "crumbling couches", delayed trains, and the lack of comforts, such as air-conditioning or functioning electrical sockets, it is recommended to pay more and travel on a newer Treno like the Freccia (Arrow) or Italo.

Here are some common sentences used in a travel context:

- **Dove è la biglietteria?**
Where is the ticket office?
- **Quando arriva il prossimo autobus?**
When will the next bus arrive?
- **Può chiamare un taxi?**

Can you call a taxi?

- **Vorrei noleggiare una macchina.**
I'd like to rent a car.
- **Qual è la prossima fermata?**
What is the next stop?

To sum up:

1. The automobile (car) is the most used means of transportation in Italy. Usually, it is possible to rent a car after arriving at the

aeroporto (airport). The English word "car" can also be translated as "auto", a shortened and common version of automobile or "macchina".

2. Taxis are not so widely used compared to other countries due to their high prices. That is why foreign tourists use them more.

3. The autobus (bus) is the cheapest option for traveling inside or outside cities. They can be called "autobus", "bus" or "pullman".

4. Although many Italians use them, the Treni (trains) are subject to a lack of quality and delays, especially the cheapest ones.

Mangiare in Italia (Eating in Italy)

Food in Italy is one of the most important aspects of Italian tradition, along with the holidays, and there are some unwritten rules about how to behave while eating and what kind of food is acceptable.

In this chapter, you are going to see how food in Italy works and the main differences with English-speaking countries like the United Kingdom and the United States. You will also see what Italians consider wrong, or even unorthodox, about food and learn the most common and essential sentences that you need to know in this particular environment.

La Colazione (Breakfast)

It can be difficult to talk about specific meals since each person is different and their habits may change.

Overall, though, there are still some established "Colazione" (breakfast) traditions followed by many Italians. Like a meal that is made of sweet-baked food and dairy, such as:

Latte   –   Milk

Cereali   –   Cereals

Cornetto   –   Croissant

Regarding croissants, Italian gives importance to the differences between an Italian "cornetto" (the famous ice cream) and an Austrian or French croissant.

Biscotti	–	Cookies
Marmellata	–	Jam
Miele	–	Honey
Caffè	–	Coffee

Of course, with "Caffè" Italians do usually mean the classic espresso in a small cup. If the "Caffè" is with milk, it will be called a "Macchiato".

Cappuccino	–	Cappuccino
Fette biscottate	–	Rusks

These are generally the food that can be found on a table during a traditional Italian "Colazione".

Children usually have breakfast with milk and cereals, biscuits or other baked pastry, while adults drink cappuccinos or coffee.

In particular, espresso is a fundamental part of many Italian people's routine. Most Italians drink one or more espressos during the day, especially at breakfast and after a meal.

It is common for waiters in restaurants to ask if you want a coffee at the end of your meal.

On the other hand, a savory breakfast is uncommon but not so rare among Italians. Usually, it consists of food like:

Tramezzino	–	Sandwich
Pizza	–	Pizza
Focaccia	–	Focaccia bread

It is not part of Italian culture to eat bacon and eggs in the morning, as they are considered main meals—although there are surely people who have this kind of breakfast.

The main difference between an Italian and American breakfast is the coffee: Italy's tradition does not, usually, include take-away coffee, and in bars, an espresso is a much more common drink at a table or bar counter. It is also served in a ceramic or glass little cup.

Now let's look at a couple of terms related to the "Colazione" and coffee.

Caffè macchiato – In the English language, it is often referred to as "Macchiato" (Stained). A macchiato is made by adding some drops of milk to the coffee. It can be caldo (hot) if the added milk has been previously boiled, or freddo (cold) if the milk was from the fridge.

The biggest difference between the two, apart from the temperature, is that the hot macchiato has foam on top due to the milk emulsion.

Caffellatte – Pay attention to this word: in English-speaking countries, it is common to ask for a "Latte" to get this drink, but if you are going to order a "Latte" in Italy, you will simply get a glass of milk.

Caffellatte is a long drink, the opposite of a macchiato, which involves adding some coffee to a cup of milk.

Il Pranzo e la Cena in Italia (The Lunch and the Dinner in Italy)

Lunch is often considered the most important meal in Italian culture. Although a hectic life has led to more and more people spending less time at the table, the tradition of gathering around the table during Sunday lunch remains strong among Italian people.

Lunch is also the most elaborate meal and is divided into several courses (Christmas and Easter traditional meals revolve around lunch).

But how is an Italian meal composed?

Antipasto – Antipasto (Appetizer) means "before the meal" and is the first course served at the table. Within time, the antipasto gained a higher value in Italian cuisine, and for this reason, it is generally offered only during special events (such as Christmas) or for lunch at a restaurant.

The appetizer can be presented in two different forms: Antipasto di terra (translated as "land-food appetizer"), which is usually composed of salami, cheese, and croutons; and the Antipasto di mare (translated as "seafood appetizer"), which is mainly fish and shellfish. Usually, the chosen kind of appetizer varies according to the daily menu, in order to follow the same concept of the next dishes.

Primo – Primo means "First", is the main course of the meal, and is usually composed of pasta, minestra, and soups. In the Mediterranean diet, pasta is an important meal, which often takes the place of the next dish since it is a high-carbohydrate meal.

Each type of pasta has its specific name and is divided into long, short, and small pasta (the latter is used for minestra).

The English word "soup" is also different in Italian culture. It can be divided into three different dishes:

> - Minestra – Obtained from cooked and blended vegetables or legumes. It can be served with or without pasta.
> - Brodo – A hot and savory liquid made by boiling different types of meat (from beef to chicken) with tortellini, a ring-shaped pasta stuffed with meat and Parmigiano cheese. Brodo can also be translated into "Broth".
> - Zuppa – A thick liquid made of fish or vegetables, usually combined with stale bread softened by the cooked soup. The word zuppa is translated into "soup", but it literally means "soaked".

These dishes are usually flavored with some grated cheese. The most loved cheese is the Parmigiano Reggiano, but other types of cheese made of cow's milk (or even sheep's milk like the Pecorino) are also used and these change depending on the Italian region and personal taste.

Secondo – The third course of the Italian meal is the "Secondo" (Second). This category includes more or less all the other dishes that are not combined with the pasta, such as meat, vegetables, and fish cooked in any way.

Sometimes the "Primo" affects the "Secondo", as in the case of the Brodo: like serving the broth as a Primo course and then the meat cooked in the broth as a Secondo meal.

Contorno (Side Dish) – This is usually served with the "Secondo" and is made up of all the food that may be combined with the main course, such as vegetables like potatoes, carrots, zucchini, or salad.

Dolce (Dessert) – This is the last course served in a traditional Italian meal. Typically, it is fresh seasonal fruit, dried fruit like nuts, almonds or walnuts (dried fruits are very common during the winter and Christmas season), and only occasionally desserts.

As previously mentioned, what you have seen so far is a complete Italian meal. However, some of these courses are skipped due to time, budget, or just desiring a light meal.

The dinner is usually the lighter meal of the whole Italian cuisine, especially because it comes after a rich meal like lunch and makes for better digestion in the evening. That is why many people split the "Primo" and "Secondo" respectively during lunch and dinner.

The same can be said for pizza, the most famous dish of Italian cuisine, which is usually reserved for dinner time.

Tradizioni a Confronto (Comparing Traditions)

Although the Italian menu on paper is nothing out of the ordinary, there are still some differences compared to other countries, which can lead to misunderstandings at a restaurant.

Here are some foreign traditions considered strange in Italy:

Drinking milk during lunch/dinner – In some countries, it is a habit to have lunch or dinner with a glass of milk. In Italy, the milk is not considered a regular lunch or dinner drink, so asking for a glass of milk during one of these two meals could cause confusion or even be denied—since it is not on the menu.

For Italians, milk is a beverage reserved for breakfast, and although there are circumstances where it is consumed during lunch or dinner, in these cases, the milk is considered a full meal as it is combined with other food, such as biscuits or cereals.

Pineapple on pizza – The hate towards this kind of pizza from Italians has reached its peak, so much so that it is a recurring joke. However, there is some truth behind the jokes: for many Italians, it is offensive to put pineapple on a pizza, and asking for it, if not on the menu, can cause the Pizzaiolo (the pizza maker) to complain as pizza is such an important dish of Italian cuisine and culture.

Water at a restaurant – In some countries, it is a common practice in restaurants to refill the customers' glasses with water every time they are empty. In Italy, it is not: when ordering, you will have to specify how many bottles of a certain drink you want (even water) and they will be brought to the table. Once finished, you can order again, but you will have to pay for every consumed bottle.

It is good to remember that the wine tradition in Italy is a source of pride for many of its inhabitants, which is why even if you cannot drink your milk while eating a plate of spaghetti carbonara, you can still enjoy some of the best wines in the world.

In addition to the dishes listed, there are dishes that Americans typically consider Italian, but are not.

Here are some examples:

Fettuccine Alfredo – This dish does not exist in Italian culture, and you will hardly see "Alfredo's name" appear on a menu—unless it is the name of the restaurant owner.

Spaghetti with meatballs – The famous spaghetti with meatballs that has become famous thanks to *Lady and the* Tramp is not Italian; it is an Italian-American recipe. In some Italian regions, such as Abruzzo, it is possible to find pasta dishes with meatballs, but they are very different from this American counterpart.

Spaghetti Bolognese – In Italy, there is a sauce called "Ragù alla Bolognese", which is simply composed of tomato sauce and ground beef or pork—so very different from the American version of the sauce.

On the other hand, some Italian traditions are strange in the eyes of a non-Italian:

The time spent around the table – As you saw before while learning how a traditional Italian meal is divided, the same tradition spends a very long time around the table speaking before, during, and after the meal. This happens mostly in Southern Italian regions; people will sit at the table chitchatting for hours after the meal ends.

Legal drinking age – Selling alcohol in the United States is permitted only to persons who have reached the age of 21. In Italy, the age is eighteen years old.

Ciambelle and Donuts – Although they are often compared to each other, the Italian ciambella is very different from the American donut. The ciambella has no icing; it is just a fritter pastry covered with sugar. Sometimes it can be stuffed with cream or jam, but it is more commonly empty.

Pagare al Ristorante (Pay at Restaurant)

So far, you have learned about meals both at home and at a restaurant, but as for the latter, there are still some differences that are worth discussing: paying the bill.

Some peculiarities could confuse a foreign tourist approaching this situation for the first time. Let's take a look at them:

The coperto – In Italy, when you eat at a restaurant, it is good to take into account the price of the "Coperto" (literally translated into "Covered"). The origin of this sort of "tax" is ancient and was a cost paid from customers for using an inn table.

The Coperto still appears on the Italian menu of many restaurants, and its price varies from €1 to €2 per person, including the cost of using the table (by tradition) and the waiters' services.

Tipping – Another big difference in restaurant services is the tip, or as called in Italian, "Mancia", left for the waiter who served you during the meal. In Italy, leaving a tip is rare and given only by the customer's discretion—unlike other countries where it is not only mandatory but also includes a minimum amount to pay.

Prices – In some countries, the prices are shown as net, i.e., the tax has not been added yet and is only totaled when paying the bill. In Italy, though, the menu shows full prices, so you do not have to worry about taking into account any tax later.

Common Sentences at the Restaurant (Frasi Comuni al Ristorante)

Now that you have seen how restaurants work, how meals are divided into certain courses, and the big differences between cultures, you will now see some useful sentences for this context:

1) Can I please order the...

Potrei ordinare il...

As you can see in this sentence, the conditional (that you already saw in the verbs dedicated chapters) was used and can be with any dish you want to order. You just have to be careful to use the right article.

For example:

Potrei ordinare la pasta?   Can I order the pasta, please?

Potrei ordinare il vino?   Can I order the wine, please?

The sentence turns out to be less friendly than the English counterpart, but in this case, it is enough to add a "Mi scusi" (Excuse me) at the beginning to make it more formal:

Mi scusi, potrei ordinare il vino?

2) This is delicious.

Questo è delizioso.

3) I would love some more of the...

Vorrei ancora un po' di...

This sentence turns out to be slightly more complicated than the previous ones, but it is easier to analyze it word by word:

(Io): implied subject – *I*

Vorrei: the conditional of the verb "to have" – *would love*

Ancora un po' – *some more*

Di – *of the* (it is not necessary to specify the article in Italian)

4) What is the best wine to go with this dish?

Qual è il miglior vino per accompagnare questo piatto?

5) How did you make...

Come hai preparato... (formal environment)

Come avete preparato... (towards a waiter)

Come ha preparato... (towards a cook)

6) Thank you for the delicious meal.

Grazie per il pasto delizioso.

In Italian, there is no habit of saying thank you after a meal (but you can still say it as good manners). On the contrary, Italians are used to saying a wish right before eating their meal, although it is considered bad manners according to the etiquette.

The wish is:

Buon appetito! Enjoy your meal!

Curiously, the literal translation of this wish is "Good appetite!"

L'Italiano e i Dialetti (Italian and its Dialects)

If your purpose is to learn the Italian language, it is good to know all the hints that exist in this language. Italy is actually a very young country, considering how recently it has been united compared to other countries like the United States, and the price of this "youth" consists of different languages and traditions within Italy.

Although Italian is recognized and taught as the national language, within the country, there are dozens of different dialects, variations of the main language based on the region to which they belong.

In many cases, Italians speak a different kind of distorted Italian words, but some other Italian regions have dialects that can also be considered real languages.

One example is Sardinia: the Italian island, known throughout the world for its beautiful coasts and high-quality cheeses, has the Sardinian language. It is a truly recognized language that can sound completely different and foreign to Italians outside of Sardinia.

Although dialects are present throughout Italy, from north to south, it is in Southern Italy where you can find great influences of these linguistic variations that can often take the place of the daily spoken Italian.

For this reason, while asking for directions in Italian, people might respond with the Italian language heavily influenced by their regional dialect/s.

While this topic is not concentrated on in this book, it is still an interesting fact to take into consideration for a non-Italian speaker.

School and Study

This chapter is essential because the scholastic and working worlds are elements that influence people's lives daily.

They are also the moments in which the knowledge of Italian plays an important role in order to carry out your job at its best and follow your education as well.

In this section, you will quickly see both the Italian school and work system, and then learn a whole sequence of sentences that can be useful at any time.

Also, be reminded that you have already seen the translation of many words related to these two worlds in one of the first chapters of the guide, but do not worry: while there is a useful list to search for any word you need, in this section, you will still analyze sentences word by word.

Let's start with the Italian school system, as each country has its differences and education systems.

The School in Italy

The Italian school begins after a child's sixth birthday. Before this, the child attends asilo (kindergarten) and before that, nursery school (asilo nido). After five years of scuole elementari (elementary school), are three years of scuole medie (middle school), until scuole superiori (high school).

If elementary and middle schools are generic, high schools are divided into dozens of options based on the subject that interests the student. There are more technical and theoretical fields, but they all last an average of five years.

At about nineteen years of age, the student can enter università (university) and choose their fields of interest. Usually, university lasts three to five years.

Knowing all this is not essential, but it is important to understand the functioning of the sentences in the next examples.

To summarize:

Asilo Nido

|

Asilo

|

Scuola elementare

|

Scuola media

|

Scuola superiore

|

Università

Studying

The verb "Studiare" (to study) was mentioned in the chapter on verbs, but now it will be detailed more specifically. Although, in general, this term can indicate the act of attending a school or being a student, in reality, it is usually used to indicate the action of studying a subject (in view of an exam, for example).

In fact, although the following sentence makes sense:

Io studio all'università.

I study at the university.

It is more common to use "Frequentare" (to attend) or more directly "Andare" (to go).

They are both verbal forms used every day, and for this reason, if you use the verb "to study", nobody would think it strange, but it is important to know this difference and not be confused.

The same sentence can be said in different ways:

Io studio all'università.	–	I study at university.
Io vado all'università.	–	I go to university.
Io frequento l'università	–	I attend university.

All three make perfect sense and are used in Italian.

In the first sentence, you see:

Io – First-person singular (I)

Studio – The verb "to studiare" (study), first-person singular

All' – The preposition between A and L' (at the)

Università – Name (University)

The second sentence works in the same way, except for the verb used, while in the third sentence, it changes the preposition from ALL to L'.

To move effortlessly in the school environment, it is good to remember that in high school and university, different manners are used as well as certain sentences that make sense only in that specific context.

Italian High School

First, most students attend public schools, as the average quality of state school education is high (although with budget cuts). For this reason, there is no clear division that can be found in other countries between private and public schools.

Regarding the etiquette that is observed, there is no obligation to wear uniforms, and students are required to address the teacher (called Professore or Professoressa – Professor) with "Lei", while teachers address the student with "Tu" (You).

(Do reread the chapter dedicated to pronouns to remember the difference between "Tu" and "Lei".)

The students are called "compagni di scuola" (classmates).

Here are some terms used in the school environment:

Volontario *[Volunteer]* – This word means the student who volunteers for an oral exam with the teacher. Students often organize themselves so that there are always volunteers, and thus are not at risk of a surprise exam.

Interrogazione *[Oral exam]* – The oral exam is one of the two methods by which the student's performance is evaluated during their time in high school. The exam consists of an oral test in which the student has to answer all of the teacher's questions.

Compito *[Written test]* – Unlike the interrogation, the written test is a test in which all of the students in the class usually take part in and allows them to obtain a grade.

Speaking of grades, it is good to remember that the Italian school environment uses a grading system from 0 to 10.

Although a 0 or a 1 grade are almost impossible to get, due to their rarity (even with a failing test it is given the minimum of 2), the maximum grade one can reach is 10 (even though is usually limited to 9). The passing grade is, therefore, 6.

Giustificazione *[Excuse Note]* – "Giustificazione" can be meant in two different ways. Usually, the "Giustificazione" is an excuse note (signed by the parent/guardian or an adult student) for a school absence. This term is sometimes also used to mean a permit to skip a test, but only when it is allowed by the professor.

Here are some more useful sentences for this context:

- **Posso andare in bagno?** – Can I go to the bathroom?

Since the school system provides a sort of hierarchy, it is usual to ask first before going to the bathroom and have a permit from the teacher. The sentence can be analyzed like this:

(Io) – As usual, it is an implied pronoun – *I*

Posso – The verb "to potere" (to can), first-person – *Can*

Andare – The infinitive form of the verb "to andare" (to go) – *To go*

Al – Preposition of A + IL – *To the*

Bagno – *Bathroom*

Since there are no interrogative sentences in Italian, the English translation is:

I can to go to the bathroom?

Of course, this sentence does not make any sense in English.

- **Che voto hai preso al compito? – What grade did you get on the exam?**

This is a classic phrase said between classmates to compare their results after a test.

Let's analyze it:

(Tu) – Implied pronoun – *You*

Che – Interrogative adjective – *What*

Voto – *Grade*

Hai – The verb "to avere" (to have), second-person singular – *Have*

Preso – Past participle of the verb "to prendere" (to get) – *Got*

Al – Preposition of A + IL – *To the*

Compito – *Written test*

Even though this sentence is largely used and perfectly correct, even in spoken Italian, the first part, "Che voto", could be replaced by "Quanto" (how much), forming the sentence:

Quanto hai preso al compito? – How much did you get on the exam?

As you can see, this sentence is much preferred in spoken Italian because it is quicker and shorter to say.

> • **Dove è la 5°B?** – Where is the classroom for the fifth year, section B?

As you can see from this question, there are numerous differences in the Italian version compared to the English one. First, you see the use of an ordinal number—one of its few uses in the Italian language.

In Italy, high schools divide their students into classes based on the school year (from one to five) they are attending. If the classes tend to be too crowded, they can be divided into two or more sections.

For this reason, in a school with few students, you will find only one class per school year, while in a very popular institution, there might be multiple, starting from the letter A onwards in alphabetical order.

The number refers to the year of the students in it, and the letter means the section among the various available in the school. A new student is thus assigned to a specific class and section.

Italian University

What are the main differences between a high school and a university?

First of all, let's continue to address the professor with "Lei", but now they also address the students with "Lei". Furthermore, the students among them are called "Colleghi" (Colleagues).

Speaking of differences with high school, the university grades are no longer expressed in tenths but marks out of thirty. This means that the maximum grade becomes 30, and the passing grade is 18.

Another typical concept of the university environment is the "Libretto Universitario" (University Booklet) where all the exams and grades obtained are written down by the professors. It is one of the most important documents during your time at university, so be careful.

No longer are written tests or oral exams spoken of; now, there are Esami d'appello ("Exam sessions") that take place at certain times of the year (usually September, January/March, and May/June).

The exam sessions are often reduced to the word "Appello", as you can see in this example:

- **Quando ci sarà il prossimo appello?** – When will the next exam call take place?

Let's analyze this sentence word by word:

Quando – Adverb – *When*

Ci sarà – The verb "to essere" (to be), future third-person singular – *Will be*

Il – Masculine determiner article – *The*

Prossimo – Adjective – *Next*

Appello – Noun – *Exam call*

Let's see a couple of sentences regarding daily university life:

- **C'è lezione domani?** – Will there be a lesson tomorrow?

The university system is based on a number of weekly lessons that may vary due to unexpected events or changes ordered by the professor. For this reason, it turns out to be an extremely useful and also frequent question for, and to ask, a student.

- **Dove è l'aula studio più vicina?** – Where is the nearest study room?

One of the most common aspects of Italian universities is study rooms. These are free access areas for students where they can spend time between classes or simply to study. In these areas, there is usually internet access, tables, chairs, and power sockets for a phone and/or laptop.

Common Questions and Sentences About Study

Now that you have seen the main differences between the school environments, let's look at more sentences that can be used for this reason:

- **Io studio all'Università di Lettere**

I study at the literature department

As seen before in this chapter, it is possible to use other verbs to understand the same sentence.

Verbs like:

1. Frequentare (to attend)
2. Essere iscritto/a (to be enrolled)
3. Andare (to go)

As a result, the interrogative form follows the same rule. The question that could be asked to those who attend university is:

- **Dove studi?** – Where do you study?

And:

- **In quale scuola vai?** – Which school do you attend?

Speaking of common questions about education, it is good to remember that these can also be placed in the past. In particular, it is common to ask what school was attended when searching for a job—in order to know if the candidate has a diploma or not.

Here are some important words to remember:

- Diploma — High school diploma
- Laurea — University Degree
- Test di ingresso — Entrance Test

Most Italian universities allow free student applications, and thus students can register at a specific faculty and with an immediate application to the chosen university.

However, certain universities require an entrance exam to send the application. This exam can be made as a mere criterion to reach in order to attend the university or as an exam to take to be accepted into a limited number's student university.

- Erasmus

This word is very common in the European university environment, particularly in Italy. The Erasmus is a study program that allows students who are part of it to study abroad during their educational path.

The question about the diploma can also be asked as:

- **Che scuola hai frequentato?** – Which school did you attend?

To which is important to reply, if owning a diploma:

- **Mi sono diplomato al liceo scientifico** – I graduated from the scientific high school

Let's analyze this sentence word by word:

(Io) – Implied subject – *I*

Mi – Personal pronoun – Me

Sono – First-person singular of the verb "to essere" (to be) – *Am*

Diplomato – Past participle of the verb "to diplomare" (to graduate) – *Graduated*

Al – Preposition of A + IL – *To the*

Liceo scientifico – Specific high school – *Scientific high school*

If you want to translate the sentence from Italian to English, it is:

I graduated myself at the scientific high school.

As you can see from the sentence just analyzed, "Diplomare" and "Laureare" (achieve a diploma or degree) are verbs that need a reflexive pronoun to express a certificate's achievement.

You also see how the sentence structure is slightly different from the original English counterpart. In fact, while in English a person graduates "from" a school, in Italian, a student graduates "at" a school.

It is also by directly using the verb "Avere" (to have), do you specify you own a diploma:

Io ho un diploma	I have a high school diploma
Io ho una laurea	I have a university degree

To sum up:

- Schools in Italy are divided into numerous institutions for students from the ages of three to four years up to twenty-four to twenty-five years.
- Attending a particular school can be expressed in three different verbal forms: "Studying" (to study), "Attending" (to attend), and "Going" (to go). All three forms have the same value and are freely used in spoken Italian.
- Grades in Italian high schools range from 0 to 10, with 6 being sufficient. In the university school system, however, the maximum grade is 30, and 18 is sufficient.
- To indicate that you have completed your studies, you can use the verb "Diplomare" or "Laureare" (to graduate – if high school or university) or directly use the verb "to have" followed by the word "Diploma" or "Graduation".

Work in Italy

Just as the school environment plays an important role in life, so does work in adulthood. Thus, the two sections you will now learn are important. In particular, they are dedicated to anyone who wants to spend more time in Italy than just a holiday.

This chapter details not only everyday sentences concerning work, but also explains what working in Italy is like. Plus, you will discover some useful words to search for and keep a job in Italy.

The Word: "Lavoro"

In English, two specific terms indicate the act of working and the work itself: the verb "to work" and the noun "job". Even "work" can be used as a noun, but between the two terms, there is a slight difference since "job" makes a greater reference to a specific profession, while "work" is a generic term.

On the other hand, in Italian, there is no such difference: the term "Lavoro" means the noun, profession, and the first-person singular of the verb "Lavorare".

Here's an example:

Io **lavoro** in pizzeria.

I work in a pizzeria.

As you can see, the word "lavoro" is used as a verbal form.

Questo è il mio **lavoro**.

This is my job.

In this second example, you find the same word again, but in this particular case, it is presented as a noun, changing its meaning—although it still concerns the working environment. Obviously, there are some synonymous that can be used instead, such as "Mestiere".

Questo è il mio **mestiere**.

This is my job.

So, which is the biggest difference between "lavoro" and "mestiere"? First of all, "mestiere" cannot be used as a verb and opposite "lavoro". While there is the verb "lavorare", there is no such verb for "mestierare".

The little difference between these two Italian words can be the same as between the English words "job" and "work". If "work" represents any activity performed to obtain remuneration, the word "job" has a more specific meaning, which refers to the profession and the role someone plays in it.

Different Kinds of Jobs in Italy

This is an important topic for anyone trying to work in the *Bel Paese* (beautiful country).

In the list below, you will find terms that have been "borrowed" from English culture and are now so integrated into daily Italian language that they have been added to Italian dictionaries.

So how is work structured in Italy? First of all, you find a division based on the working week:

- Part-time

This English word joined the daily spoken Italian language many years ago. This term refers to a job with a maximum of twenty hours of weekly work divided over various days. This kind of work is often given to students or people who don't have more time to commit to longer hours of work.

- Full time

In this case, the workweek incorporates thirty-eight to forty hours divided into various days (for example, five eight-hour days).

Unlike other countries, it is good to remember that, in Italy, there is no law (at the moment) that provides for a minimum wage. Even if there are labor unions that promise to protect the worker's rights, this involves the possibility of running into job proposals with extremely low hourly wages.

Work in Italy can further be divided into two categories.

The first is the regular job, which is regulated and registered thanks to a contract signed by the two parties with established hours, the duration of the work, and, obviously, its remuneration.

On the other hand, we find the so-called "Lavoro in nero" (uncalled work) that indicates an illegal working condition in which a contract does not protect the worker and, therefore, is subject to sudden changes in schedules, duration, and pay. This type of work is also illegal due to a lack of work safety (so be very careful if you encounter this type of work in Italy!).

An additional division can be made according to the duration of the work contract.

In this particular case, there are two kinds of contracts:

- **Lavoro a tempo determinate** – Temporary Job

This kind of work contract means a short duration (usually a few months), and at its end, the contract can be renewed or annulled. This contract is very common and is usually used for testing a worker's abilities before a permanent job contract.

- **Lavoro a tempo indeterminate** – Permanent Job

This contract is the goal of many workers: with it, there is no contract end date, and thus, there is greater security and stability for the employee.

A third division of jobs is seasonal work (Lavoro stagionale): these are job positions that mainly open up in the summer (waitresses, lifeguards, guides, etc.) in response to tourism, and which are closed for autumn. For this reason, they do not give great stability to workers.

Talking At Work

The ability to communicate within a work environment is important as it is the best way to carry out your job without problems, as well as establish a good relationship with colleagues, clients, and employers.

Here are some common sentences in this environment:

"Hai controllato i tuoi turni lavorativi?"

"Have you checked your work shifts?"

As in many other parts of the world, there are many jobs in Italy where employees are asked to do certain shifts, which can change from day to day or week to week. "Il turno" (the shift) thus becomes an important aspect of the working environment.

"Puoi sostituirmi al mio turno a lavoro?"

"Can you replace me for my shift at work?"

This is a sentence you will hear more often than you would like: the willingness among colleagues to cover themselves in difficult moments. Although it can be annoying sometimes, it is what allows work to run perfectly.

"Posso avere una settimana di ferie?"

"Can I have a week off?"

Holidays are accrued while working during the year. The employees can miss work for a certain number of days and still get paid.

Talking About Work

If it is important to talk with other people during your shift, usually, our job can be a topic of conversation and common in any context as well.

Let's see how to ask and reply to questions related to work:

"Il mio lavoro è fare il cameriere."

"My job is to be a waiter."

With this sentence, you can immediately indicate your job, even if it may look too forced compared to a more natural sentence like:

"Io sono un cameriere."

"I'm a waiter."

This option flows better, yet it can be sound a bit cold, so that is why the best option is a compromise:

"Lavoro come cameriere."

"I work as a waiter."

Often during the conversation, for how long you have done the job or activity is also added so a complete sentence could be:

"Lavoro come cameriere al Bar Fragola da due anni."

"I've been working as a waiter at Bar Fragola for two years."

Let's analyze the sentence word by word:

(Io) – Implied subject, as Italian practice – *I*

Lavoro – The first-person singular present of the verb "lavorare" (to work) – *work*

Come – Adverb – *as*

Cameriere – Noun – *Waiter*

Da – Temporal preposition – *since*

Due – Number – *two*

Anni – Object – years

If, unfortunately, you are unemployed, and are looking for a job, use the sentence:

"Sto cercando lavoro come cameriere."

"I'm looking for a job as a waiter."

Or maybe you would like to look for a job in a certain environment:

"Sto cercando lavoro in centro città."

"I'm looking for a job in the city center."

If instead, you want to ask another person about their current working condition, it is obvious to ask if they are currently working. Usually, if you are not sure of the answer, it is good practice to ask only after getting into the topic:

"Stai lavorando, al momento?"

"Are you working at the moment?"

If you know that a person has a job, your question would be about the job:

"Qual è il tuo lavoro?"

"What is your job?"

Or even asking where the person is working:

"Dove lavori in questo periodo?"

"Where do you work now?"

Studying is the way to obtain a good job, and this is why so many people are getting an education in order to achieve that. Most people have a dream job, so that could be a good conversation topic.

"Che lavoro vorresti fare?"

"Which kind of job would you like to do?"

It is clear that all the sentences listed are suggestions for starting a conversation, but also to provide more words that you could insert in the dedicated section at the beginning of the book.

Usually, questions may appear that concern certain aspects of working life. One of the most classic questions is:

"Dove lavori?" – "Where do you work?"

And the reply is:

"Io lavoro in…" – "I work in…"

Then add the place where you are working. In this case, you are not talking about the company name, but rather the generic place where you work.

Here are some examples:

un ufficio	–	an office
un negozio	–	a shop
- un ristorante	–	a restaurant
- una banca	–	a bank
- una fabbrica	–	a factory
- un call center	–	a call center

Work Environment Related Words

There are several words related to the work environment, and knowing them is important to work in Italy.

Here are a couple of examples:

Curriculum

Originally a Latin word, this is an extremely common word in the working environment, and not only in Italy; it is spread all over the world. This document is a report of all previous experience, both in terms of education and work that can be fitting to obtain a certain job position.

Although it is not accepted, or even legal in other countries, in Italy, it is often asked to attach a photo to the curriculum, especially for jobs that require public interaction.

Stipendio/Busta paga – *Salary/Pay*

Of course, this also plays a fundamental role in the work environment. The salary is generally based on both hourly or monthly income. "Busta paga" is a synonym for "Salary" in most sentences.

Connected to this topic, you can find the term "Straordinari":

Straordinari – *Overtime*

Curiously, the word "Straordinari" means extraordinary and is usually used to describe people with exceptional power or with a unique talent. On the other hand, in a working environment, the word "Straordinari" means working over the usual shift to gain a higher income.

Pensione – *Retirement*

This word indicates the period of life at the end of one's working years, where you are going to obtain a monthly income thanks to the contributions paid during your working years.

Disoccupato/a – *Unemployed*

This is a condition in which a person does not work.

Licenziare – *To fire*

As you may have understood from the translation above, this is the verb most feared by every worker and indicates when someone is removed from their employment.

HACCP

In Italy, in many jobs, it is necessary to obtain this particular certificate (HACCP – Hazard Analysis and Critical Control Points) to work.

Some jobs involve contact with (or simply the presence of) food. There are different levels, and once the certificate is obtained, it is possible to work in the specific sector.

To sum up:

- The word "lavoro" can refer to the verb "lavorare" (to work) or the noun "lavoro" (job) itself. As for the noun, there is an alternative found in the word "mestiere" (job), but it cannot be used as a verbal form.
- Jobs in Italy are divided into different categories: part-time and full-time. These are also based on shifts of twenty and forty weekly hours.
- If the type of work is divided according to the contract's length, you have the "lavoro a tempo determinato" (temporary job) and the "lavoro a tempo indeterminato" (permanent job).

Relationships in Italy

How can we interact with our loved ones? What are the most common sentences used among people who love each other? And which terms are important to know in this context?

Throughout this chapter, you will find out how relationships work in Italy, firstly, by starting with one of the most important and commonly used sentences in the world...

I Love You

It is significant to focus on this expression because, in the Italian language, it is used in a specific context only; while in English, it has a much wider use. In English, "I love you" can be said to a partner or a friend, as it can mean both romantic love and friendship.

On the contrary, in Italian, there are two different sentences for expressing the different sentiments:

"Io ti amo"   –   "I love you"

"Io ti voglio bene"   –   "I love you"

As previously mentioned, in English, the sentence can have the same meaning, while in Italian, they are used in certain and different contexts.

In fact, "Ti amo" is a sentence generally used only concerning a person you are romantically involved with. A partner, girlfriend, husband—overall, the expression "Ti amo" is used towards anyone, no matter their gender since it does not change while addressing a female or male.

Whereas "Ti voglio bene" indicates a more general love, which is not necessarily a romantic one. So, although couples can also use it, this expression is used for friends and family as well.

But be careful: the verb "Amare" (to love), used in the first sentence, can be said to any person you are attached to; only the expression "Ti amo" is reserved for a romantic partner.

Now you are going to see the verb's conjugation, and then some sentences in which the verb "Amare" is given to any other person you are not romantically attached to.

Here is the present form of "Amare":

Io amo	I love
Tu ami	You love
Lui ama	He loves
Lei ama	She loves
Noi amiamo	We love
Voi amate	You love
Loro amano	They love

After seeing the conjugation, let's see some sentences:

- **"Io ti amo"** – "I love you"

As mentioned, overall, this sentence is reserved for a partner; however, it does not mean that it cannot be used towards friends or family, but it may sound too strong and even strange in these contexts.

In these cases, it is much better to use the alternative, "Volere".

How is this verb built? This is the verb "volere" (to want) followed by the word "bene" (good).

For example:

"Ti voglio bene."

Can be literally translated into:

"I want you good."

And, obviously, it does not make any sense since (as seen before) the correct translation is "I love you."

Anyway, the verb "Amare" can be used in other contexts too:

- **"Lui ama suo padre"**   –   "He loves his father"

Although it has been said that "I love you" is usually reserved only for a romantic interest, the verb "Amare" can also be used in other contexts. In this particular case, it makes sense to use this verb.

To better understand this concept, let's take a clearer example: in the following two sentences, Marco will say (in one) to his mother that he loves her. Then (in two) he will tell someone else that he loves his mother:

Marco (verso la madre): "Io ti voglio bene."

Marco (towards his mother): "I love you."

Marco (verso l'amico, parlando della madre): "Io amo mia madre."

Marco (to his friend, speaking of his mother): "I love my mother."

As you can see, in the first case, the word "voler bene" is used, while in the second, it is still acceptable to use the verb "Amare".

However, what is said in this part of the guide it is not a strict rule. It is not like if a person said "Ti amo" towards their father they would get arrested. But in daily spoken Italian language, it can sound odd since another word is used for that.

The same happens when talking with friends.

Other Words to Express "Amore"

Just like in other languages, even in Italian, there are other words used as alternatives for meaning love:

Sono pazzo di te – *I'm crazy about you*

As with the English word, even in Italian "Pazzo" means crazy. This sentence indicates a feeling of very strong love toward someone, but beware: there are two other words to indicate an erratic behavior, such as "Folle" and "Matto", but they cannot usually replace "Pazzo" in a sentence involving love. Although, in Italy, there is a popular love song called "Cuore Matto" (roughly translated as "Mad Heart").

So, adding the word "Pazzo" make the sentence's meaning a lot stronger:

Sono pazzo di gelosia.   –   I'm mad jealous.

This indicates a strong jealousy. However, if the word "pazzo" is not followed by any kind of sentiment towards someone, like in the first sentence, it just means a feeling.

Sono cotto di te   –   I'm cooked of you (literal) – I have fallen for you (meaning)

It is obvious how the literal translation does not make any sense at all. The meaning is similar to the previous sentence, although "Essere cotto" (I have fallen for you) indicates the first stage of love—when you are starting to feel interested in someone.

The word "Cotta" (that has been used as a verb in a previous sentence) can be translated into English with "Crush".

Basically, you can express the same concept with a sentence like:

Ho una cotta per te – I have a crush on you

As you can see, in this case, the literal translation turns out to be the correct one, and there are very few differences between the Italian and the English versions.

Although, in English, there are even two different words for expressing the same concept, the Italian word remains the same.

In the Italian one, you do not find the subject (I) because, as you already learned, it is implied. Another difference is the preposition used in the second to last word. English uses the word "On" that can be translated into "Su" in Italian. While, in Italian, the preposition used is "Per", which is translated into "For".

Another difference between English and Italian culture is the importance hidden behind the phrase "Ti amo" – I love you. Although how much weight this sentence has and what is the right moment to say it in a relationship is an extremely personal and subjective element (and therefore it is not possible to draw up a general rule). Generally, in Italy, it has much less importance than its American counterpart.

Though its meaning and the right moment to say it in a relationship are both personal matters (and it is not possible to make up a general rule about it), usually, in Italy, the words have less importance than in many other English-speaking countries, like the United States.

It is very common to see how important this aspect is in movies and TV Series, while in Italy, it is just a natural consequence of a strong love relationship between two people.

The Engagement in Italy

Another big difference between English and Italian cultures is based on the engagement party. When two people's relationship goes to the next step, it is common, in the United States, to hold an engagement party to announce the engagement to others and celebrate it.

This tradition in Italy, however, it is not so common; it is almost non-existent because couples would rather celebrate their relationship with marriage.

However, the word "Fidanzarsi" (to get engaged) exists in Italy, even if its initial meaning, which was very similar to the English one, has fallen into disuse. Nowadays it simply indicates two people with a romantic relationship, but without being promised to each other or with the need for an engagement ring.

The Marriage in Italy

Italian culture has changed radically through the centuries and even if it is a now a laic country, it is still difficult for many people to forget its Christian's roots. Although marriage is a legal act that recognizes the couple as such, most of the first marriages are celebrated inside churches (especially the ones from the spouses' town) and followed by a rich and very feast-like wedding lunch.

Despite this, marriages that distance themselves from Christian ones (especially marriages after a divorce and not accepted by the Church) became established in Italian culture. For this reason, they are not held in churches but other places, like a town hall.

In the Italian tradition, the bride and groom exchange the "Fede" (Wedding Ring), which is traditionally made of gold of different colors and silver, rather than diamond and other gemstones rings.

Curiously, the word "Fede" both means the wedding ring and the word "faith", highlighting the Christian origin of marriage in the country.

Throwing rice at the just married couple while they are leaving the church after the ceremony is also common and brings good luck to the couple.

Over time, the married couple will celebrate the "wedding anniversary" based on the day they were married. The "wedding anniversary" classification has an ancient origin, dating back to the Ancient Romans and is common around the world, and, of course, in Italy.

This sort of ranking starts from a minimum of one year to a maximum of 75 years, and the most important (and celebrated) in Italy are:

25 anni – Nozze d'argento	*25 years – Silver Wedding*
50 anni – Nozze d'oro	*50 years – Gold Wedding*
60 anni – Nozze di diamante	*60 years – Diamond Wedding*
75 anni – Nozze di Platino	*75 years – Platinum Wedding*

With the increase of divorces and marriages celebrated by people of an older age compared to the past (once people used to get married at only eighteen), these kinds of anniversaries are becoming more and more rare.

To sum up:

- "I love you" is usually translated into two different sentences: "Ti amo" when it is said to a romantic interest, and "Ti voglio bene" when it is said to friends or relatives.
- Despite this, the verb "Amare" can be used indiscriminately towards anyone. For example: "Amo i miei amici." – ("I love my friends.").
- Other words can express the feelings of romantic love, such as "Sono pazzo di te." ("I am crazy about you.") and "Sono cotto di te." ("I have a crush on you.").
- The engagement, in Italy, is not celebrated as much as in other countries, and although the word "Fidanzarsi" lost its initial meaning (translated as "being engaged"), in the current Italian language, it is just used for people in a love relationship.
- In Italy, marriage still has a very important role among many people and tradition, especially for its Christian origin. It is quite common also to celebrate the wedding anniversary through the years and assign a symbolic material to certain years of marriage.

Le Feste Italiane (The Italian Holidays)

For those planning a trip to Italy as tourists or who even want to live in Italy, holidays affect many aspects of life like work, school, and people's interactions. Specifically, there are many religious, non-religious, ancient, or quite new holidays that it is good to know in order not to disrespect the Italian culture and integrate into the country.

Dicembre 8 (December 8)

Christmas is the most famous holiday in the world. It is celebrated in many countries, and with a different meaning: some religiously celebrate Christmas, others treat it as a romantic holiday (like in Japan), and others still see Christmas as a more commercial activity.

In Italy, Christmas is both commercial and religious. For now, let's look at the latter.

Since Christmas in Italy mainly celebrates the birth of Jesus Christ, December 8 is dedicated to the immaculate conception that revolves around the Virgin Mary. Traditionally, it is the day for starting to decorate the Christmas tree and setting up the "Presepe".

The "Presepe" is an exhibition of objects that recreate the nativity scene; it can be minimal with just the figures of Joseph, the Virgin Mary, and Jesus in the stable, or more complex with also the city of Bethlehem. While the Christmas tree is very common among people, the Presepe is slowly falling in disuse due to its strong Christian roots. Despite this, it is often a live exhibition, with actors and real animals, of the nativity scene and is called "Presepe vivente" (live nativity scene).

This kind of holiday does not have specific wishing, although it is impossible to hear:

"Buona festa della Madonna." – "Happy Madonna's holiday."

On December 8, usually, students and workers have the day off.

Natale e Santo Stefano (Christmas and Saint Stephan)

This chapter section lists the typical customs that most Italian families practice during a holiday. Of course, every person is different, so everyone has their own point of view about holidays and way to celebrate them. This is going to be a whole picture of the Italian culture and thus is easy to understand.

Christmas eve is celebrated on December 24. Overall, it is not considered a real holiday, so many people work on this day. Italians are more used to starting the celebrations during the evening with the "Cenone" (translated as "Big dinner").

According to its Christian origins, Christmas eve is the period spent waiting for Jesus' birth, accompanied by a fish dinner. This tradition has influenced Italian society so much that even restaurants have, usually, only fish menus on Christmas eve. After dinner, Italian people are split about the traditions: some wait until midnight to exchange gifts and wishes, while others postpone the celebration to the next day.

Then, December 25 comes and Christmas! It is an established Christian tradition to attend the celebration in the city or town's church on Christmas morning. However, it is also common to see the religious function commemorated by the Pope himself on the TV.

Curiously, despite Italy's religious significance, more and more people are leaving their religion, although most Italian people still take part in the Christmas morning liturgy as per tradition. The Mass is usually followed by Christmas lunch, a hearty meal with the family. In fact, it is common to say:

Natale con i tuoi; Pasqua con chi vuoi – Christmas with your family; Easter with whomever you want

Which other sentences can come in handy in this situation? And what kind of sentences are better to wish a merry Christmas to people around you? Usually, there are two wishes:

"Buon natale!"   – "Merry Christmas!"

"Auguri!"   – "Best wishes!"

While the first one is a wish that can only be used at Christmas, "Auguri" is largely used for every holiday and festivity, from birthday to Easter, and kept its meaning. Basically, it is a generic wish, while "Buon Natale" is just for Christmas.

Speaking of Christmas, there is another important figure of this holiday. If morning mass represents the Christian's soul of the holiday, Santa Claus represents the most commercial one:

Babbo Natale – *Santa Claus*

The name is made of the word Babbo (Dad) and Natale (Christmas). The English translation is, thus, "Father Christmas".

Once Christmas is over, it is **December 26** or **Santo Stefano** (Saint Stephen). This day is still considered a holiday, although it does not have any particular meaning compared to the UK and the Commonwealth countries' Boxing Day. Santo Stefano is another chance to eat together with family, and, typically, the lunch consists of leftovers from Christmas lunch.

Ultimo Dell'anno e Capodanno (New Year's Eve and New Year)

The last day of the year and the first day of the next year are both celebrated around the world, but how are they celebrated according to the Italian tradition?

Usually, the Last of the Year (last day of the year) is spent at someone's will—given that there is no moral rule that requires them to spend it with family. This is why many groups of friends organize booking houses and getaways for the night.

Unlike the other holidays, December 31 is not a national holiday, so it is a working day—although there is no school as most schools close a few days before Christmas and reopen on January 7.

Tradition has it that you should wait for the "last of the year" with dinner and, just like in the case of Christmas Eve, has a typical dish to serve: the "zampone" with lentils. It is coarsely chopped pork spiced and inserted into the paw of the same animal. This dish, accompanied by lentils, is said to bring good luck.

At this point, the end of the year is expected, with the classic countdown to the fireworks and "Spumante" (sparkling wine).

The phrase in this case (apart from the classic "Auguri", which always goes well) is:

"Buon anno nuovo!"   –   "Happy new year!"

Usually, this sentence can be shortened to:

"Buon anno!"   –   "Happy (new) year!"

These kinds of wishes are often exchanged with handshakes, hugs, and kisses based on the relationship between people.

As in many other countries, there are traditions and superstitions associated with this holiday even in Italy, among which can be mentioned:

I buoni propositi del nuovo anno – The new year's resolutions

Even if it is disappearing with time, the habit of making a good intentions list with the purpose of motivating yourself for a better year than the previous one is still quite common among Italian people—although it is also very common to forget these good intentions, too, so much that it is mocked by many.

Another superstition based on the "year's end" is how an action done on this day will be repeated for the whole next year. For example, it is common to think that if a person falls on New Year's Eve, then they will keep falling throughout the new year.

Finally, let's look at the traditional holiday Italian food. As mentioned regarding the "Zampone", most Italian culture revolves around meals. Every part of the holiday is combined with a typical dish and dessert, usually only eaten during this specific period of the year.

What are the most common new year's eve and new year desserts? They are typically the same, eaten during Christmas, and the most common ones are two desserts that split Italian people's tastes.

First, is the Pandoro, a tall soft cake decorated with icing sugar. Second, is the Panettone, a sort of sweet bread loaf containing raisins, candied fruit, or even chocolate. They are both originally made in the north of Italy.

Italy does not have a typical hot beverage, such as eggnog (zabaione in Italian), like in English-speaking countries, but it is very common to drink hot chocolate during the winter season and sparkling wine on Christmas and New Year's Eve.

Epifania e la Befana (Epiphany and the Befana)

On January 6, the second holiday of the year arrives, which has a double meaning: it is both religious and commercial.

From an exclusively Christian's point of view, the "Epifania" (Epiphany) is the manifestation of Christ's divine powers. However, this holiday is mainly known as the "Befana" (Hag), which is celebrated on the same day. This holiday is aimed at children and involves giving them a large sock from the Befana. The contents of this sock may change depending on the child's behavior: if they were good, the sock is filled with various kind of sweets; if they were bad, the sock is filled with coal.

The Befana is depicted as an old witch wearing shredded clothes riding a broom. It is clear that she is strongly inspired by Santa Claus (as he appears once a year bringing gifts to good children and coal to bad children).

This holiday is only compared to Christmas since it is well-established in Italian culture by centuries. The Befana can also be found in a common nursery rhyme:

La Befana vien di notte

con le scarpe tutte rotte

con le toppe alla sottana:

Viva, viva la Befana!

La Befana comes at night

With completely broken shoes

with the patches on the skirt:

Long live the Befana!

Related to the Epiphany, another well-known saying is:

L'Epifania tutte le feste si porta via – *The Epiphany takes all the holidays away*

Naturally, this saying refers to the fact that the Epiphany is the last of a long series of holidays starting from December 8, so it works as an end to all the festivities. There aren't any particular wishes during this holiday, so it is okay just to use "Best wishes". However, you do occasionally hear, "Buona Befana!" (translated as "Good Hag!").

Carnevale (Carnival)

"Carnevale" (Carnival) traditionally begins with the Epiphany's conclusion and ends on the Tuesday before the "Mercoledì delle ceneri" (Ash Wednesday), which is the Wednesday preceding Easter. This holiday does not have any public days and, usually, it is just a way to let children dress up as books, comics, movies characters, or even with traditional masks.

Carnevale and its masks are different from region to region, with the masks based on fictional characters. The most famous ones are Pulcinella (Neapolitan mask) and Arlecchino (Venetian mask).

A popular thought was that the Carnevale's loud noises, colors, and music were needed to banish the darkness and the cold of winter, to pave the way for spring.

During these celebrations, carnival floats are commonly seen passing along Italian streets. Usually, the carnival floats look satirical, even irreverent, or are a true piece of art. Also, it is common, especially among children, to dress up as fictional characters and throw confetti in the streets.

As mentioned, Carnevale is strongly influenced by the region it is celebrated in, even the typical sweets and desserts may vary from region to region, but typically, the most famous Carnevale's sweets are the Chiacchiere (Chit-chat), a sweet pastry fritter covered with icing sugar and perfect for getting the right amount of energy to celebrate Carnevale during the cold season.

Carnival does not have any specific wishes.

Pasqua e Pasquetta (Easter and Easter Monday)

Right after Carnevale, is Pasqua (Easter) that does not have a specific day for being celebrated. Technically speaking, Pasqua is celebrated on the first Sunday after the first spring full moon, but luckily, there is no need to be an astronomer to know when Easter will be celebrated: just take a look at the calendar.

Pasqua is a public holiday, which means students and some workers have several days off. Its origins lie in Christianity, although Pasqua now has a more commercial purpose.

From a purely Christian point of view, Pasqua celebrates the resurrection of Christ and the next day, Pasquetta (Easter Monday), is called "Lunedì dell'angelo" (Angel Monday) and celebrates the meeting between the angel and the women at Jesus' tomb. Traditionally, Pasqua is celebrated with different religious rites more or less followed by the Italian population. Sunday is generally spent at home with family, while the next day is dedicated to picnics, excursions, and outdoor activities.

On the other hand, the more commercial soul of this holiday, just as with Babbo Natale and Befana, involves giving presents, usually to younger family members. In this case, the most common Pasqua gift are big eggs made of different types of chocolate, which contain surprises like toys or jewelry.

Originally, the eggs were just painted regular eggs that symbolized rebirth, but through time, this tradition evolved into the exchange of chocolate eggs and is celebrated by almost everyone in Italy.

Compared to other countries, in Italy, there is no tradition of "looking for eggs" nor the concept of the "Easter Bunny"—although it is common to give rabbits made of chocolate as a gift, even though they just represent fertility and rebirth.

In this case, it is possible to wish:

Buona Pasqua! – *Happy Easter!*

Or just:

"Auguri!" – *Best wishes!*

Concerning the traditional Italian cuisine during Easter, there is the habit of eating lamb on Sunday, which originates from the Christian side of the holiday and the redeeming nature of the animal according to Christianity. As for the desserts, besides the chocolate eggs and rabbits, it is common to eat the "Colomba" (Dove), an iced-sugar baked cake with almonds made into the shape of the bird.

Both Easter and Easter Monday are national holidays in Italy.

Festa Della Donna (Women's Day)

The Festa Della Donna (International Women's Day) is celebrated on **March 8** in honor of the social conquests achieved by women over the years. In Italy, it is common practice for men to give mimosa flowers to women they are attached to (like family members or love interests), but also as a polite gesture to female colleagues and classmates.

Obviously, in this case, the wishes are only reserved for women:

"Buona Festa Della Donna." – "Happy Woman's Day."

During this holiday, it is quite common to organize women-only dinners, and even restaurants, bars, and nightclubs have special promotions for women.

However, it is not recognized as a public holiday.

Festa Del Papà (Father's Day)

March 19 is Festa Del Papà (Father's Day), which celebrates fathers. Children usually give presents to their fathers on this day.

It is important to note that this day changes from country to country. Italy shares this date with countries like Spain, Bolivia, and a handful of other countries, while the Festa Del Papà's date changes into the third Sunday of June in other countries.

Festa Della Liberazione (Liberation Day)

This is the first Italian historical celebration and takes place on April 2, the day when Italy celebrates the liberation's anniversary from the fascist regime and Nazi occupation. It is recognized as a national holiday during which schools are closed and, usually, people do not work.

No special wishes or traditions are considered since it is a fairly recent celebration, and overall, it is a holiday that is meant to be spent doing outdoor activities, such as picnics.

Festa Dei Lavoratori (Workers' Day)

As in other countries of the world, May 1 in Italy is Festa dei Lavoratori (Workers' day). It is celebrated to honor workers' rights and to remember the sacrifices made in order to obtain them. It is recognized as a public holiday, so schools are closed and, obviously, workers have the day off.

Festa Della Mamma (Mother's Day)

The Festa Della Mamma (Mother's Day) is celebrated on **May 10**. Although it is not recognized as a public holiday, on this day, it is customary to celebrate every mother and give them gifts.

Sometimes the celebration is also extended to grandmothers.

Festa Della Repubblica (Republic Day)

On **June 2,** Italy celebrates the Festa Della Repubblica (Republic Day) in honor of the referendum held on the same day in 1946. On that date, Italian people went to vote on still being under a monarchy or becoming a republic. With 54 percent of the votes, Italy became a republic, and for this reason, June 2 is recognized as a public holiday by the state.

There are not any particular wishes for this holiday.

Ferragosto

Ferragosto is celebrated on **August 15**. It is a holiday of ancient origin, since Ancient Rome, made for giving a day of rest from the scorching summer period. It is recognized as a public holiday and traditionally celebrated by eating outdoors, hiking, going to the beach, or doing any other outdoor activities.

Curiously, Italians used to wish "Buon Ferragosto" (Happy August 15) rather than wishing "Auguri" (Best wishes) because it is not a real celebration—but more an opportunity to enjoy some rest, especially a day off from work, during summer.

Halloween

As in other countries, especially the English-speaking ones, Halloween is celebrated in Italy on **October 31.** Although this holiday became popular thanks to movies and television, it still a fairly new celebration in Italian culture.

It is still not a habit for Italian children to do "trick-or-treat" in the streets to get sweets, but it is seen as an occasion to dress up children as fictional characters like during Carnevale (Carnival).

On the other hand, radical Christians in Italy are strongly against this holiday since it is seen as blasphemous.

Halloween is not a public holiday.

Ognissanti e Commemorazione Dei Morti (All Saints' Day/All Souls' Day)

"Ognissanti", or also called "Tutti i Santi", (All Saints), is a Christian holiday on **November 1** in which all the saints are celebrated, even those not canonized. It is recognized as a public holiday, so a day off school and, usually, work. There is not a specific tradition to follow, except for Christian's processions towards the cemeteries to bless the tombs.

The "Commemorazione dei Morti" (All Souls' Day), or more commonly called "Giorno dei Morti", (Day of the Dead), is celebrated the following day, on **November 2**. Although this is not a public holiday like Ognissanti, on this day, many people honor the dead by visiting cemeteries and bringing them flowers.

In both cases, there are no particular wishes.

Santi e Patroni in Italia (Saints and Patron Saints in Italy)

Given the strong Christian traditions in Italy's past, you may have noticed that Santi (Saints) are very important. Every Italian town and city has a Santo Patrono (Patron Saint) to represent them, and on the day that Santo Patrono is celebrated, it is considered a public holiday, so schools and some stores are closed.

The cultural importance of Santi Patroni and Santi-related celebrations change from place to place and region to region. For example, in Southern Italy, celebrating the Santi has an important impact on the cities' traditions, and on people living in the cities, much more than in other parts of Italy.

Proverbi (Proverbs)

In the previous chapter, many Italian figures of speech were detailed. Given that Italy is a multicultural peninsula, thanks to its many regions, the figures of speech also vary from area to area.

In this chapter, proverbs, the other side of the coin, will be discussed. The well-known proverbs have popular origins and are rooted over time. They stem from oral tradition and convey a teaching so that other people can learn from it.

Proverbs of this type are a powerful tool in the hands of those who want to learn the Italian language: it is much easier to learn words when the message they transmit is interesting. For this reason, the original proverb is offered, then its translation and meaning. A good way to remember these proverbs is to try to associate the English equivalent with the Italian proverb.

Modi Di Dire e Frasi Fatte (Common Sayings and Set Phrases)

This section is quite long, but you don't need to learn it all at once. Just like the dedicated words chapter, the main purpose is to give you a point of reference for all the dialects and phrases that cannot be translated literally. Just think about the common saying: "Like shooting fish in a barrel." If you tried to translate it into Italian, it would make no sense. However, if you learn the meaning of a certain common saying instead, then it will be easier to recognize, and you can use it in spoken Italian too.

Why are common sayings so important?

> 1. If you do not know them, you will not understand a sentence's meaning.

> 2. If you use a common saying, the impression you give of your mastery of Italian will improve drastically.

Of course, it is impossible to list all the Italian ways without making thousands of chapters out of them, so only the most popular and used ones are listed.

Let's start:

Abbaiare alla luna (*to bark at the moon*). Useless complaints because we are not heard or the person we are talking to do not have any interest in hearing us; just like a dog that barks at the moon.

Abbassare la cresta *(to lower the crest).* Don't be too cocky; be humbler instead. In fact, the crest stated in the common saying is the same as a chicken.

Abboccare all'amo *(to bite the hook).* Fall into a trap or provocation.

Andare a braccetto *(go hand in hand). Get along.*

Andare a letto con i polli *(go to bed with the chickens).* Going to bed early. This common saying takes its origin from an old tradition that keeps going on in Italy even nowadays. Chickens have the habit of retreating into the henhouse as soon as the sun goes down and wake up at dawn. This is why the farmers used to go to bed very early (as the chickens do) and woke up just as early.

Andare a tentoni *(to go while groping).* Not having clear ideas. The common saying represents the act of stretching out the arms and touching things while in the dark because it is impossible to see.

Andare a vuoto *(to go empty).* Cannot do it; failing; do not succeed.

Andare a zonzo *(to go for a stroll).* Walking aimlessly, just for fun or for passing the time.

Andare in bestia *(to become a beast).* Raging over something like a beast; losing self-control; getting angry; becoming violent.

Andare in bianco *(to go in white).* Another common saying for failure.

Andare in vacca *(to go in cow).* Getting into bad conditions or ruining everything.

Arrampicarsi sugli specchi *(to climb the mirrors).* Making useless attempts or working hard for nothing in an already useless challenge.

Aspettare al varco *(to wait at the gate).* Waiting for someone while hiding; also be ready to face them as soon as they are near.

Attaccare bottone *(to stick a button).* Starting a conversation with someone.

Avere la coda di paglia (*to have a tail made of straw*). Feeling judged and attacked for doing something wrong.

Avere una fifa blu (*to have a blue fear*). Having a great fear of something. Curiously, the word "blue" (blu) states sadness in the English language, while in Italian, it states fear.

Avere fegato (*to have liver*). Being brave. The common saying's origins are from the Greek myth of Prometheus, the titan who took the fire from the gods to give it to human beings. Because of that, Prometheus was bound to a rock, and his liver was eaten every day by an eagle. Then, the liver would grow back in order to be eaten the next day again.

Avere culo (*to have butt*). Being lucky.

Avere gli occhi foderati di prosciutto (*to have the eyes covered by ham*). Don't see the evidence.

Avere il pollice verde (*to have the green thumb*). Being extremely gifted at taking care of plants and flowers.

Avere la luna storta (*to have the crooked moon*). Being moody, unreasonably irritable, and ready to fight. A little trivia: the character Remus Lupin from the fantasy saga *Harry Potter* is also called "Moony", while in the Italian version of the books, he is called "Lunastorta".

Avere la pelle d'oca (*Goose bumps*). Shiver in cold or fear. In the English language, there is a variation of this common saying involving another animal than the goose: having chicken skin.

Battere il ferro finché è caldo (*to beat the iron while it's still hot*). Knowing how to take advantage of good opportunities and start something when the situation is favorable.

Battere la fiacca (*to beat the weariness*). Being unenthusiastic and lazy.

Bruciare le tappe (*to burn the stages*). Proceed at a fast pace, quickly overcoming obstacles, and having no hesitation.

Cadere dalla padella nella brace (*fall from the pan to the grill*). Worsening a situation; finding an alleged remedy that, instead, soon turns out to be worse than the problem.

Calzare a pennello (*wear as a brush*). Wearing something perfectly; being the perfect size.

Cercare il pelo nell'uovo (*to search the hair in the egg*). Being picky.

Cercare rogne (*to look for trouble*). Looking purposely for difficult and risky situations.

Cercare un ago in un pagliaio (*look for a needle in a haystack*). Sentence used to indicate a desperate and impossible challenge.

Chiudere un occhio (*to close one eye*). Pretending not to know something.

Cogliere con le mani nel sacco (*to catch someone with his hands in the bag*). Surprise someone in the act.

Conoscere i propri polli (*to know your chickens*). Knowing well the people you are involved with.

Contare quanto il due di briscola (*to have the same value as the two in the game Briscola*). Do not be relevant. This common saying came from the popular Italian card game, Briscola, in which the ace is the card of maximum value while the two is worth nothing (so much that it is always discarded while playing with three other players)

Dar del filo da torcere (*giving some thread to twist*). Make something, usually a challenge, difficult to others to not be defeated yet.

Dare i numeri (*giving numbers*). Looking crazy; saying and doing something incoherent; talk nonsense.

Dare il benservito *(pink slip)*. Throw someone out; fire someone from work; abandon someone.

Dare un colpo al cerchio e uno alla botte *(hit both the circle and the barrel)*. Distribute appropriately praise or blame, reasons or wrongs, in order not to displease anyone; carry on two deals, taking care of them alternately; try to juggle without displeasing anyone; do not take a clear position.

Darsi la zappa sui piedi *(hit ourselves with the hoe)*. To reason; to bring evidence against one's assumption; to harm oneself unintentionally.

Dormirci sopra *(sleeping on it)*. Postpone a decision by sleeping on it and thinking about it with a fresher mind.

Entrare negli anta *(entering the forty)*. Turn forty.

Essere al verde *(being at green)*. Do not have any money or do not have something in particular anymore.

Essere baciato dalla fortuna *(being kissed by luck)*. Being extremely lucky. It is based on how luck is usually depicted as a blindfolded woman. So being kissed by a woman who cannot see it is considered unique.

Essere in alto mare *(being on open sea)*. Being far from a solution to a problem or something's conclusion. Just like being in a boat on the open sea, maybe during a storm.

Essere in una botte di ferro *(being in an iron barrel)*. Being in a situation of tranquility; being faultless; or, usually, just being safe.

Essere in vena *(being on vein)*. Feeling full of strength or creativity; overall, being in the best condition to do something.

Essere l'ultima ruota del carro *(being the last wheel of the cart)*. Being the least important person in a group.

Essere negato *(being hopeless)*. Being completely unsuitable; not being accepted at all (for an activity or discipline).

Essere sano come un pesce *(being as healthy as a fish)*. Having good health.

Essere un figlio di papà *(being a father's son)*. It is said of a young person who leads a comfortable life or who makes their way through economic and social position, authority, or prestige, being protected by their father.

Essere una frana *(being a landslide)*. Being unable to achieve something.

Essere una spugna *(being a sponge)*. Being a drunk; a heavy drinker.

Far buon viso a cattivo gioco *(making good faces while playing dirty)*. Getting used to the good in unpleasant situations.

Far secco *(dry someone)*. Killing someone.

Far vedere i sorci verdi *(let others see the green rats)*. Make others angry or even scaring someone and creating a series of difficulties.

Fare cilecca *(misfire)*. Missing life's goals; failing.

Fare di ogni erba un fascio *(make each bundle a bundle)*. Not knowing how to distinguish between totally different things; having strong prejudices; comparing different things.

Fare il buono e il cattivo tempo *(doing good and bad)*. Exercise power over a group of people.

Fare la cresta su qualcosa *(cresting on something)*. Increase the price of something to gain an advantage.

Fare la nanna *(doing the nanna)*. Sleeping. A common saying, especially by children.

Farla finita *(get it over with)*. Stop something immediately.

Farla franca *(doing it candid)*. Being able to get away with impunity; do an unlawful and reprehensible action without being caught.

Gettare la polvere negli occhi a qualcuno *(throwing dust into someone's eyes)*. Deceive someone.

Gettare la spugna *(throwing the sponge)*. Giving up on something.

Indorare la pillola *(gild a pill)*. Making something less bitter; mitigate displeasure with appropriate words; prettify.

Lasciarci le penne *(lost the feathers)*. Suffer serious harm or literally dying.

Leccarsi i baffi *(lick the mustaches)*. Feeling pleasure while eating something delicious.

Leccarsi le ferite *(lick the wounds)*. Seek comfort in disappointment or failure; comfort ourselves.

Legarsela al dito *(tying to the finger)*. Hold a grudge; promising revenge.

Levare le tende *(remove the tents)*. Leaving a place.

Mandare a monte *(sending to mountains)*. Let something fail; prevent the realization of something.

Mandare a quel paese *(sending to the town)*. To send someone away in a bad way; get rid of it quickly.

Mangiare la foglia *(eating the leaf)*. Understanding the situation; understanding the hidden meaning of a certain message; realizing that things are not as they look.

Metterci una pietra sopra *(put a rock over it)*. Getting definitely over something.

Mettere i bastoni tra le ruote *(put sticks through wheels)*. Get in the way.

Mettersi le mani nei capelli *(putting hands through the hair).* Despair.

Molto fumo e poco arrosto *(much smoke and little roast).* A lot of appearance and little substance.

Nella botte piccola ci sta il vino buono *(in the little barrel there is the finest wine).* A common saying used to praise a person of little height that might feel inferior to those who are taller.

Non aver peli sulla lingua *(do not have hair on your tongue).* To express oneself frankly even at the cost of being judged critical and rude.

Non cavar un ragno dal buco *(do not pull out any spiders from a hole).* Get nothing despite the efforts; do not finish anything.

Non svegliare il can che dorme *(do not awake the sleeping dog).* Do not tease who looks dangerous.

Pagare alla romana *(paying like a Roman).* Dividing the paying bills or paying your part of the bill.

Parlare al vento *(speak to the wind).* Speaking while being ignored.

Passare un brutto quarto d'ora *(spending an awful quarter of an hour).* Being in an awful situation.

Perdere il pelo ma non il vizio *(losing the fur but not the bad habits).* Do not believe in any people changing.

Piangere lacrime di coccodrillo *(crying crocodile tears).* Too late to regret something.

Predicare bene e razzolare male *(preach good but rummage through badly).* Saying always the right thing but, actually, acting in a mean and disrespectful way.

Prendere un granchio *(taking a crab).* Misunderstanding something big.

Saperne una più del diavolo *(knowing better than the devil).* Being very smart.

Tutto fa brodo *(anything goes).* An unstable economic situation and using the last resources for doing something.

I Proverbi Più Famosi (The Most Famous Proverbs)

Le bugie hanno le gambe corte. – *Lies have short legs.*

Lies are discovered immediately; they have short legs and cannot go far. Curiously, the proverb that lies have a long nose is far more common. This second version comes from the spread of the novel *Pinocchio* in Italy (in Collodi).

Non è tutto oro quel che luccica. – *Not all that glitters is gold.*

Not all beautiful things are, in the end, the best. A proverb that warns of pure appearance, seeking a deeper meaning.

Anche l'occhio vuole la sua parte. – *The eye also wants its part.*

Even the outward appearance affects the judgment of things or people. Even if the outward appearance should be less important than what we have inside, it would be hypocritical to claim that it has no weight in our choices.

Morto un papa se ne fa un altro. – *When a Pope dies, another one is appointed.*

No one is irreplaceable. This proverb comes from the practice of appointing a Pope after the death of his predecessor, with the famous smoked ceremony announcing the new pontiff.

Chi sa fa e chi non sa insegna. – *Who knows how to do it, does it. And who does not know to do it, teaches.*

More and more people are teaching how to do something without having an idea of how to do it. Who can do something, does it. Whoever cannot do it, starts talking.

Lontano dagli occhi, lontano dal cuore – *Out of sight out of mind.*

Many people believe that distance strengthens love, and sometimes it is true. But often staying away also makes love dim.

Chi ha i denti non ha pane, e chi ha pane non ha i denti. – *He who has teeth has no bread, and he who has bread has no teeth.*

The only people who truly appreciate something are those who don't have it but would like to have it.

A buon intenditor, poche parole. – *Few words to the wise.*

Who can listen does not need too many words, just as those who are ready to hear do not need any cry.

Fare il passo più lungo della gamba. – *Take a step longer than the leg.*

Don't calculate the risks and costs of an action well overestimating your capabilities.

Uomo avvisato mezzo salvato. – *Forewarned is forearmed.*

Seeing a danger still gives us the chance to avoid it—if we know how to seize the opportunity.

Chi semina vento raccoglie tempesta. – *Who seeds wind shall harvest storm.*

A concept very similar to that of Karma. Who perpetuates evil deeds will be repaid with the same coin.

Vivi e lascia vivere. – *Live and let live.*

A proverb that preaches tolerance.

Il gioco è bello quando dura poco. – *The game is nice when it doesn't last long.*

Even the best things must end before they become annoying. Too much too bad, using another figure of speech.

Tra moglie e marito non mettere il dito. – *Don't put your finger between husband and wife.*

Even if the intent is positive, it is not good to interfere in a relationship between two other people.

Ne uccide più la lingua che la spada. – *The pen kills more people than the sword.*

An invitation not to underestimate the strength and consequences that certain words can have.

A caval donato non si guarda in bocca. – *Don't look a gift horse in the mouth.*

A gift must be accepted without any reservation and without evaluating its value. The proverb stems from the habit of checking the teeth of a horse before purchasing it to evaluate its health.

L'erba del vicino è sempre più verde. – *The neighbor's grass is always greener.*

It is easier to appreciate what others have rather than what we have.

Meglio soli che male accompagnati. – *Better alone than in bad company.*

It is necessary to carefully choose the people around us, as not all company is worthy of others.

Il mondo è fatto a scale. C'è chi scende e c'è chi sale. – *The world is made up of stairs. There are those who descend, and those who ascend.*

There are times when it seems that everything goes wrong, but (like a series of stairs) life offers both ascents and descents; you have just to overcome the moment.

L'amore non è bello se non è litigarello. – *Love is not good if there are no arguments*

In a good report, there is a discussion, even a heated one, between two partners.

Chi è causa del suo mal pianga sé stesso. – *Who causes his own illness will cry himself.*

When we are the cause of our misfortunes, we can only reproach ourselves. This proverb has ancient origins and is a reinterpretation of a verse of the "Divine Comedy" by Dante Alighieri.

Chi troppo e chi niente. – *There are those who have too much and those who have nothing.*

Luck is unfairly distributed.

Chi si loda si imbroda. – *Whoever praises himself gets messed up.*

Literally: "He who weaves his praise ends up in the broth." Those who praise themselves too much end up damaging themselves.

Chi dorme non piglia pesci. – *Who sleeps does not catch fish.*

The fisherman who falls asleep does not notice the fish that bites. A proverb that warns against idleness and laziness.

Dagli amici mi guardi Iddio; che dai nemici mi guardo io. – *God protect me from friends; I take care of my enemies.*

From an enemy, you know what to expect; it is the betrayal of a friend that hurts the most.

Altezza mezza bellezza. – *Being tall means already being half beautiful.*

A typical proverb said by those who are tall and want to taunt those who are shorter, who respond with:

Nella botte piccolo, c'è il vino buono. – *In the small barrel, there is good wine.*

Precisely because the smaller the barrel, in general, the more the wine is prized.

Non è bello ciò che è bello ma è bello ciò che piace. – *What is beautiful is not beautiful, but what is pleasing is beautiful.*

There is no single ideal of beauty; it is subjective. Curiously, there is a dialect variant that is known throughout the country: "Ogne scarrafone è bell 'a mamma soja", which literally means "Every cockroach is beautiful for its mother", a proverb that also indicates the infinite love of mothers.

Il riso abbonda sulla bocca degli stolti. – *Laughter abounds on the mouth of fools.*

Laughing without demeanor is a symptom of rudeness and stupidity.

Sbagliando si impara. – *You learn by making mistakes.*

We must value our mistakes because we can learn and improve from them. There is a popular (grammatically wrong) variant that is "Nessuno nasce imparato" or "No one is born learned".

Chi disprezza compra. – *He who despises buys*

Often, those who speak ill of something are actually much closer to it than one would think.

Chi si fa i fatti suoi campa cent'anni. – *Who does his business, lives for a hundred years.*

The real elixir of long life is not to pay attention to others and to live thinking of our own facts.

Occhio non vede, cuore non duole. – *Eye does not see; heart does not hurt.*

If you don't know that a fact has happened, you can't suffer from it.

Rosso di sera, bel tempo si spera. – *Red sky at night, hopefully good weather the next day.*

It is a popular belief that when the sky takes on reddish shades at sunset, the day that follows will be characterized by good weather.

Il lupo perde il pelo ma non il vizio. – *The wolf loses the hair but not the vice.*

Beware of trusting those who have shown themselves to be negative: it is difficult to really change.

Oggi a me domani a te. – *Today to me, tomorrow to you.*

Life is a wheel, and everyone has positive and negative moments.

Ogni lasciata è persa. – *Every opportunity left is lost.*

We must never postpone when we are faced with an occasion because it is not said that this will recur in the future.

L'ospite è come il pesce: dopo tre giorni puzza. – *The guest is like fish: after three days it stinks.*

Guests are more welcome if their visits don't last too long.

Can che abbaia non morde. – *Barking dog does not bite.*

Often those who show themselves to be the most violent and aggressive are actually less dangerous than ever.

La via dell'Inferno è lastricata di buone intenzioni. – *The road to Hell is paved with good intentions.*

Probably one of the most beautiful proverbs of all: mistakes are often made or wrong things done, shielding behind good intentions.

Non si può avere la botte piena e la moglie ubriaca. – *You can't have your cake and eat it too.*

You can't have everything. The literal translation means "You can't have the barrel full of wine and the wife drunk at the same time".

Tra il dire e il fare c'è di mezzo il mare. – *Between saying and doing there is the sea.*

Everyone is good at words, but only some act. There is a big difference between saying something and doing it.

Chi va con lo zoppo, impara a zoppicare. – *Who goes with the lame, learns to limp.*

It is very easy to learn from others, especially the negative aspects.

Chi si accontenta gode. – *Whoever is satisfied, enjoys it.*

Rather than always looking at what we do not have, we should enjoy what we have and be satisfied with it. There is a very famous song in Italy, "Vasco Rossi", where these words are found, even if they are later denied.

Finché c'è vita c'è speranza. – *As long as there is life, there is hope.*

We must never lose hope. This proverb has ancient origins: in Latin, there was a similar phrase, "Spes ultima dea" referring to the goddess of Hope, who remained even when all the others left the Earth.

Natale con i tuoi; Pasqua con chi vuoi. – *Christmas with your family; Easter with whomever you want.*

This was mentioned in the Italian holidays section. Christmas, by tradition, is spent with family; Easter, on the other hand, can be spent with friends and acquaintances.

Il buon giorno si vede dal mattino. – *The good day starts in the morning.*

A good start is often a good omen for everything to continue in the best way.

I soldi non fanno la felicità. – *Money does not buy happiness.*

Although wealth is a dream shared by all, money does not make us happy (as demonstrated by unhappy millionaires who live a life of extremes).

Il bue dice cornuto all'asino. – The ox says horned to the donkey.

There are those who criticize the faults of others without realizing that they have the same (and often worse) faults. In Italian, "Cornuto" is a fairly serious offense, as it means having been betrayed by your wife.

Chi troppo vuole nulla stringe. – *Who wants too much, gets nothing.*

A proverb similar to that of "Chi si accontenta gode" that once again underlines the importance of appreciating what one has.

Chi rompe paga e i cocci sono i suoi. – *Who breaks pays and the pieces are his.*

If you break an object, you have to pay for it, and at most, you can keep the broken object. This is practically an unwritten rule of many Italian shops and, in fact, the proverb is also taught to small children so that they do not break anything.

Tentar non nuoce. – *There's no harm in trying.*

Rather than doing nothing, it is always better to try.

Se non è zuppa è pan bagnato. – *If it's not soup, it's wet bread.*

This is a proverb that could confuse a person who is learning Italian for the first time, but fortunately, "zuppa" has already been mentioned. This is a soup with stale bread, which is why the proverb means: "Two things are the same even if apparently different".

Tra i due litiganti il terzo gode. – *Between two parties, the third gains.*

When two people argue, there is always a third that takes advantage of the situation.

Tutto fumo e niente arrosto. – *All smoke and no roast.*

Often referred to a person who appears to be exceptional but who turns out to be less than they seemed to be.

Fortunato al gioco, sfortunato in amore. – *Lucky at cards, unlucky in love.*

If a person proves lucky in the game (often cards), then they will be unlucky in love. Often the reverse phrase is also used and is a typical Italian belief.

Si stava meglio quando si stava peggio. – *It was better when it was worse.*

A nostalgic phrase that indicates that when everything seemed worse than today, we actually lived better. Often, in Italy, it is used to allude to old political administrations.

Al cuore non si comanda. – *You can't control your heart.*

The heart does not follow reason but one's feelings. This proverb is often used to justify an apparently impossible love.

Chi trova un amico trova un tesoro. – *Whoever finds a friend finds a treasure.*

A friend is far more precious than any other treasure. Little curiosity: there is a movie with this title of a famous couple composed by Bud Spencer and Terrence Hill.

Non svegliar il can che dorme. – *Do not awaken a sleeping dog.*

Do not provoke those who are calm and placid but potentially dangerous. There is a variable of this proverb that says: "Non c'è peggior cattivo di un buono che diventa cattivo", or "There is none so bad than a good person who becomes bad". Also, in this case, the importance of not provoking others is underlined.

Chi cerca, trova. – *Who seeks, finds.*

If you want to get something, don't just sit still. This proverb has a similar meaning to that of "He who sleeps does not catch fish".

È inutile piangere sul latte versato. – *It is useless to cry over spilled milk.*

After making a mistake, it is useless to cry and despair.

Chi tace acconsente. – *Whoever keeps silent, agrees.*

A proverb against those who do nothing but then complain. If you remain silent, you are an accomplice to what has happened.

L'abito non fa il monaco. – *The dress does not make the priest.*

It is not our appearance that tells us who we are, but what we have on the inside. Similar in meaning is "Non si giudica un libro dalla copertina", which translates as: "You don't judge a book by its cover".

Paese che vai usanza che trovi. – *Country you go, custom you find.*

Never has a proverb proved to be more suited to such a manual: each country has its customary uses. There is a second proverb with a similar meaning, "Mogli e buoi, dei paesi tuoi", which translates as: "Wives and oxen from your countries".

Chi fa da sé fa per tre. – *Those who act alone are worth three.*

Act on your own and roll up your sleeves without waiting for them to help you guarantees the best result.

Non tutte le ciambelle escono con il buco. – *Not all donuts come with a hole.*

It is not certain that everything ends as you expect.

Non tutto il male vien per nuocere. – *Not all evil comes to harm.*

Sometimes what appears to be a negative event actually conceals a benefit.

Una mela al giorno leva il medico di torno. – *An apple a day keeps the doctor away.*

One of the most famous proverbs in Italy: by eating an apple a day, thanks to its beneficial effects, you remain healthy and keep the doctor away.

Una rondine non fa primavera. – *A swallow does not make spring.*

Swallows are very present in Italy and often coincide with the arrival of spring. But a single swallow does not mean that spring has arrived.

Quando il gatto non c'è i topi ballano. – *When the cat is not there, the mice dance.*

When no one is in control, everyone does what they want.

Meglio tardi che mai. – *Better late than never.*

A proverb that is found in many other countries too: it is never late to start; it is always better than to do nothing.

Non c'è peggior sordo di chi non vuol sentire. – *There are none so deaf as those who will not hear.*

It is needless to talk to those who don't want to listen.

La gatta frettolosa fece i gattini ciechi. – *The hasty cat made the kittens blind.*

Doing things in a hurry never leads to positive results.

La fortuna aiuta gli audaci. – *Fortune favors the bold.*

Luck is more benevolent towards those who conquer it. This sentence has an ancient origin, deriving from the Latin expression of Virgil: "Fortuna audaces iuvat".

Meglio un uovo oggi che una gallina domani. – *Better an egg today than a chicken tomorrow.*

An immediate certainty is better than future uncertainty.

Chi va piano va sano e va lontano. Chi va forte va alla morte. – *Who goes slow and steady wins. Whoever goes fast goes to death.*

Better to do things calmly and prudently. The saying is often associated with the fable of the rabbit and the turtle, where the latter manages to win by going slowly and without stopping.

Ride bene chi ride ultimo. – *Laughs best who laughs last.*

A temporary victory is not necessarily a definitive one.

Part 2: Italian Phrase Book

*2500 Super Helpful Phrases and Words
You'll Want for Your Trip to Italy*

Introduction

This is a short presentation of the Italian language. Thinking that you are supposed to learn as you go, you will find short bits of grammar and vocabulary here and there while taking a trip to Italy. Although, initially, you will find some basic information to help you through the rest of the book. In the First Section of the book, you will find an essential and easy description of how to read (Chapter 1), how to count and handle money (Chapter 2), how to talk about weather and time (Chapter 3), how to have a simple conversation with somebody you just met (Chapter 4), and how to ask questions politely (Chapter 5), in Italian.

In the Second Section, you will take a trip to Italy. This trip will give you the chance to learn new words while picking up pieces of grammar (grammar tips) on the way. You will first travel to Italy (Chapter 6), either by airplane or by other means of transportation, and then you will choose your favorite kind of accommodation and go around visiting museums, going shopping, and enjoying the Italian cuisine (Chapter 7). This trip will end with a linguistic overview of the Italian culture, delivered the way your grandparents would have delivered it: through old tales or proverbs and idioms (Chapter 8).

As anticipated, after the trip to Italy, you will find a section of Essential Grammar (Chapter 9). This is the grammar you need for the trip and a little bit more. At the end of the book, you will have the Essential Vocabulary (Chapter 10) that you found in this book, which will enable you to search both in Italian to English and in English to Italian.

Chapter 1 - Letters and Words

There is bad news and good news when you learn how to read in Italian. The bad news is that quite a few letters are pronounced differently from how you would pronounce them in English. The good news is that there are very few rules (five!) and they ALWAYS (with few exceptions) apply.

There are only five **vowels** in Italian:

A as in father

E as in bed

I as in pizza

O as in go

U as in rule

Vowels are always pronounced (never silent) and in the same way. Sometimes vowels appear one after the other, and you should always, at least, try to pronounce them all one after the other. This may be an entertaining challenge, like in *aiuole* (*flower beds*), the Italian word that carries all five vowels.

As for **consonants**, this is when the rules apply to **three** of them (c, g, h). The easy one is h, which is always silent, even in foreign words like *hotel* and *hamburger*. C and g are pronounced differently depending on what comes before or after them; they behave similarly when followed by vowels or h.

Five rules for reading:

1) C before vowels and h:

C is hard as in *cat* before a, o, u, and h:

casa (*house*), **cosa** (*thing*), **culla** (cradle), **chitarra** (guitar), **che** (which)

C sounds like *ch* in *chat* before i and e:

ciao (*hello/goodbye*), **cena** (*dinner*), **Cina** (*China*), **cioccolata** (*chocolate*), **ciuccio** (*pacifier*).

2) G before vowels and h:

G is hard as in *good* before a, o, u, and h:

gatto (*cat*), **gola** (*throat*), **gusto** (*flavor*), **ghetta** (*gaiter*), **ghiaccio** (*ice*)

G is pronounced like j in *jacket* before i and e:

giacca (*jacket*), **gioco** (*game*), **giusto** (*correct*), **gelato** (*ice cream*), **gita** (*trip*)

C and G sound different in three more cases:

3) C after S:

sc is hard as in *scout* before a, o, u, and h:

scatto (*click*), **scossa** (*shake*, [electric] *shock*), **scuola** (*school*), **schiaffo** (*slap*), **scherzo** (*joke*)

sc sounds like *sh* in *sheet* before i and e:

scialle (*shawl*), **scena** (*scene*), **sci** (*ski*), **sciocco** (*silly*), **sciupato** (*damaged*)

4) g before n:

gn like in ***gnocchi*** (*gnocchi*), ***bagno*** (*bathroom*), ***sogno*** (*dream*) sounds like the **gn** in *lasagna*

5) g before l:

gl like in *figlio* (*son*), *foglio* (*sheet*) sounds like **ll** in *million*

Otherwise, as you will see in the next section, consonants are usually pronounced as in English, with the exception of *r*, which is thrilled as in ***bravò!***

The Alphabet

The Italian alphabet has only 26 letters, 5 vowels, and 21 consonants. The letters J, K, X, Y, and W only appear (more and more often nowadays) in foreign words.

A as in *father* (***padre***)

B as in *banana* (***banana***)

C as in *cat* (***gatto***) or *chocolate* (***cioccolato***)

D as in *dice* (***dado***)

E as in *bed* (***letto***)

F as in *flower* (***fiore***)

G as in *good* (***buono***) or *jacket* (***giacca***)

H **always silent**

I as in *pizza* (***pizza***)

L as in *letter* (***lettera***)

M as in *mother* (***madre***)

N as in *nonna* (***grandmother***)

O as in *opera* (***opera***)

P as in *peach* (***pesca***)

Q as in *queen* (***regina***)

R as in *bravo* (**bravò**)

S as in *sound* (**suono**)

T as in *turtle* (**tartaruga**)

U as in *rule* (**regola**)

V as in *valley* (**valle**)

Z as in *zone* (**zona**)

Expected and unexpected hiccups:

Doubles

As letters are (almost) always pronounced in the same way and each sound is (almost) always written in the same way, you can and must rely on what is written. Every letter matters, even when the same one is repeated like in the case of "*a double*": "**una doppia**". Few consonants can be doubled, and they are not pronounced twice; they are simply longer than usual. It matters as much as the difference between:

casa (*home*) and **cassa** (*register*), **caro** (*dear*) and **carro** (*wagon*), **polo** (*pole*) and **pollo** (*chicken*), **fato** (*fate*) and **fatto** (*done*), **ano** (*anus*) and **anno** (*year*), **nono** (*ninth*) and **nonno** (*grandfather*).

Word stress

You can get by without knowing where to stress a word, at the beginning, in the middle, at the end—everybody who makes an effort will understand you. As in English, you cannot tell where to stress a word from how it is written. But you can guess! Most Italian words are stressed on the second to last syllable: *casa, banana.*

This could be tricky for an English speaker since English long words are usually stressed on the first syllable (*station, hospital, restaurant,* etc.), and usually, their Italian counterparts are stressed on the penultimate (one before last) syllable: ***stazione, ospedale, ristorante.*** This pattern is so frequent that Italians pronounce foreign words the same way and will say ***hamburger*** (with a silent h!).

You also can rely on one (and only) clue given by an accent on the last vowel for words that are stressed on the last syllable: *città* (*city*), *comò* (*chest of drawers*), etc., and it luckily distinguishes *papà* (*dad*) from *Papa* (*Pope*).

Chapter 2 - Numbers and Money

In this chapter, you will find the Italian number system and learn how to use cardinal and ordinal numbers. Cardinal numbers express amounts; ordinal numbers refer to an ordered sequence. Cardinal numbers refer to amounts; for example, when you need to say you need *five* (***cinque***) tickets for the train or you would like to buy *four* (***quattro***) apples or order *two* (***due***) glasses of wine. Ordinal numbers are further needed when you need to understand when to take a turn at the *second* (***seconda***) street, or that your seat is on the *third* (***terza***) row or your room is on the *fifth* (***quinto***) floor.

Cardinal numbers

Like in most languages, you need to memorize the first few numbers, and then it becomes easier to discover a system to be able to say any number.

When you pronounce the numbers' names, remember that there are only five **vowels** in Italian (A as in father, E as in bed, I as in pizza, O as in go, U as in rule) and you need to pronounce them all one after the other!

0 *zero*

1 *uno*

2 *due*

3 *tre*

4 *quattro*

5 *cinque*

6 *sei*

7 *sette*

8 *otto*

9 *nove*

10 *dieci*

11 *undici* (*un-* stands for *uno* and *-dici* for *dieci*)

12 *dodici*

13 *tredici*

14 *quattordici*

15 *quindici*

16 *sedici*

17 *diciassette*

18 *diciotto*

19 *diciannove*

After 19, you can easily put together the numbers once you know the tens, hundreds, and so on. As an example, here are the "twenties":

20 *venti*

21 *ventuno*

22 *ventidue*

23 *ventitré*

24 *ventiquattro*

25 *venticinque*

26 *ventisei*

27 *ventisette*

28 *ventotto*

29 *ventinove*

The tens:

10 **dieci**, 20 **venti**, 30 **trenta**, 40 **quaranta**, 50 **cinquanta**, 60 **sessanta**, 70 **settanta**, 80 **ottanta**, 90 **novanta**

The hundreds:

100 **cento**, 200 **duecento**, 300 **trecento**, 400 **quattrocento**, 500 **cinquecento**, 600 **seicento**, 700 **settecento**, 800 **ottocento**, 900 **novecento**

The thousands:

1000 **mille**, 2000 **duemila**, 3000 **tremila**, 4000 **quattromila**, 5000 **cinquemila**, 6000 **seimila**, 7000 **settemila**, 8000 **ottomila**, 9000 **novemila**

As you would have noticed, when there is only one thousand, the word is **mille,** but when there is more than one, the word is **mila**.

After the *thousands*, there are the *millions* (**un milione, due milioni,** *tre milioni*...) and the *billions* (**un miliardo, due miliardi**...).

Ordinal numbers

The first ten ordinal numbers are not systematic, but from the eleventh on, you may just drop the last vowel of the original number and attach -esimo: **undic-i** (*eleven*) becomes **undic-esimo** (*eleventh*).

Primo (*first*), **secondo** (*second*), **terzo** (*third*), **quarto** (*fourth*), **quinto** (*fifth*), **sesto** (*sixth*), **settimo** (*seventh*), **ottavo** (*eighth*), **nono** (*ninth*), **decimo** (*tenth*).

Undicesimo (*eleventh*), **dodicesimo** (*twelth*), **tredicesimo** (*thirteenth*), quattordicesimo (fourteenth), quindicesimo (fifteenth), sedicesimo (sixteenth), diciassettesimo (seventeenth), diciottesimo (eighteenth), diciannovesimo (nineteenth).

Ventesimo (*twentieth*), **ventunesimo** (*twenty-first*), **ventiduesimo** (*twenty-second*)...

trentesimo (*thirtieth*), **quarantesimo** (*forthieth*), **cinquantesimo** (*fiftieth*)... **centesimo** (*hundredth*), **milleimo** (*thousandth*).

GRAMMAR TIP – GENDER AND NUMBER in articles and ordinal numbers

Italian words end differently depending on whether they are feminine or masculine and singular or plural. Most of the time, the last vowel for the feminine singular is -a, feminine plural is -e, masculine singular is -o, masculine plural is -i.

Gender and number show in the articles:

la for *the* (feminine singular)

le for *the* (feminine plural)

una for *a* (feminine singular)

alcune for *some* (feminine plural)

il/lo, *the* singular (masculine singular)

i/gli, *the* plural (masculine plural)

uno/un for *a* (masculine singular)

alcuni for *some* (masculine plural)

When a determiner ending with a vowel (*la*, *le*, **una**, *lo*) is followed by a word beginning with a vowel, the determiner loses its vowel, and its loss is marked by an apostrophe: *la estate* becomes *l'estate* (*the summer*). The exception is for **uno**: the vowel disappears, but no apostrophe marks its place (**un amico**, *a friend* [masculine]).

Ordinal numbers follow this rule too:

Feminine:

La prima bambina (*the first girl*)

Le prime bambine (*the first girls*)

Masculine:

Il primo bambino (*the first boy*)

I primi bambini (*the first boys*)

Some singular masculine words end in -e and their plural counterpart ends in -i:

Mese (*month*) and **mesi** (*months*)

Money (i soldi)

Italy is in the Eurozone, and, like the other 19 of the 28 member states of the European Union, adopted the euro* (code: **EUR**) as its official *currency* (**valuta**). The Greek epsilon (€) and the first letter of the word Europe inspired the € symbol. The euro *banknotes* (**banconote**) are issued in €500, €200, €100, €50, €20, €10, €5. Each banknote (**banconota**) has its own color and is dedicated to an artistic period of European architecture. There are no *bills* (**banconote**) for 1 and 2 euros, but *coins* (**monete**). The euro is divided in 100 *cents* (**centesimi**) and coins are issued for 50c, 20c, 10c, 5c, 2c, and 1c.

*The word euro is written in the same way in Italian and English but it's pronounced quite differently! Remember every vowel is pronounced in the same way one after the other: 'e' as in *bed*, 'u' as in *rule*, 'r' as in *bravo,* and 'o' as in *go*.

Paying for something

Quant'è? for *how much is it?*

È costoso for *it is expensive*

È economico for *it is cheap*

Accettate carte di credito? for *do you accept credit card?*

Posso pagare con il bancomat? for *may I pay with my debit card?*

Posso pagare in dollari? For *may I pay with dollars?*

Certo, accettiamo carte di credito for *of course, we accept credit cards*

Prego, firmate la ricevuta for *please, sign the receipt*

Accettiamo solo contante for *we accept only cash*

Ho i traveller's cheque for *I have traveler's checks*

Posso farti un assegno? For *can I write you a check?*

Usually, *cash* (*i contanti*) is preferred over the *credit* (*carta di credito*) or *debit card* (*bancomat*). Also, when you buy anything in Italy, they are required by law to give you a *receipt* (*una ricevuta*).

> **GRAMMAR TIP: the conjugation of the verb *comprare* (to buy), *vendere* (to sell) and *pagare* (*to pay*)**

Italian regular verbs conjugate for every person and tense: the form changes depending on who performs the action and when. There are three groups of regular verbs, and you can recognize them by the last three letters in their infinitive form. The first group ends in -are, like *comprare* (*to buy*) and *pagare* (*to pay*), the second group ends in –ere, like *vendere* and *spendere* (*to spend*), and the third group ends in –ire, like *partire* (*to leave*). When you conjugate a verb, it loses the infinitive ending (-are, -ere or -ire) and gains the end for a person in a particular time (present, past, future...). Usually, there are six different endings for six different persons: *io* (*I*), *tu* (*you*), *lei/lui* (*she/he*), *noi* (*we*), *voi* (*you* many) and *essi/loro* (*they*). Given that every person ends differently, in Italian, it is not important to mention the pronoun (*io, tu, lei, lui...*) and it can be simply dropped! When it comes to money, the verbs you may need most frequently are *vend-ere* (*to sell*), *compr-are* (*to buy*) and *pag-are* (*to pay*).

Present of *comprare* (*to buy*):

Io compro *(i.e., compr-o)* for *I buy*

Tu compri *(i.e., compr-i)* for *you buy*

Lei/lui compra *(i.e., compr-a)* for *s/he buys*

Noi compriamo *(i.e., compr-iamo)* for *we buy*

Voi comprate *(i.e., compr-ate)* for *you* (many) *buy*

Essi/Loro comprano *(i.e., compr-ano)* for *they buy*

Present of **vendere** (*to sell*):

Io vendo *(i.e., vend-o)* for *I sell*

Tu vendi *(i.e., vend-i)* for *you sell*

Lei/lui vende *(i.e., vend-e)* for *s/he sell*

Noi vendiamo *(i.e., vend-iamo)* for *we sell*

Voi vendete *(i.e., vend-ete)* for *you* (many) *sell*

Essi/loro vendono *(i.e., vend-ono)* for *they sell*

Present of **pagare** (*to pay*)

Io pago for *I pay*

Tu paghi for *you pay*

Lei/lui paga for *she/he pays*

Noi paghiamo for *we pay*

Voi pagate for *you (many) pay*

Essi/loro pagano for *they pay*

Other relevant verbs related to money are:

Chiedere in prestito for *to borrow*

Incassare un assegno for *to cash a check*

Costare for *to cost*

Girare un assegno for *to endorse*

Cambiare for *to change*

Prestare for *to lend*

Ordinare for *to order*

Dovere for *to owe*

Rimborsare for *to refund*

Risparmiare for *to save*

Spendere for *to spend*

Trasferire del denaro/dei soldi for *to transfer money*

At the bank (*in banca*) or the ATM

You can find an *ATM* (*il bancomat*) right outside or after the first door of a bank as well as at the airport or station. It is not common to find one in a store!

Dov'è il bancomat? For *where is the cash machine?*

ATMs usually allow you to choose your language, but there are keys on the board that may be in Italian only: *esatto* (*exact*), *conferma* (*confirm*), *esegui* (*enter*), *annulla/annullare* (*cancel*).

Dov'è la banca? For *where is the bank?*

Vorrei aprire un conto corrente for *I would like to open an account*

Vorrei fare un prelievo for *I would like to make a withdrawal*

Vorrei fare un versamento for *I would like to make a deposit*

Ho perso il mio bancomat for *I lost my debit card*

Ho perso la mia carta di credito for *I lost my credit card*

La mia carta non funziona for *my card does not work*

La mia carta è stata smagnetizzata for *my card has been deactivated*

La mia carta è stata rubata for *my card has been stolen*

La mia carta è stata trattenuta dal bancomat for *my card has been eaten by the ATM*

Il conto for *the account*

Il saldo for *the balance*

La banca for *the bank*

Il conto bancario for *the bank account*

La banconota/le banconote for *the bill or banknote*

I contanti for *cash*

Il cambio for *the exchange*

Il resto for *the change*

L'assegno/gli assegni for *the check*

Il conto for *the bill*

La carta/le carte di credito for *the credit card/cards*

Il cliente for *the client*

Il dollaro/i dollari for *the dollar/dollars*

Le spese for *the expenses*

L'interesse/gli interessi for *the interest/interests*

Il tasso d'interesse for *the interest rate*

Il prestito for *the loan*

Il vaglia postale for *the money order*

Il beneficiario/i beneficiari for *the payee/payees*

Il pagamento/i pagamenti for *the payment/payments*

La percentuale/le percentuali for *the percentage*

L'assegno personale for *the personal check*

Il prezzo/i prezzi for *the price/prices*

Il rimborso for *the refund*

Lo stipendio/gli stipendi for *the salary*

Le spese for *the spendings*

Il prelievo/i prelievi for *the withdrawal/withdrawals*

At currency exchange or exchange bureau (il cambiavalute)

You can change currency (*la valuta*) at most banks (*banche*), or you can find a currency exchange counter at the airport (*aeroporto*), station (*stazione*), and in some hotels (*alberghi*) and stores (*negozi*).

Beware that a currency exchange or bureau de change (*il cambiavalute*) is a business that makes its profit by buying foreign currency and then selling the same currency at a higher exchange rate. Sometimes you might want to ask whether they are charging you a *commission* or *fee* (*commissione*) or a *surcharge* (*un sovrapprezzo*) on the *purchase* (*acquisto*) or *sale* (*vendita*) of your money. Usually, the closer the buying and selling rates, the fairer the currency exchange.

Quant'è il cambio? For *how much is the exchange rate?*

Vorrei cambiare 100 dollari in euro for *I would like to change 100 dollars in euro*

Quant'è la commissione? For *how much is your fee/commission?*

Vorrei comprare/vendere degli euro for *I would like to buy/sell some euros*

Vorrei comprare/vendere dei dollari for *I would like to buy/sell some dollars*

Vorrei banconote di piccolo/grosso taglio for *I would like small/big bills*

Vorrei banconote di taglio misto for *I would like mixed bills*

Mi può cambiare queste banconote? for *could you break this in smaller bills?*

Chapter 3 - Time and Weather

In this chapter, we will use the number system to learn how to talk about time. In Italian, *time* and *weather* are expressed by the same word, *tempo*. Indeed, they are strictly connected as weather (*tempo*), and the temperature (*temperatura*) usually changes during the day (*giorno*), the months (*mesi*), the seasons (*stagioni*).

What time is it?

Times goes by in *ore* (*hours*), *minuti* (*minutes*), *secondi* (*seconds*), and a day (*giorno*) lasts 24 hours. It starts at *mezzanotte* (*midnight*), goes to *l'una* (1 a.m.), then *le due* (2 a.m.), then *le tre* (3 a.m.), and so on until **le ventitré e cinquantanove** (*23:59* or *11:59 p.m.*).

To ask and tell about time, you use the third person of *essere* (*to be*); the person will be either singular (*è* for *is*) or plural (*sono* for *are*) depending on the time. If it is one o'clock, then you will use the singular *è* (it is only one!); otherwise, you will use the plural *sono* (it is more than one!!).

Che ora è? or *Che ore sono?* for *what time it is?*

È l'una or *sono le due* for *it is 1 o'clock* or *it is two o'clock*

Sono le quattro e trenta minuti for *it is four-thirty*

Sono le diciassette e quarantacinque minuti e dieci secondi for *it is 5:45:10 p.m.*

Instead of the minutes, you can say what fraction of the hour it is: *un quarto* (*a quarter*), *mezza* (*a half*), *tre quarti* (*three quarters*). As in English, you use *e* (*and*) between the number and the portion of the hour:

Sono le undici e un quarto/ e mezza/ e tre quarti for *it is 11 and a quarter/and a half/and three quarters*

You can also say how many minutes to the hour:

Mancano dieci minuti alle quattordici for *ten to 2 p.m.*

Sono 5 all'una for *it is 5 to 1 a.m.*

Manca un quarto alle dieci for *it is a quarter to 10 a.m.*

In Italy, they use the 24-hour system, but you can use the 12-hour system and indicate which part of the day you are referring to:

la mattina for *the morning*

il pomeriggio for *the afternoon*

la sera for *the evening*

la notte for *the night*

Che ore sono?

Sono le due di notte for *it is two in the morning (a.m.)*

Sono le dieci del mattino for *it is 10 in the morning (a.m.)*

Sono le quattro del pomeriggio for *it is four in the afternoon (p.m.)*

Sono le 7 di sera for *it is 7 p.m.*

Sono le 11 della notte for *it is 11 p.m.*

GRAMMAR TIP: the use of *di* (*of*) with an article

The preposition *di* (*of*) indicates possession like *la casa di Matteo* (*the house of Matteo*). When followed by an article, they blend:

Di + *la* = *della* (*of the* – feminine singular)

Di + *le* = *delle* (*of the* – feminine plural)

Di + *il* = *del* or *di+lo*= *dello* (*of the* – masculine singular)

Di + *i* = *dei* or *di* + *gli* = *degli* (*of the* – masculine plural)

The days of the week

In Italian, the days of the week (*i giorni della settimana*) are not capitalized, they are all masculine but for Sunday, and they do not require a preposition in a sentence: *il lunedì* (*Monday*), *il martedì* (*Tuesday*), *il mercoledì* (*Wednesday*), *il giovedì* (*Thursday*), *il venerdì* (*Friday*), *il sabato* (*Saturday*), *la domenica* (*Sunday*).

Il lunedì vado in palestra, for *on Monday I go to the gym*

Vado a teatro sabato sera for *I go to the theater on Saturday evening*

To ask about the day of the week, you use *che giorno*, *what day*:

Che giorno è oggi? for *what day is today?*

Oggi è martedì. for *today is Tuesday*

What's the date?

In Italian, you use the ordinal number to refer to the first of any month and the cardinal number to refer to all the other days.

Il primo gennaio, but il *due/tre/quattro/cinque/... gennaio*

Usually, to say a date, you use *il* (*the*) followed by the number of the day like *primo*, *due*, *tre*... and by the preposition *di* (*of*) and the month:

Il primo di gennaio (*January*), *febbraio* (*February*), *marzo* (*March*), *aprile* (*April*), *maggio* (*May*), *giugno* (*June*), *luglio* (*July*), *agosto* (*August*), *settembre* (*September*), *ottobre* (*October*), *novembre* (*November*), *dicembre* (*December*).

To mention a date in the past, however, you may just say the number, the month, and the year: *il **quattro novembre 1974**, the fourth of November 1974*. To mention a year, though, in Italian, you say the whole number without breaking it into two parts.

1950 **millenovecentocinquanta** (*nineteen fifty*)

1999 **millenovecentonovantanove** (*nineteen ninety-nine*)

2020 **duemila e venti**

Il calendario delle feste

Italy has been a Catholic country for a long time and many holidays are Catholic, but not all!

The first holiday of the year is *the 1st of January* for **Capodanno** (literally the 'head of the year') or **primo dell'anno**. As part of the Catholic festivities, the sixth of January is *Epiphany* (**Epifania**), and sometime in the spring, two days celebrate *Easter* (**Pasqua**) and *Easter Monday* (**Lunedì dell'Angelo**).

After Easter, a series of non-religious national holidays follow and these are observed by most of the population as well. The 25th of April is the *Liberation Day* (**la Festa della Liberazione**) of Italy from the Nazi occupation in 1945. Italy celebrates *International Workers' Day* (**la festa dei lavoratori**) on the 1st of May, like in most countries, instead of Labour Day and people usually simply call it **il Primo Maggio**. June second is *Republic Day* (**la Festa della Repubblica**) to remember when, in 1964, Italy voted in favor of a Republic instead of a Monarchy.

In the summer, on August 15th Italians celebrate both the **Ferragosto** and the *Assumption* (**l'Assunzione**). The first was introduced by the emperor Augustus in 18 BCE as "Festivals [Holidays] of the Emperor Augustus" to celebrate the harvest and the end of a long period of intense agricultural labor, and, over time, became a long weekend (**ponte di ferragosto**); the second is the bodily taking up of the Virgin Mary into Heaven at the end of her earthly life.

Then, in the Fall, is *All Saints' Day* (**Tutti i Santi** or **Ognissanti**) on November 1st, the *Immaculate Conception* (**l'Immacolata Concezione**) on December 8th and *Christmas Day* (**Natale**) and *Saint Stephen Day* (**Santo Stefano**) on December 25th and 26th respectively.

Surprisingly, for many travelers, is the extent to which a holiday impacts everything: transportation, stores, restaurants, and schools and students. So much that if you are planning to arrive on a major holiday, you may want to make sure there will be transportation to take you from the airport to your hotel, or how much the surcharge would be.

Che festa c'è il 6 gennaio? For *what holidays is on the 6th of January?*

Siete aperti per le feste? For *are you open during the holidays?*

Buone feste! for *Happy holidays!*

Buon Natale! for *Merry Christmas!*

Buon Capodanno! Or *Felice anno nuovo!* for *Happy New Year*

GRAMMAR TIP: the conjugation of the verb *celebrare* (*to celebrate*), present, past and future

You may like to use the verb **celebrare** (*to celebrate*) to refer to the holidays as well as all kinds of celebrations: birthdays, graduations, weddings, etc. As in English, you can always opt out and just use the verb **fare** (*to do*).

Come celebrerai le feste? For *how will you celebrate the holidays?*

Cosa fate per le feste? For *what are you doing for the holidays?*

Simple Present:

Io celebro for *I celebrate*

Tu celebri for *you celebrate*

Lei/lui celebra for *she/he celebrate*

Noi celebriamo for *we celebrate*

Voi celebrate for *you* (many) *celebrate*

Essi/loro celebrano for *they celebrate*

Present Perfect:

Io ho celebrato for *I celebrated*

Tu hai celebrato for *you celebrated*

Lei/lui ha celebrato for *she/he celebrated*

Noi abbiamo celebrato for *we celebrated*

Voi avete celebrato for *you* (many) *celebrated*

Essi/loro hanno celebrato for *they celebrated*

Future:

Io celebrerò for *I will celebrate*

Tu celebrerai for *you will celebrate*

Lei/lui celebrerà for *she/he will celebrate*

Noi celebreremo for *we will celebrate*

Voi celebrerete for *you* (many) *will celebrate*

Essi/loro celebreranno for *they will celebrate*

*In Italian, the present perfect is used (sometimes erroneously) more frequently as a past than a present perfect. And it happens that Italians would say *io ho fatto* when you say *I did*, and *io sono andato* when you say *I went*.

Speaking of time: how old are you?

To ask *how old are you?* you need to ask for how many years:

Quanti anni hai? for *how old are you?*

Io ho 5 anni for *I am 5 years old*

Quanti anni avevi nel 2001? for *how old were you in 2001?*

Quanti anni avrai l'anno prossimo? for *how old will you be next year?*

GRAMMAR TIP: the conjugation of avere

The verb *avere* (*to have*) is irregular, as in English and, as in English, is normally used to indicate possession or as an auxiliary for the past and conditional. In Italian, the two most frequent past tenses are the present perfect and the imperfect. You use the present perfect for actions completed (finished!) in the recent past and the imperfect for ongoing or habitual actions in the past: *mentre bevevo il caffè, ho finito i miei compiti* (*while I was drinking my coffee, I finished my homework*).

Simple Present:

Io ho* for *I have*

Tu hai* for *you have*

Lei/lui ha* for *she/he has*

Noi abbiamo for *we have*

Voi avete for *you have*

Loro/essi hanno* for *they have*

Present perfect:

Io ho avuto for I had

Tu hai avuto for *you had*

Lei/lui ha avuto for *she/he had*

Noi abbiamo avuto for *we had*

Voi avete avuto for *you* (many) *had*

Essi/loro hanno avuto for *they had*

Imperfect:

Io avevo for *I had*

Tu avevi for *you had*

Lei/lui aveva for *she/he had*

Noi avevamo for *we had*

Voi avevate for *you* (many) *had*

Essi/loro avevano for *they had*

Future:

Io avrò for *I will have*

Tu avrai for *you will have*

Lei/lui avrà for *she/he will have*

Noi avremo for *we will have*

Voi avrete for *you* (many) *will have*

Essi/loro avranno for *they will have*

*Remember the *h* is always silent

Essential vocabulary to speak and ask about time:

Quando? for *when?*

Ieri (*yesterday*), *oggi* (*today*), *domani* (*tomorrow*)

Quando arrivate in Italia? for *when do you arrive in Italy?*

Siamo arrivati ieri for *we arrived yesterday*

Arriviamo oggi for *we arrive today*

Arriveremo domani for *we will arrive tomorrow*

Che/Quale? for *which/on which?*

Che/quale giorno/giorni for *which day/days*

Che/quale settimana/settimane for *which week/weeks*

Che/quale mese/mesi for *which month/months*

Che/quale anno/anni for *which year/years*

In quale? for *in which?*

In quale secolo/secoli for *in which century/centuries*

In quale stagione? for *in which season?*

Prima/dopo for *before/after*

Presto/tardi for *early/late*

Mai/sempre for *never/always*

Piu tardi for *later*

A volte for *sometimes*

Qualche volta for *some times*

Una volta for *once*

Due volte for *twice*

Tre volte for *three times*

Più o meno for *more or less* (*sono più o meno le sei* for *it's six more or less*)

Circa for *about*

Weather (tempo) and climate (il clima)

Italian has one word, *tempo*, for both *time* and *weather*. Indeed, the weather does change in time with the *seasons*, *le stagioni* (singular: *la stagione*).

L'inverno, gli inverni for *the winter/winters*

La primavera, le primavere for *the spring/springs*

L'estate, le estati for *the summer/summers*

L'autunno, gli autunni for *the autumn/autumns*

When you ask and talk about the weather, you use either *essere* (*to be*) or *fare* (*to do*): apparently, the weather "does" itself.

L'inverno è freddo for *the winter is cold*

La primavera è fresca for *the spring is cool/crisp*

L'estate è calda for *the summer is hot*

L'autunno è piovoso for *the autumn is rainy*

Or

In inverno fa freddo for *in the winter is cold*

In estate fa caldo for *in the summer is hot*

To ask how the weather is, you always use *fare* (*to do*), but to answer, you can use either *fare* or *essere*:

Che tempo fa? for *how is the weather?*

Fa bello/brutto for *the weather is good/bad*

È bello/brutto for *the weather is good/bad*

Weather and temperature

Italy uses the metric system and temperatures are expressed in *Celsius scale* (**Scala Celsius**), which is divided into *centigrade degrees* (**gradi centigradi**). With this system, water freezes at **zero** °C (*zero*) and boils at **cento** °C (*100*). Temperatures range between -10 °C (14 °F), to 0 (32 °F) and 10 °C (50 °F) during winter and between 20 °C (68 °F) and 40°C (104°F) during the summer.

Another difference is that, in English, the temperature *is*, while in Italian, *ci sono* (*there are*) degrees of temperature:

Qual è la temperatura oggi? For *what's the temperature today?*

Quanti gradi ci sono fuori? For *what's the temperature* (literally: how many degrees there are) *outside*?

Ci sono 21 (ventuno) gradi celsius (circa 70 gradi Fahrenheit) for *it's 21 degrees celsius (about 70 Fahrenheit)*

Essential vocabulary to talk about the weather

Bel tempo for *it's good weather*

Brutto tempo for *it's bad weather*

Il cielo for *the sky*

Il sole for *the sun*

La brina for *the frost*

La pioggia for *the rain*

La grandine for *the hail*

Il temporale for *the storm*

La neve for *the snow*

Il ghiaccio for *the ice*

La nebbia for *the fog*

La foschia for *the haze/mist*

Il lampo for *lightning*

La rugiada for *the dew*

Il vento for *the wind*

L'arcobaleno for *the rainbow*

Il sole for *sun*

La nuvola/le nuvole for *cloud/clouds*

Piove for *it's raining*

Diluvia for *it's pouring*

Grandina for *it's hailing*

Nevica for *it's snowing*

È umido for *it's humid*

È nuvoloso for *it's overcast*

C'è il sole for *it's sunny*

C'è il vento for it's windy

C'è la nebbia for it's foggy

C'è la pioggia for it's rainy

C'è burrasca for *it's stormy*

Ci sono lampi e tuoni for *lightning and thunder*

Piove a catinelle for *it rains cats and dogs*

GRAMMAR TIP: the use and conjugation of fare (to do)

Io faccio for *I do*

Tu fai for *you do*

Lei/lui fa for *she/he does*

Noi facciamo for *we do*

Voi fate for *you* (more than one) *do*

Loro/essi fanno for *they do*

Fare is a very useful word, especially in fixed expressions that might be tricky for an English speaker:

Fare il biglietto for *to buy a ticket*

Fare un viaggio/una gita for *to take a trip/an excursion*

Fare una passeggiata for *to take a walk*

Fare la fila for *to wait in line*

Fare una fotografia for *to take a picture*

Fare finta for *to pretend*

Far vedere for *to show*

Fare tardi for *to be late*

Fare presto for *to be quick*

Fare alla romana for *to go Dutch*

Fare la spesa for *do the shopping*

Fare le spese for *to go shopping*

Fare il pieno for *to fill up the gas tank*

Fare colazione for *to have breakfast*

Fare la doccia for *to have a shower*

Chapter 4 - Greetings, Salutations, and Introductions

Now you can read and use very frequent common phrases and learn how to meet with people.

Greetings, pleasantries, and salutations

Salve for *hello*

Buon giorno for *good morning*

Buon pomeriggio for *good afternoon*

Buona sera for *good evening*

Buona notte for *goodnight*

Arrivederci for *so long*

A presto for *see you soon*

A domani for *until tomorrow*

Ciao for *hello* and *goodbye*

Grazie for *thank you*

Prego for *you are welcome*

Benvenuto for *welcome*

Signorina for *signorina*

Signora for *Mrs*

Signore for *Mr*

Signori for *Mr and Mrs*

Introductions and basic conversation

For a basic conversation, you need three verbs: ***chiamarsi*** (*to be named, to be called*), ***essere*** (*to be*) and ***stare*** (*to be, to stay*).

When introducing yourself or somebody else, you use the verb ***chiamarsi*** (literally: *to call oneself*).

GRAMMAR TIP: how to conjugate a verb

In Italian, verbs change their ending depending on the person (who performs the action). There are six persons: ***io*** (*I*), ***tu*** (*you*), ***lei/lui*** (*she/he*), ***noi*** (*we*), ***voi*** (*you* – more than one) and ***loro/essi*** (*they*). ***Chiamarsi*** is a very particular verb, and when you use it, it divides itself into ***chiamare*** (*to call*) and ***-si*** (*oneself*) and both change depending on the person:

Io mi chiamo means *my name is* (literally: *I call myself*

Tu ti chiami for *your name is* (literally: *you call yourself*)

Lei/lui si chiama for *her/his name is* (literally: *she/he calls herself/himself*)

Noi ci chiamiamo for *our names are* (literally: *we call ourselves*)

Voi vi chiamate for *your names are* (literally: *you call yourselves*)

Loro/essi si chiamano for *their names are* (literally: *you call yourselves*)

Mi chiamo Lara for *my name is Lara*

Lei come si chiama? for *what is your name?* (formal)

Tu come ti chiami? *for what is your name?* (informal)

You can alternatively use the verb *to be* (***essere***) for introductions:

Buon giorno, noi siamo la signora e il signor White. Voi come vi chiamate?

Good morning, we are Mrs. and Mr. White. What's your name? (formal)

Noi siamo Marco e Maria, i cugini di Francesco.

We are Marco and Maria, Francesco's cousins.

GRAMMAR TIP: the conjugation of *essere* **(***to be***), present, past and future**

This verb, like in English, is highly irregular and most needed:

Present:

Io sono for *I am*

Tu sei for *you are*

Lui/lei è for *she/he is*

Noi siamo for *we are*

Voi siete for *you (more than one) are*

Essi/loro sono for *they are*

Past:*

Io sono stato for *I was*

Tu sei stato for *you were*

Lei è stata/lui è stato for *she/he was*

Noi siamo stati for *we were*

Voi siete stati for *you* (many) *were*

Essi/loro sono stati for *they were*

Future:

Io sarò for *I will be*

Tu sarai for *you will be*

Lei/lui sarà for *she/he will be*

Noi saremo for *we will be*

Voi sarete for *you* (many) *will be*

Essi saranno for *they will be*

* the past is rendered with the most frequently used past tense rather than correctly translated with the less frequently used preterit *(io fui, tu fosti, lei/lui fu, noi fummo, voi foste, essi furono)*, especially in the north of Italy.

Sometimes *families* (***famiglie***) gather together and you may need to introduce yours or understand the relationship between whoever is being introduced to you:

Buongiorno, io sono Marco, questa è mia moglie, Marcella, e questi sono i nostri figli, Pietro e Luca.

Good morning, I am Marco, this is my wife, Marcella and these are our sons, Pietro and Luca.

Famiglia (la famiglia, le famiglie) for *family, families*

Moglie (la moglie, le mogli) for *wife, wives*

Marito (il marito, i mariti) for *husband, husbands*

Madre (la madre, le madri) for *mother, mothers*

Padre (il padre, i padri) for *father, fathers*

Figlio (il figlio, i figli) for *son, sons*

Figlia (la figlia, le figlie) for *daughter, daughters*

Fratello (il fratello, i fratelli) for *brother, brothers*

Sorella (la sorella, le sorelle) for *sister, sisters*

Zia (la zia, le zie) for *aunt, aunts*

Zio (lo zio, gli zii) for *uncle, uncles*

Cugina (la cugina, le cugine) for *cousin, cousins (feminine)*

Cugino (il cugino, i cugini) for *cousin, cousins (masculine)*

Nipote (il nipote, i nipoti) for *nephew, nephews and grandson, grandsons*

Nipote (la nipote, le nipoti) for *niece, nieces and granddaughter, granddaughters*

Nonna (la nonna, le nonne) for *grandmother, grandmothers*

Nonno (il nonno, i nonni) for *grandfather, grandfathers*

Suocera (la suocera, le suocere) for *mother-in-law, mother-in-laws*

Suocero (il suocero, i suoceri) for *father-in-law, father-in-laws*

Nuora (la nuora, le nuore) for *daughter-in-law, daughter-in-laws*

Genero (il genero, i generi) for *son-in-law, son-in-laws*

These are the common replies when being introduced or answering to an introduction:

Piacere di conoscerti/conoscerla for *pleased to meet you (informal/formal)*

Molto piacere for *very pleased [to meet you]*

Piacere for *pleased [to meet you]*

As in English, during introductions, you can reply asking how they are, and to do so, you use **stare** (literally *to stay*):

Come stai/sta? for *how are you?* (informal/formal)

Io sto bene e tu? for *I am well and you?*

Noi stiamo bene e voi? for *we are well and you?*

Bene grazie e tu/lei? for *well, thank you, and you?* (informal/formal)

Or you may want to say **molto bene** (*very well*), **meglio** (*better*) **non c'è male** (*not bad*), **così così** (*so and so*), **non bene** (*not well*), **male** (*badly*).

If you want to say more about how you are, you may need to use *essere*: ***sono riposato/stanco*** (I am rested/tired), ***sono malato/guarito*** (I am sick/healed), ***sono raffreddato*** (*I have a cold*)...

GRAMMAR TIP: the conjugation of *stare* (*to be, to stay*)

Io sto bene for *I am well*

Tu stai bene for *you are well*

Lui/lei sta bene for *she/he is well*

Noi stiamo bene for *we are well*

Voi state bene for *you (many) are well*

Essi/loro stanno bene for *they are well*

Stare is also used in a series of very frequent fixed expressions:

Stare zitta for *to be quiet*

Stare attento for *to pay attention*

Stare con qualcuno for *to be in a relationship with*

Stare fermo for *to keep still*

Stare fuori for *to be outside*

Stare a pennello for *to fit like a glove*

Stare in guardia for *to be on one's guard*

Stare in piedi for *to be standing*

As in English, you can also ask *how is it going* saying:

Come va? for *how is it going?* or *how are you?*

Va bene/benissimo for *it is going well/very well* or *I am well/very well*

Va tutto bene for *all is going well*

Grazie for *thank you*

Prego for *you're welcome*

Per favore for *please*

Certo for *sure/of course*

Dica for *please, tell me*

Non parlo italiano [molto bene] for *I do not speak Italian [very well]*

Per favore, potrebbe parlare lentamente? for *could you, please, speak slowly?*

Può ripetere, per favore? for *could you repeat, please?*

Non capisco for *I do not understand**

Capisco for *I understand*

Cosa significa? for *what does that mean?*

Come si dice/si chiama questo in italiano? for *how do you say this in Italian?*

Potrebbe scrivermelo? for *could you please write this down for me?*

Parli inglese? For *do you speak English?*

C'è qualcuno che parla inglese? For *does anybody speak English?*

Per favore, potrebbe parlare inglese? For *could you please speak English?*

*To make a negative sentence in Italian, you only need to place the word *non* (*not*) before the verb.

GRAMMAR TIP: the conjugation of *parlare* (*to speak*), *scrivere* (*to write*), *ripetere* (*to repeat*), *capire* (*to understand*)

Simple Present of *parlare* (*to speak*):

Io parlo for *I speak*

Tu parli for *you speak*

Lei/lui parla for *she/he speaks*

Noi parliamo for *we speak*

Voi parlate for *you* (many) *speak*

Essi/loro parlano for *they speak*

Simple Present of *scrivere* (*to write*):

Io scrivo for *I write*

Tu scrivi for *you write*

Lei/lui scrive for *she/he writes*

Noi scriviamo for *we write*

Voi scrivete for *you* (many) *write*

Essi/loro scrivono for *they write*

Simple Present of *ripetere* (*to repeat*):

Io ripeto for *I repeat*

Tu ripeti for *you repeat*

Lei/lui ripete for *she/he repeats*

Noi ripetiamo for *we repeat*

Voi ripetete for *you* (many) *repeat*

Essi/loro ripetono for *they repeat*

Simple Present of *capire* (*to understand*):

Io capisco for *I understand*

Tu capisci for *you understand*

Lei/lui capisce for *she/he understand*

Noi capiamo for *we understand*

Voi capite for *you* (many) *understand*

Essi/loro capiscono for *they understand*

GRAMMAR TIP: *can (posso)* and *could (potrei)*

When you ask for something, as in English, in Italian, you can either use **posso?** (*can I?*) or **potrei?** (*could I?*) depending on the circumstances and how polite you would like to be. As in English, they are both followed by the infinitive form of a verb: **posso ripetere** (*I can repeat*) or **potrei ripetere** (*I could repeat*), **puoi ripetere** (*can you repeat?*) or **potresti ripetere** (*could you repeat?*).

Simple Present:

Io posso for *I can*

Tu puoi for *you can*

Lei/lui può for *she/he can*

Noi possiamo for *we can*

Voi potete for *you* (many) *can*

Essi/loro possono for *they can*

Present conditional:

Io potrei for *I could*

Tu potresti for *you could*

Lei/lui potrebbe for *she/he could*

Noi potremmo for *we could*

Voi potreste for *you* (many) *could*

Essi/loro potrebbero for *they could*

Present perfect:

Io ho potuto for *I could (in the past)*

Tu hai potuto for *you could*

Lei/lui ha potuto for *she/he could*

Noi abbiamo potuto for *we could*

Voi avevte potuto for *you* (many) *could*

Essi/loro hanno potuto for *they could*

Present perfect conditional:

Io avrei potuto for *I could have*

Tu avresti potuto for *you could have*

Lei/lui avrebbe potuto for *she/he could have*

Noi avremmo potuto for *we could have*

Voi avreste potuto for *you* (many) *could have*

Essi/loro avrebbero potuto for *they could have*

Future:

Io potrò for *I will be able to*

Tu potrai for *you will be able to*

Lei/lui potrà for *she/he will be able to*

Noi potremo for *we will be able to*

Voi potrete for *you* (many) *will be able to*

Essi/loro potranno for *they will be able to*

Chapter 5 - Asking Questions

In this chapter, you will find what words better translate the English question words in different situations. And you will learn how to ask questions politely and give (unfortunately) negative answers.

GRAMMAR TIP: the conditional is polite!

To ask for something politely, when ordering at a restaurant, on the plane, buying tickets, asking for directions, in Italian, you use the conditional of *volere* (*to want*), which corresponds to using *would*, but often translates as *would like*:

Present Indicative:

Io voglio for *I want*

Tu vuoi for *you want*

Lei/lui vuole for *she/he wants*

Noi vogliamo for *we want*

Voi volete for *you* (many) *want*

Essi/loro vogliono for *they want*

Present Conditional:

Io vorrei for *I would*

Tu vorresti for *you would*

Lei/lui vorrebbe for *she/he would*

Noi vorremmo for *we would*

Voi vorreste for *you would*

Essi/loro vorrebbero for *they would*

GRAMMAR TIP: the conjugation of *scusarsi* (*to apologize*)

As in English, another way to be polite is to excuse yourself. **Scusarsi** is a reflexive verb like **chiamarsi** (*to be named*) and has two parts: the infinitive **scusarsi** breaks into the verb stem (*scus-*) and the reflexive pronoun (*-si*). Both change for each person! The pronoun is placed in front of the verb, which is conjugated like a regular verb ending in -are (as if it was **scusare**, which means *to excuse*). Basically, **scusarsi** (*to apologize*) in Italian, matches *to excuse oneself.*

Simple present:

Io mi scuso for *I apologize*

Tu ti scusi for *you apologize*

Lei/lui si scusa for *she/he apologizes*

Noi ci scusiamo for *we apologize*

Voi vi scusate for *you* (many) *apologize*

Essi/loro si scusano for *they apologize*

Mi scusi, sa dirmi dove, quando, perché...?

Excuse me, can you tell me where, when, why...?

What

There are three different ways to ask *what*: *che, cosa,* and *che cosa*. When it is possible to substitute *what* with *which,* you can use *che*; otherwise, you use either *che cosa* or *cosa.*

Che giorno è oggi? for *what day is today?*

Che ora è? for *what time is it?*

Che cosa/cosa c'è da mangiare al ristorante? for *what is there to eat at the restaurant?*

Che cosa/Cosa fanno nel pomeriggio? for *what do they do in the afternoon?*

Cos'è questo/quello? for *what is this/that?*

Cosa vorresti fare? for *what would you like to do?*

Who

The word *chi* corresponds to the word *who*:

Chi sei? for *who are you?*

Chi sono questi bambini? for *who are these children?*

Chi è la ragazza con Paolo? for *who is the girl with Paolo?*

Where

You use *dove* for *where*:

Dove sono i nostri posti? for *where are our seats?*

Dov'è il teatro/la stazione/il ristorante...? for *where is the theater/the station/the restaurant?*

How?

Come is used to translate *how* and is used with *essere* to find out how people or things are:

Com'è la pizza? for *how is the pizza?*

Com'è la vacanza? for *how is the vacation?*

Come sono le spiagge? for *how are the beaches?*

Come stai? for *how are you?*

Come sta? for *how is she/he?*

Come stanno i tuoi genitori? for *how are your parents?*

As you saw in Chapter 2, *come* (*how*) with *chiamarsi* (*be named, be called*) is used to ask somebody's name: *come ti chiami?* for *what's your name?* and *mi chiamo Mario* for *my name is Mario*

Why?

Perché is used for both *why* and *because*:

Perché ridi for *why are you laughing?*

Perché andate in Italia for *why are you going to Italy?*

Perché suoni la chitarra for *why do you play the guitar?*

Perché è divertente for *because it is funny*

Perché i nostri genitori vivono in Italia for *because our parents live in Italy*

Perché mi piace for *because I like it*

When

Quando is used for *when*:

Quand'è il concerto? for *when is the concert?*

Quando parte il treno? for *when does the train leave?*

How much and how many

Quanto is used for *how much,* refers to a quantity, and varies with gender:

Quanto costa? for *how much does it cost?*

Quant'è? for *how much is it?*

Quant'è il vestito/il biglietto/il cambio? for *how much is the dress/the ticket/the exchange rate?*

Quanto pesa? for *how much does it weigh?*

Quanto dura? for *how long does it last?*

Quanto denaro hai? for *how much money do you have?*

Quanta pizza vuoi? for *how much pizza would you like?*

Quanti is used for *how many* and it varies with gender too:

Quante figlie avete? for *how many daughters do you have?*

Quanti figli avete? for *how many sons do you have?*

Which

Which is either ***quale*** for *which one* or ***quali*** for *which ones* and both can be replaced by ***che***:

Quale giorno parti? for *on which day do you leave?*

Quale pizza vuoi? for *which pizza do you want?*

Quale è la capitale d'Italia? for *which [city] is the capital of Italy?*

Quali mesi sono freddi? for *which months are cold?*

Quali gusti ti piacciono? for *which flavors do you like?*

Che giorno parti? for *on which day do you leave?*

Che pizza vuoi? for *which pizza do you want?*

Che gusti ti piacciono? for *which flavors do you like?*

Is there / are there?

Often in English, *is there? are there?* are used to ask for something that you are looking for, like a restaurant, bathroom, or taxi. The words ***c'è*** and ***ci sono*** correspond to the English *there is* and *there* *are* respectively. These words are used in the same order to both state there is something there and to ask: is there something? A rising tone for the question makes the difference:

C'è un ristorante vicino all'albergo for *there is a restaurant close to the hotel*

Ci sono dei negozi vicino alla stazione for *there are some stores nearby the station*

C'è un ristorante vicino al teatro? for *is there a restaurant close to the theater?*

Ci sono dei negozi vicino al museo? for *are there some stores nearby the museum?*

Ecco

The word ***ecco*** matches the English *here is* and *here are* (also *there is* and *there are*) and might be a likely answer to an *is there/are there* question:

Ci sono ancora due biglietti per il film? for *are there still two tickets for the movie?*

Ecco i biglietti for *here are the tickets*

C'è ancora un tavolo per quattro? for *is there still a table for four?*

Ecco il vostro tavolo for *here is your table*

Ecco il ristorante! for *here is the restaurant!*

Ecco il giornale! for *here is the newspaper!*

Ecco i calzini! for *here are the socks!*

Eccomi for *here I am*

Eccoti for *here you are*

Eccola for *here she is*

Eccolo for *here he is*

Eccoci for *here we are*

Eccovi for *here you (many) are*

Eccoli for *here they are*

GRAMMAR TIP: Negative sentences

To make a negative sentence in Italian, you only need to place the word *non* (*not*) before the verb:

Non c'è acqua nel bagno for *there is no water in the bathroom*

Non ci sono asciugamani nel bagno for *there aren't any towels in the bathroom*

Non ci sono elefanti allo zoo? for *aren't there elephants at the zoo?*

Mi scusi, c'è un bagno? for *excuse me, is there a bathroom?*

No, non c'è for *no, there is not*

Ci sono ancora dei biglietti per il concerto? for *are there still tickets for the concert?*

No, non ce ne sono più for *no, there aren't any more*

This is true for any kind of sentence:

Non c'è il sole for *it is not sunny*

Non piove for *it is not raining*

Chapter 6 - Traveling

Imagine that you are on your first trip to Italy, and pick up as many words and grammar as you can on your way there. Most people use an *airplane* (***aeroplano***) *to fly* (***volare***) there in as little time as possible. Otherwise, to get there or travel around Italy, you may end up using different *forms of transportation* (***mezzi di trasporto***), like *trains* (***treni***), *busses* (***autobus***), *ferries* (***traghetti***) or *rental cars* (***macchine a noleggio***). Last, but not least, you will probably go around a lot during your visit on *foot* (***a piedi***) and by *public transportation* (***trasporto pubblico***), like busses, *taxis* (***taxi***) and *steamboats* (***vaporetti***)—if you travel to Venezia.

Flying

On the plane

When you step on the plane on your way to Italy, you will show your *boarding pass* (***carta d'imbarco***) to *the flight attendant* (***l'assistente di volo***). She or he will point you to your *seat* (***il sedile***, ***il posto***) or your *seats* (***i sedili***, ***i posti***). Once you found your seat, you may need to first find some room for your *carry-on* (***il bagaglio a mano***).

Dove posso sistemare il mio bagaglio a mano?

Where could I put my carry-on?

Usually, you should put your carry-on in the *overhead compartment* (**nella cappelliera**) and your personal belongings, whether it is your purse (**borsetta**) or messenger bag (**borsa a tracolla**), *under the seat in front of you* (**sotto al sedile di fronte**). Sometimes, this may be more challenging than foreseen and you might need to ask:

Mi scusi mi può aiutare a sistemare il mio bagaglio?

Excuse me, could you help me with my luggage?

When everyone is all aboard and in their assigned seats, *the pilot* (*il pilota*) will give her/his greetings and announcements and the flight attendants (**gli assistenti di volo**) will participate in the (nowadays media delivered) *instructions in case of emergencies* (**istruzioni in caso di emergenza**) and make sure you know where the *emergency exits* (**uscite di emergenza**) and the *life-vests* (**giubbotti di salvataggio**) are.

Getting ready:

As soon as all passengers are on board (sometimes earlier), they will be advised to take their *seats* (**posti a sedere**) and fasten *their seatbelts* (**le loro cinture di sicurezza**). To prepare for *the take off* (*il decollo*), they will also be asked *to turn their electronics off* (**spegnere i dispositivi elettronici**), close the seat *table* (**tavolo**) in front of them, and put their *seat back* (**schienale**).

The *take off* (*il decollo*):

Quando decolliamo? for *when do we take off?*

Quando decolleremo? for *when will we take off?*

Quando siamo decollati? for *when did we take off?*

Siamo decollati alle 9 e 30 for *we took off at 9:30*

Siamo decollati con mezz'ora di ritardo for *we took off half an hour late*

Siamo decollati in anticipo for *we took off early*

Ho paura di volare for *I am afraid to fly*

While flying:

There are so many questions you may need to ask or things you need to say during your flight. In case you would like to start practicing, here are a few:

Cabina for *cabin*

Il vassoio for *the tray*

Potrei avere un bicchier d'acqua? for *may I have a glass of water?*

Vorrei una spremuta d'arancia for *I would like an orange juice*

Potrei avere qualcosa da mangiare? for *may I have something to eat?*

Quando verrà servita la cena/il pranzo/la colazione? for *when will dinner/lunch/breakfast be served?*

Cosa c'è per cena/pranzo/colazione? for *what are the options for dinner/lunch/breakfast?*

Io (non) ho un pasto speciale for *I (don't) have a special meal*

Ho ordinato un pasto per bambini/ragazzi for *I ordered a meal for children (0-24months/2-12years old)*

Ho ordinato un pasto... for *I ordered a... meal*

Vegetariano asiatico for *asian vegetarian*

Kosher for *kosher*

Musulmano for *muslim*

Indù for *hindu*

Leggero for *bland*

Senza glutine for *gluten free*

Ipocalorico for *low calories*

Ipocolesterolemico or **a basso contenuto di colesterolo** for *low cholesterol*

Iposodico for *low salt*

Senza lattosio for *lactose free*

A base di pesce for *fish*

Vegano for *vegan*

Vegetariano for *vegetarian*

Dov'è il bagno? for *where is the bathroom?*

Potrei avere un fazzoletto? for *may I have a tissue?*

Potrei avere un analgesico? for *may I have a painkiller?*

Ho bisogno di sgranchirmi le gambe for *I need to stretch my legs*

Non mi sento bene for *I don't feel well*

Ho freddo, ha una coperta per favore? for *I am cold, may I have a blanket please?*

Siete pregati di allacciare le cinture di sicurezza for *please, fasten your seatbelts*

La mia cuffia non funziona for *my headset does not work*

Sono previste turbolenze for *we are expecting turbulence*

Landing in Italy

Atterraggio for *landing*

Quanto manca all'atterraggio? for *how long before the landing?*

Quando atterreremo? for *when will we land?*

A che ora atterreremo? for *what time will we be landing?*

Saremo in ritardo/in anticipo for *ee will be late/early*

Saremo in ritardo/in anticipo? for *will we be late/early?*

Atterrare for *to land*

Siamo in fase di atterraggio for *we started landing*

L'aereo atterrerà tra mezz'ora for *the plane will land in half an hour*

Quando attereremo? For *when will we be landing?*

Dov'è il ritiro bagagli? for *where is the baggage claim?*

Controllo passaporti for *passport control*

The good news about landing in Italy is that you do not need to fill in any form on the plane before landing. They will still check your *passport/passports* (***passaporto/passaporti***) and you will still have to go through custom, where they will ask you if there is *anything* you need *to declare* (***qualcosa da dichiarare?***).

Il mio bagaglio è stato danneggiato for *my luggage has been damaged*

Il mio bagaglio è andato perso for *my luggage has been lost*

Ho perso il volo di coincidenza for *I missed my connection*

Ho perso il mio passaporto for *I lost my passport*

Ho perso il mio biglietto aereo for *I lost my ticket*

Ho perso la mia carta d'imbarco for *I lost my boarding card*

Mi sono perso for *I am lost*

How to leave the airport:

You can leave an airport in many different ways: taxi (***taxi***), shuttle (***shuttle***), busses (***bus***), train (***treno***), rental car (***macchina a noleggio***), steamboat (***vaporetto***).

You can find a taxi at the *taxi rank* (***parcheggio dei taxi***) right outside the airport, where you will probably also find all the shuttles and local busses. Local buses are very *inexpensive* (***economici***) and connect the airports with major cities, also with small towns, and may be the right choice for many locals. They are usually divided into *urban* (**urbano**) and *suburban* (**interurbano** or **extraurbano**) lines, and you might need to buy tickets in advance at the *newstand* (**il giornalaio**). Shuttles are usually quite efficient and drivers usually sell *tickets* (**biglietti**) themselves. Airport shuttles are highly developed and convenient for rail travelers and few airports (Roma Fiumicino, Milano Malpensa and Torino Caselle) are directly connected to the *railway network* (**rete ferroviaria**).

Taking off from Italy

When you are taking off from Italy, instead of landing, the main task is to wander the airport (**muoversi nell'aeroporto**), check in, go through security (**la sicurezza**), and board at the right gate. After some shopping (and alast Italian espresso!), you will probably be ready *to leave* (**partire**).

GRAMMAR TIP: the conjugation of *partire* (*to leave*) and *arrivare* (*to arrive*), present, past and future

The two most important verbs when traveling are **partire** (*to leave*) and **arrivare** (*to arrive*).

As a reminder, verbs end differently for different persons. In Italian, there are three possible infinitive endings or conjugations: -are, -ere, and -ire. The infinitive form of a verb (i.e. **partire** -*to leave*) loses its ending, which coincides with the last three letters (i.e., *-ire* for **partire**). You will always have the first part of the verb, like part- or arriv-, and then add the person. Persons are the same for verbs of the same conjugations, but may differ for persons of verbs belonging to different conjugations:

Voi arriv-ate for *you* (many) *arrive* is different from *voi corr-ete* for *you* (many) *run* and *voi part-ite* for *you* (many) *leave*.

Simple present of **partire** (*to leave*):

Io parto for *I leave*

Tu parti for *you leave*

Lei/lui parte for *she/he leaves*

Noi partiamo for *we leave*

Voi partite for *you leave*

Essi/loro partono for *they leave*

Present perfect* of *partire* (*to leave*):

Io sono partito for *I have left*

Tu sei partito for *you have left*

Lei è partita / lui è partito for *she/he has left*

Noi siamo partiti for *we have left*

Voi siete partiti for *you* (many) *have left*

Essi/loro sono partiti for *they have left*

The future of *partire* (*to leave*):

Io partirò for *I will leave*

Tu partirai for *you will leave*

Lei/lui partirà for *she/he will leave*

Noi partiremo for *we will leave*

Voi partirete for *you* (many) *will leave*

Essi/loro partiranno for *they will leave*

Simple present of *arrivare* (*to arrive*):

Io arrivo for *I arrive*

Tu arrivi for *you arrive*

Lei/lui arriva for *she/he arrive*

Noi arriviamo for *we arrive*

Voi arrivate for *you arrive*

Essi/loro arrivano for *they arrive*

Present perfect* of *arrivare* (*to arrive*):

Io sono arrivato for *I have arrived* (*I arrived*)

Tu sei arrivato for *you have arrived* (*you arrived*)

Lei è arrivata/lui è arrivato for *she/he has arrived* (*she/he arrived*)

Noi siamo arrivati for *we have arrived* (*we arrived*)

Voi siete arrivati for *you* (many) *have arrived* (*we arrived*)

Loro/essi sono arrivati for *they have arrived* (*they arrived*)

The future of *arrivare* (*to arrive*):

Io arriverò for *I will arrive*

Tu arriverai for *you will arrive*

Lei/lui arriverà for *she/he will arrive*

Noi arriveremo for *we will arrive*

Voi arriverete for *you* (many) *will arrive*

Loro/essi arriveranno for *they will arrive*

*In Italian, the present perfect is used more frequently (sometimes erroneously) as a past rather than a present perfect. And it happens that Italians would say **ho fatto** when you say *I did*, and **sono andato** when you say *I went*.

Trains

The majority of Italian trains and railway are owned and managed by a state company, **Le Ferrovie dello Stato** Italiane, and there are other (also public) regional agencies that operate on the Italian network. For both, it is possible to book trips and purchase tickets and passes online at trenitalia.com, which has a very functional English version.

High speed trains (**treni ad alta velocità**, AV -formerly Eurostar Italia) connect major cities, such as Roma, Firenze, Bologna, Milano, Torino, Venezia, Napoli, Salerno, within a few hours and are quite comfortable. A *reservation* (**prenotazione**) for an *assigned seat* (**posto assegnato**) is required for these trains at a small commission. There are three kinds of high speed trains, from the fastest: *il Frecciarossa* (*Red arrow*), *il Frecciargento* (*Silver arrow*), and *il Frecciabianca* (*White arrow*).

Intercity trains (*Intercity IC*) are the next fastest trains and connect cities and towns off the main network during the day. The *night trains* (*Intercity Notte ICN*) have sleeper compartments (*vagoni letto*) and washrooms (*bagni*), but no showers on board.

Regional services both fast (*regionale veloce RGV*) and slow (*regionale REG*) connect the smaller stations between cities. Trains of regional agencies are connected and shown on Trenitalia; their tickets can also be purchased at the local newsstand or tobacco store.

At the station

In almost every train station (*stazione dei treni*), no matter how big or small, there will be a *ticket booth* (*una biglietteria automatica*) where you can plan your trip, reserve a seat, buy your ticket or print a ticket you bought online. You are required *to stamp/validate* (*obliterare*) your ticket before getting on the train; otherwise, there is always the ticket inspector (*il controllore*) who will issue you a fine (*una multa*). The reason is that for regional services there is no date or time on the ticket and the same ticket could be used multiple times if not stamped. The only exception are the tickets with a seat reservation because they have a precise date for a determined train.

The *validating machines* (*le obliteratrici*) are usually located close by the ticket booth, before the *tracks* (*binari*) and on the *platform* (*la pensilina*).

Different panels by the tracks will show the *schedules* (*gli orari*) of the closest departures (*partenze*) and arrivals (*arrivi*). For every train, you will see the time and *platform* (*binario*).

You can always go to the *ticket office* (*biglietteria*) and speak with the *clerk* (*addetto*) if you want to make sure to have the right tickets for your destination.

Buongiorno, vorrei un biglietto di sola andata per Venezia Centrale

Good morning, I would like a one-way ticket for Venezia Centrale

Buongiorno vorremmo due biglietti di andata e ritorno per Roma Termini

Good morning, we would like two round trip tickets for Roma Termini

Local busses

Travel by bus in Italy lets you reach destinations which, due to Italy's geography, are not connected to the rail network. There are always regional public busses (*autobus interurbani*) which connect train stations, airports to cities (*città*), and small villages (*paesi*). You can buy the tickets for these busses either at the bus station (*stazione degli autobus*) or at a newsstand (*giornalaio*) of ticket booths (*biglietterie automatiche*) at the train station or at the airport. Often, not always, you can also buy the ticket on the bus. Other private bus providers offer low cost bus tickets, offering convenient connections with Italy and connecting Italy to many European destinations.

Car rentals

Public transportation in Italy is quite efficient, and while it is great, you still must stick to a schedule, and the busses and trains only take you so far. Renting a car (*noleggiare una macchina*) in Italy will provide you with the freedom of moving at your pleasure and is a wonderful way to see the country. You can drive up to the mountains (*montagne*), see quaint villages (*paesi pittoreschi*), drive past cliff-side vineyards (*vigne*), find a random castle (*castello*), stop by the hidden beach (*spiaggia*) you would have otherwise never spotted, and more.

There are few things to remember when renting a car in Italy. You can book your car online, in English, and it will probably be cheaper.

Second, the majority of the rental cars have a standard shift with *manual transmission* (**cambio manuale**). If you need or want an *automatic* (**cambio automatico**), you need to specify and probably reserve it quite far in advance. As anywhere, you can find the major *rental companies* (**compagnie/agenzie di autonoleggio**), some European, and some Italian ones.

As anywhere else, you will have to choose which *kind of car* (**tipo di macchina**) you want, which may depend on where you are going, how *many suitcases* (**quante valigie**) you have, and how many *passengers* (**passeggeri**) there will be.

As far as the *insurance* (**assicurazione**) is concerned, you need to remember that the *deductible* (**franchigia**) is the limit or the most that the *insurance company* (**compagnia assicurativa**) will reimburse you in case of *damage* (**danno**). The rest of the amount will be on you. A more expensive option will cover the damage completely. This option is often referred to as **kasko** in Italy, even when provided by a different company.

Companies offer many different kinds of rentals: by *hour* (**orario**), by *day* (**giornaliero**), by *week* (**settimanale**), by month (**mensile**). You can even still choose between limited and unlimited miles (**chilometraggio limitato** o **illimitato**). Then you can choose to add some optional features to your rental: a *navigation system* (**sistema di navigazione**), the *prepay fuel* (**pieno prepagato**), a *car seat* (**seggiolino**) or a *booster* (**adattatore**).

Distances in Italy are measured in *meters* (**metri**) and *kilometers* (**chilometri**) rather than *feet* (**piedi**) and *miles* (**miglia**). Approximately, a *meter* (**un metro**) corresponds to *three feet* (**tre piedi**) and *one mile* (**un miglio**) corresponds to *one kilometer and a half* (**un chilometro e mezzo**). Exactly, *one foot* (**un piede**) is 0.3 meters (**metri**) and one mile equals 1.6 kilometers, so you will probably think places are further away than they really are if you are looking at their distance in kilometers.

If you do not choose prepaid fuel, you need to remember to *fill the tank* (***fare il pieno***) before returning your *rental car* (***macchina a noleggio***). The petrol/gas prices might look quite low, but keep in mind that in Italy—and pretty much the entire world—*gasoline* (***benzina***) is sold by the *liter* (***litro***) rather than the *gallon* (***gallone***). You need *four and a half liters* (***quattro litri e mezzo***) for one gallon. The price is quite variable in Italy as well—just remember that you might need four times more then what you expect to fill the tank! Also, there might be a pay station shared by a couple of numbered *pumps* (***pompe***), but it may only take debit cards (***bancomat***) and no credit cards (***carte di credito***). Usually, these machines take *cash* (***contanti***), though, in *bills* (***banconote***).

The usual speed limit in a *town* (***paese***) or *city* (***città***) or any populated area (***centro urbano***) is 50km/h, (i.e., *50 kilometers per hour – cinquanta chilometri all'ora*), which is 31 miles per hour. The **strade extraurbane secondarie** (*secondary state roads*) are main roads that connect cities, towns, and airports, and the usual speed limit is 90 km/h. These roads used to be called **strade statali** (***SS***), **strade regionali** (***SR***) or **strade provinciali** (***SP***), and they are all marked by one of those initials and a number. There are also **strada extraurbana principale** or **superstrade** (*principal state road* and Italian equivalent for expressway). These roads are directly controlled by the Italian government or by the regions—there is no toll and the general speed limit is 110 km/h. Access restrictions on these expressways are the same as those for *highways* (***autostrade***). Italian Highways (***autostrade italiane***) are marked with the letter A and a number, and are managed by the government (Ministero delle Infrastrutture e dei Trasporti) who impose a *toll* (***pedaggio***). There are two kinds of toll. The *closed toll system* (***a sistema chiuso***) is more common and requires one to take a ticket when entering the highway and to pay at the exit. The amount you will be charged is proportional to the distance you traveled, the vehicle you drove, and the highway you drove on. You can also purchase the automatic system (Telepass) that will detect your entrance and exit and automatically charge you and skip the lines. There is also an *open system* (***sistema aperto***) on few minor portions, by which everybody pays a fixed amount regardless of distance and vehicle. The speed limit on highways is normally 130 km/h (81 miles per hour), but varies with the weather and experience: with rain and snow it can reduce to 110 km/h, with fog to 50 km/h and new drivers need to drive with a 110km/h limit for three years.

Buongiorno vorrei noleggiare una macchina

Good morning I would like to rent a car

Buongiorno ho prenotato una macchina a noleggio

Good morning I reserved a rental car

Che tipo di macchina vorreste?

What kind of car would you like?

Waterways

Italy is a *peninsula* (***penisola***) with many *islands* (***isole***), and most of its borders are in the sea. Many ferries (***traghetti***) connect Italy with other countries: Spagna, Francia, Croazia, Grecia, Tunisia, Marocco, and Algeria are some of them. Plus a network of ferries and hydrofoils connect the islands and the mainland to the islands, like la Sicilia, la Sardegna, le Isole Eolie, le Isole Tremiti, le Isole Pontine, Pantelleria, Capri, Ischia, and l'Isola d'Elba. Also, major Cities, like Venezia, Genova, Napoli, and Trieste, are destination points for *cruises* (***crociere***).

GRAMMAR TIP: the conjugation of *imbarcarsi, to board*

When you travel by boat, as on a plane, you *board* (***imbarcarsi***)

Simple Present:

Io mi imbarco for *I board*

Tu ti imbarchi for *you board*

Lei/lui si imbarca for *she/he boards*

Noi ci imbarchiamo for *we board*

Voi vi imbarcate for *you* (many) *board*

Loro/essi si imbarcano for *they board*

Present perfect:

Io mi sono imbarcato for *I boarded*

Tu ti sei imbarcato for *you boarded*

Lei/lui si è imbarcato for *she/he boarded*

Noi ci siamo imbarcati for *we boarded*

Voi vi siete imbarcati for *you* (many) *boarded*

Essi/loro si sono imbarcati for *they boarded*

Future:

Io mi imbarcherò for *I will board*

Tu ti imbarcherai for *you will board*

Lei/lui si imbarcherà for *she/he will board*

Noi ci imbarcheremo for *we will board*

Voi vi imbarcherete for *you* (many) *will board*

Essi/loro si imbarcheranno for *they will board*

Essential vocabulary:

Viaggiare in nave for *to travel by boat*

Avere mal di mare for *to be seasick*

Sbarcare for *to disembark*

Imbarcarsi for *to embark*

Salpare for *to sail*

Porto for *port*

Darsena for *harbor*

Terminal traghetti *for ferry terminal*

Crociera *for cruise*

Traversata *for crossing*

Passeggero a piedi *for foot passenger*

Mare calmo *for calm sea*

Mare agitato *for rough sea*

Capitano *for captain*

Membro dell'equipaggio *for member of the crew*

Cabina *for cabin*

Ponte *for deck*

Ponte per le auto *for car deck*

Passerella *for gangway*

Banco delle informazioni *for information desk*

Scialuppa di salvataggio *for lifeboat*

Giubbotto di salvataggio *for life jacket*

Salvagente *for life belt*

Types of vessel (**tipi di imbarcazione**):

Traghetto (adibito a trasporto auto) *for car ferry*

Nave da crociera for *cruise ship*

Traghetto *for ferry*

Hovercraft *for hovercraft*

Barca a remi *for rowboat*

Barca a vela *for sailboat*

Veliero *for sailing ship*

Motoscafo *for motorboat*

Aliscafo for hydrofoil

Vaporetto *for steamboat or waterbus (in Venice)*

Zattera *for raft*

Sailing

If you decide *to go sailing* (***andare in barca a vela***), you may like to know a few essential words before *boarding* (***imbarcarsi***). The *starboard* is to the right (***tribordo)***, and *port* to the left (***babordo***). The *bow* or front of a *boat* (***barca***) is called ***prua***; the *stern,* ***poppa,*** and the *helm,* ***timone***. When you take the helm (***stare al timone*** or, figuratively, ***prendere il comando***, *to take command*) as ***capitano*** and ***navigatore***. The *crew* (***l'equipaggio***) may consist of one *sailor* (***marinaio***) or more (***marinai***), and they *hoist* (***issare***) and *lower* (***calare***) the *sails* (***le vele***) in *calm* (***mare calmo***) and *rough seas* (***mare mosso***). There may be a ***mozzo*** (*ship's boy*) or a ***cambusa***, which could be either a *boat's galley* or the *on-board cook.*

On foot

In Italy, you will often find yourself walking around and looking for the next *museum* (***museo***), *café* (**caffè** or **bar**), *restaurant* (***ristorante***), *ice cream store* (***gelateria***), a particular *store* (***negozio***) and probably your *hotel* (***albergo***). You may also need to find your way within a building: a *shopping mall* (***centro commerciale***), a big museum, an *aquarium* (***acquario***) or an *airport* (***aeroporto***)!

You may ask where to find what you are looking for:

Mi scusi sa dov'è la stazione? for *excuse me, do you* (formal) *know where the station is?*

Scusa, sai dov'è la stazione? for *excuse me, do you* (informal) *know where the station is?*

Certo, la stazione è di fronte all'albergo for *of course, the station is in front of the hotel*

Your destination may be *far* (**lontano**) or *close by* (**vicino**) or simply *over there* (**laggiù**) as different adverbs of place indicate.

Location adverbs

Qui, **qua** for *here*

Lì, **là** for *there*

Vicino for near, close

Lontano for far

Di fronte for in front of

Davanti for facing, in front of

Dietro for behind

Accanto for next to

A destra for on the right

A sinistra for on the left

Dentro for inside

Fuori for outside

Sopra for on, above

Su for up, on

Sotto for under, below

Giù for down, under

Intorno for around

Via for away

Quassù for up here

Quaggiù for down here

Lassù for up there

Laggiù for down there

Qui vicino for close by

Lì vicino for over there

Qui sopra for up here

Qui sotto for down here

Lì sopra for up there

Lì sotto for down there

Lì in cima for on top over there

Lì in fondo for down there

Possible destinations that you might need to reach are:

Il museo for *the museum*

Il teatro for *the theater*

Il ristorante for *the restaurant*

Il bar for *the coffee shop*

La fermata dell'autobus for *the bus stop*

Il parcheggio dei taxi for *the taxis*

L'ospedale for *the hospital*

La farmacia for *the pharmacy*

La stazione della polizia for *the police station*

Il pronto soccorso for *the emergency room*

Asking for directions on the street

You might need to know how to ask for directions, to understand the directions and find your way. To do that you need a few words that point (*indicare*) to where things are (adverbs of place) and a few verbs that help you navigate (*andare*/to go, *proseguire*/to continue, *girare*/to turn, s*voltare*/to turn, *salire*/to go up, *scendere*/to go down, *tornare*/to return).

Mi scusi sa indicarmi...? for *excuse me, do you know how to point me to...?*

Mi scusi mi potrebbe indicare...? for *excuse me, could you* (formal) *point me to...?*

As you saw in Chapter 5, a polite way to ask a question is by using the conditional of *volere* (*to want*):

Mi scusi, vorrei andare... for *excuse me, I would like to go....*

Another possibility is to use *dovere* (*to have to*) to indicate that you need to go somewhere and you can either use it in the present simple, since you must go in that particular place, or you can use the conditional, if it is not absolutely necessary or if you need to go there but you still want to be polite:

Mi scusi, devo andare alla stazione... for *excuse me, I have to go to the station*

Mi scusi dovrei andare alla stazione.... for *excuse me, I should go to the station*

Deve andare prima a destra al primo semaforo e poi a sinistra alla farmacia

You have to turn right at the traffic light and then left at the pharmacy

GRAMMAR TIP: the conjugation of *dovere* (*to have*)

Dovere (*to have to*) is also very commonly use in giving directions: *deve girare prima a sinistra e poi a destra* (*you have to turn first left and then right*). So you may like to have its conjugation for the Simple Present and the Simple Present Conditional for every person (you may find the imperfect, the present perfect and the future in Chapter 14).

Simple Present

Io devo for *I have to*

Tu devi for *you have to*

Lei/lui deve for *she/he has to*

Noi dobbiamo for *we have to*

Voi dovete for *you* (many) *have to*

Essi/loro devono for *they have to*

Simple Present Conditional

Io dovrei for *I should*

Tu dovresti for *you should*

Lei/lui dovrebbe for *she/he should*

Noi dovremmo for *we should*

Voi dovreste for *you* (many) *should*

Essi/loro dovrebbero for *they should*

Mi scusi dovrei andare al museo d'arte moderna

Excuse me, I should go to the modern art museum

Deve andare sempre dritto fino alla stazione, poi deve girare a sinistra e proseguire per due isolati

You have to go straight until the station, then you have to turn left and keep going for two blocks

There might be more things that *you have to* (***tu devi***) to do in order to reach your destination:

Attraversare la strada for *to cross the street*

Prendere il sottopassaggio for *to take the underpassage*

Attraversare il ponte for *to cross the bridge*

In the unfortunate event that who is giving you directions will not use ***dovere*** followed by the infinite of one of the movement verbs, or that you want to repeat the directions to double-check whether you understood, you might need to know the Simple Present of the most common ones:

Simple present of **andare** (*to go*):

Io vado for *I go*

Tu vai for *you go*

Lei/lui va for *she/he goes*

Noi andiamo for *we go*

Voi andate for *you* (many) *go*

Essi/loro vanno for *they go*

Simple present of **proseguire** (*to continue*):

Io proseguo for *I continue*

Tu prosegui for *you continue*

Lei/lui prosegue for *she/he continue*

Noi proseguiamo for *we continue*

Voi proseguite for *you* (many) *continue*

Essi/loro proseguono for *they continue*

Simple Present of **girare** (*to turn*)

Io giro for *I turn*

Tu giri for *you turn*

Lei/lui gira for *she/he turns*

Noi giriamo for *we turn*

Voi girate for *you* (many) *turn*

Essi/loro girano for *they turn*

Asking for directions in a building

When inside a building, you might need a few more words to wander about on different floors and specific destinations:

Prendere l'ascensore for *to take the elevator*

Prendere le scale mobili for *to take the escalator*

Salire le scale for *to go up the stairwell*

Scendere le scale for *to go down the stairs*

Bus & Metro

Extensive metros (***metropolitane***) exist in Rome, Milan, Naples, and Turin, with smaller metros in Genoa and Catania. The *Minimetrò* in Perugia connects the train station with the city center.

Cities and towns of any size have an efficient ***urbano*** (*urban*) and ***extraurbano*** (*suburban*) bus system. Services are generally limited on Sundays and holidays.

Purchase bus and metro tickets before boarding and validate them once on board. Passengers with unvalidated tickets are subject to a fine (between €50 and €110). Buy tickets from a *tabaccaio* (tobacconist's shop), newsstands, ticket booths, or dispensing machines at bus and metro stations. Tickets usually cost around €1 to €2. Many cities offer good-value 24-hour or daily tourist tickets.

Taxi

You can catch a taxi at the official ranks outside most train and bus stations, or simply call for a radio taxi. Every city has its own company and different phone number. Radio taxi meters start running from when you have called rather than when you are picked up. Usually, taxi drivers accept *cash* (***contanti***) and do not have much *change* (***resto***). The best way to handle the destination is to have the precise address in Italian (possibly written). Extra charges are common for suitcases and trips outside the city border during the night. *A tip* (***una mancia***) may be nice, but not necessary; usually, it consists of a few euros or the change (***il resto***) if it is in that range.

Buongiorno vorrei andare in Via Roma 15

Good morning, I would like to go to Via Roma 15

Grazie, tenga il resto

Thank you, keep the change

I vaporetti di Venezia

A special case – Venice

Venezia (*Venice*) is built on an *archipelago* (*arcipelago*) of 118 islands (*isole*) connected by 400 bridges (*ponti*) over 177 canals (*canali*). The adjoining Ponte della Libertà and a railroad connect Venezia with the mainland. Beyond a parking facility (Piazzale Roma) and the train station (Venezia Santa Lucia), transportation is entirely on water or foot. This is the largest urban car-free area in Europe.

The classic Venetian boat is the *gondola* (plural: *gondole*), although it is now mostly used for tourists, or weddings, funerals, or other ceremonies, or as *traghetto/i* (*ferry/ferries*) to cross the Grand Canal instead of a nearby bridge.

The main public transportation means are motorized *waterbuses* (*vaporetti*), which use regular routes along the Grand Canal and between the city's islands. There are many authorized vendors in the historical centre of Venezia, where you can buy the tickets and learn about the routes.

Dove posso comprare i biglietti per il vaporetto? for *where can I buy the tickets for the waterbus?*

Quale vaporetto mi porta in Piazza San Marco? for *which waterbus takes me to Piazza San Marco?*

Quale vaporetto mi porta a Murano, Burano, e Torcello...? for *which waterbus takes me to Murano, Burano, and Torcello?*

Quale vaporetto va alla Biennale/ai Giardini? for *which waterbus goes to the Biennale/to I Giardini?*

Quando arriva il prossimo vaporetto? for *when does this waterbus arrive?*

Quanto tempo ci mette il vaporetto per andare all'aeroporto? for *how long does the waterbus take to get to the airport?*

Quanto spesso passa questo vaporetto per l'aeroporto? for *how often does the waterbus to airport come?*

Car

Driving around can be marvelous, whether you own or rent a car. You need to find parking and fill the tank at the gas station for *gas* (**benzina**). You might also have to go to the car wash. If something happens to the car, you might have to call a *tow truck* (**carro attrezzi**).

La strada for *the road*

La via for *the street*

La piazza for *the square*

Il semaforo for *traffic light*

La rotatoria for *rotary*

L'incrocio for *intersection*

Il vigile urbano for *traffic policeman*

L'isolato for *block*

La stazione di servizio for *service station*

L'autolavaggio for *car wash*

Vai dritto for *go straight*

Gira/svolta a destra for *turn right*

Gira/svolta a sinistra for *turn left*

Inverti la marcia for *reverse*

Fai retromarcia/fai marcia indietro for *reverse*

Fai un'inversione ad U for *take a U-turn*

Torna indietro for *go back*

Alla rotatoria prendi la prima, seconda, terza, quarta... uscita for *at the rotary, take the first, second, third, fourth... exit*

Prendi la prima strada a destra for *take the first street on the right*

Al semaforo gira a sinistra for *at the traffic light turn left*

Chapter 7 - Visiting

*Hotels (**albergo**, **alberghi**)*

When you arrive in Italy, you might just want to get to *your hotel room* (***la tua stanza d'albergo***) to take a shower (***doccia***) and a nap (***pisolino***). Hotels in Italy work as in the rest of the world. There are different kinds of hotels marked with more or less stars (***stelle***), and different kinds of *rooms* (***stanze***) for different budgets. Some may have *swimming pools* (***piscina***, ***piscine***), *gyms* (***palestra***, ***palestre***), *free breakfast* (***colazione inclusa***), a *restaurant* (***ristorante***) and an *in-house bar* (***bar***). Others may not even have an *elevator* (***ascensore***).

Usually, though, a *single room* (***stanza singola***) is for one person only, *a double room for single use* (***stanza doppia a uso singolo***) is a room that is big enough for two people, but since only one person is using it, there is a lower price. A double room of any kind is for two people, but double bedrooms often have two *twin beds* (***letti singoli***), which can be made up as two beds or put together to make a king-size bed. If a room has one *double bed* (***letto doppio***), it is usually queen-size. Rooms never have two double beds as is common in the USA.

---

*Small hotel (**pensione**)*

A smaller, family owned and managed hotel is traditionally called **pensione**. They usually have a cozy warm atmosphere, and there is a less formal relationship between hosts (**albergatore**) and guests (**ospite, ospiti**). Traditionally, the only option would have been to have one meal per day (**mezza pensione**), but even these kinds of accommodations have evolved and offer, nowadays, more comforts, like a spa or gym, etc.

*Hostels (**ostello, ostelli**)*

Hostels are a good option if you do not mind *sharing* (**condividere**). Though, these facilities (both around the world and in Italy) have moved from strictly *dorm-style* (**stile dormitorio**) *bunks* (**letti a castello**) only for young people to historical buildings with smaller or private rooms with separate bathrooms and no age restrictions. If so, you still have the opportunity to use a shared kitchen (**cucina**) and living space (**salotto**). A hostel should offer accommodation on a budget, with the possibility of creating a familiar atmosphere among the guests.

Bed and Breakfasts

Bed and Breakfasts in Italy do not traditionally have a great reputation: many cheap hotels call themselves B&Bs if they include some kind of breakfast (**colazione**) in the price of the room. If you are really looking for the more traditional version of a B&B, you will want to find out exactly what breakfast consists of. Some Italian B&Bs serve nothing more than a typical Italian breakfast: **caffè e pasticcini** or **pane e marmellata** (coffee and pastry or bread and jam). Since Italians are not generally a breakfast culture, they are not exactly splashing out a big breakfast spread. You might find a fridge in your room stocked with *fruit* (**frutta**), *yogurt* (**yogurt**), and the makings for coffee, or you may find some pastry and bread and jam in a common area and that will be the *breakfast* portion. You may book a B&B and then find it is really just a budget hotel that provides a simple buffet breakfast.

Agriturismo (farm holiday)

The usual translation for **agriturismo** (*farm holiday*) may be misleading. **Agriturismo** is a special kind of accommodation offered in a family-owned farm, where you can enjoy the food produced by the farm and activities especially organized for the guests. You might be able to go camping, enjoy locally produced food, oil or wine tasting (**degustazioni**), go trekking, horseback riding, kayaking, canoeing, etc. Often the accommodation is quite similar to a bed and breakfast, with a private room (**stanza singola** or **doppia** –*single* or *double room*) and a *shared bathroom* (**bagno condiviso**), usually with at least one *meal* (**pasto incluso**) per day.

*Convents and Monasteries (**conventi e monasteri**)*

Historically, Italy has been largely a Catholic country and unsurprisingly is full of convents and monasteries, some of which have a long history of opening their doors to *pilgrims* (**pellegrini**)— and for some, that has a modern twist. Some convents and monasteries now play host to not only pilgrims but *travelers* (**viaggiatori**) of any sort. You can find these kinds of accommodations both in cities and in the countryside, and they are often incredibly *cheap* (**economici**). They are also notoriously safe places to stay, which used to be very appealing to female travelers (either **pellegrine** or **viaggiatrici**). There might be few catches— staying in a convent can include having a *curfew* (**coprifuoco**), participating in *prayer times* (**preghiere**), or separate sleeping quarters for men and women.

*Villas and Other Vacation Rentals (**Ville e altri affitti per le vacanze**)*

If you decide on a longer stay or are part of a larger group (especially with young kids), you might like to rent a *house* (**casa**), an *apartment* (**appartamento**) or a *villa* (**villa**).

*Camping (**campeggio**)*

Camping is very popular in Italy with a very large number of official sites (*campeggio*) in operation, where you can stay for a nominal fee (***tassa giornaliera***), usually charged per person daily. A complete list of camping sites with a location map is issued free by the Federazione Italiana del Campeggio e del Caravanning (Federcampeggio).

Dining and drinking

In Italy, there are three main meals: *la prima colazione* (*breakfast*), *il pranzo* (*lunch*), and *la cena* (*dinner*). After these, children usually have a *snack* (***una merenda***) in the *morning* (***al mattino***) and or in the *afternoon* (***pomeriggio***). As an adult, you may need a *break* (***una pausa***) for a *coffee* (***caffè***) or *tea* (*tè* or ***the***) in the morning and/or in the afternoon, or you might like to have an *aperitif* (***aperitivo***) before dinner.

Usually, breakfast is served from 7 a.m. till 9 a.m., lunch from 12 p.m. to 2 p.m. (or 14:00) and dinner from 7 till 11 p.m. (23:00) at least. In between, you may have a snack in pastry shops or a cafè.

The traditional Italian breakfast at home is *bread and jam* (***pane e marmellata***) with *coffee* (***caffè***)—often it is *bread* (***pane***), *butter* (***burro***), and *jam* (***marmellata***), and there is *milk* (***latte***) in the coffee, so to have a ***caffellatte***. It is possible to have breakfast at a bar. An Italian bar is not a pub or bar in the American sense; it is more like a small coffee shop, where you can have an espresso (and every possible variation), tea, sodas, and pastries. Many like to have their breakfast at the bar, and the standard is an *espresso* (***un caffè***) with a *croissant* (***cornetto***).

You can find a *continental breakfast* (***colazione continentale*** or ***colazione all'americana***) almost anywhere and you can order *eggs* (***uova***) *scrambled* (***strapazzate***), *fried* (***fritte***), or *hard-boiled* (***sode***) with or without *a piece of toasted bread* (***una fetta di pane tostato***). You might also find *pancakes* (***frittelle***), *cereals* (***i cereali***), *yogurt*, and *seasonal fruit* (***frutta di stagione***).

Colazione (la colazione, le colazioni) for *breakfast*

Caffè (il caffè, i caffè) for *coffee*

Zucchero (lo zucchero) for *sugar*

Latte (il latte) for *milk*

Panna (la panna) for *cream*

Tè (il tè) for *tea*

Tazzina (la tazzina, le tazzine) for *small cup*

Tazza (la tazza, le tazze) for *cup*

Miele (il miele) for *honey*

Cornetto (il cornetto, i cornetti) for *croissant*

Cereali (i cereali) for *cereals*

Biscotti (il biscotto, i biscotti) for *cookies*

There are many different places where you can have lunch and dinner. The *restaurant* (**ristorante**) is a formal place that may or may not specialize in a particular kind of food, like those that mainly serve *fish* (**ristorante di pesce**) or *meat* (**ristorante di carne**) or *vegetarian food* (**ristorante vegetariano**). *Trattorie* are less formal venues with authentic regional food, which used to be a family-owned version of a diner. A *pizzeria* usually has a *brick oven* (**forno a legna**) and serves mainly pizza, but you can also find the main traditional Italian dishes. Sometimes, on the road, there are small shops where you can find *pizza al taglio* (*pizza by the slice*). In those places, you can either eat it quickly there standing or take it to go. *Osteria* is the closest to a tavern or corner pub, serving snacks, appetizers, simple dishes, and wine in an unpretentious venue. Although, if you would like to have a good *glass of wine* (**bicchiere di vino**) and eat some delicatessen, you might have better luck in an *Enoteca*. Enoteca literally means "collection of wine", and in these venues, you can buy bottles of wine or just enjoy a few glasses of your choice.

Instead, if you are out in the country, you may decide to stop by an *agriturismo*, a farm that the owners have decided to partially use for accommodation purposes. There you will only find food made from the produce, eggs, meat, and often wine and olive oil that is fresh off the farm.

A *paninoteca* is the Italian answer to American fast food. It literally means "collection of *sandwiches* (*panini*)" and this is the main theme, but you are not expected to eat fast and go, and everything will be cooked and made on the spot. A *Rosticceria* sells whole rotisserie chickens and a variety of ready-to-eat meals for takeout at a fair price. There are also establishments (*tavola calda*) where you can find pre-made dishes (often local specialties); these are usually self-serve, cafeteria-style venues.

Lastly, when looking for a snack or a dessert after dinner, you can always stop by a homemade *ice-cream parlor* (*Gelateria*).

Ordering food

Restaurants, osterie, pizzerie, and so on usually do not have different *menus* (*menù*) for lunch and dinner. Either way, menus are usually divided in sections that reflect the course of an Italian meal: *antipasto* (appetizer), *primi* (*first courses*), *secondi* (*second courses*), *contorni* (*side dishes*), *frutta* (*fruit*), *dolci* (*dessert*). Appetizers may be *warm* (*caldi*) or *cold* (*freddi*), usually the cold ones are not cooked. *The first course* (*il primo*) might be further divided into *soups* (*zuppe* or *minestre*), rice dishes (*risotti*), and *pasta dishes* (*pasta*). *The second course* (*il secondo*) may also have subsections for *meat* (*carne*) and *fish* (*pesce*).

In the unfortunate event that the English menu went missing or you would like to try ordering from the Italian menu, here is some essential "menu vocabulary":

Essential vocabulary

Menù for *menu*

Antipasto for *appetizer*

Primi piatti for *first course*

Zuppa for *soup*

Minestra for *soup*

Brodo for *broth*

Secondi piatti for *second course*

Contorni for *side dishes*

Insalata for *salad*

Verdure for *vegetables*

Verdure grigliate for *grilled vegetables*

Verdure al forno for *baked vegetables*

Patate (la patata, le patate) for *potatoes*

Pesce (il pesce, i pesci) for *fish*

Trota (la trota, le trote) for *trout*

Salmone (il salmone, i salmoni) for *salmon*

Aragosta (l'aragosta, le aragoste) for *lobster*

Branzino (il branzino, i branzini) for *European Seabass*

Gambero *(il gambero, i gamberi) for prawn or shrimp*

Polpo *or* **Polipo** for *octopus*

Spada *(pesce spada)* for *swordfish*

Tonno (il tonno, i tonni) for *tuna*

Carne *(la carne, le carni)* for *meat*

Manzo for *beef*

Cinghiale for *boar*

Pollo for *chicken*

Tacchino for *turkey*

Coniglio for *rabbit*

Selvaggina for *game*

Going shopping

Like in the rest of the world, you can buy almost everything everywhere and find clothes in supermarkets or food in bookstores. However, in Italy, you can still find many specialized stores that will sell only what they were traditionally meant to sell. There are stores dedicated to *general food* (*i negozi di generi alimentari*) or specialize in a particular kind of food:

Macelleria (la macelleria, le macellerie) for *the butcher*

Pescheria (la pescherie, le pescherie) for *the fish market*

Salumeria (la salumeria, le salumerie) for *cold cuts, cheese, olives*

Fruttivendolo (il fruttivendolo, i fruttivendoli) for *fruit and vegetables*

Pasticceria (la pasticceria, le pasticcerie) for *bakery* for pastry

Panetteria (la panetteria, le panetterie) for *bakery* for bread and cookies

Panificio (il panificio, i panifici) for *bakery* for bread and cookies

Fornaio (il fornaio, i fornai) for *bakery* for bread and cookies

Enoteca (l'enoteca, le enoteche) for *wine dealer*

And more stores:

Tabaccheria (la tabaccheria, le tabaccherie) for *tobacco shop*

Libreria (la libreria, le librerie) for *book store*

Cartoleria (la cartoleria, le cartolerie) for *stationary store*

Profumeria (la profumeria, le profumerie) for *perfume store*

Negozio di abbigliamento (il negozio, i negozi) for *store for clothing*

Farmacia (la farmacia, le farmacie) for *pharmacy*

Drogheria (la drogheria, le drogherie) for *drugstore*

Just remember—when leaving a store, as you would do in English—to say: ***Grazie e arrivederci*** (*thank you, see you soon*) or ***Grazie e buona giornata*** (*thank you and have a good day*).

Groceries

If you need to buy groceries (***fare la spesa***), you can choose to go to the *supermarket* (***il supermercato***) and fill your *basket* (***cestino***) or *cart* (***il carrello***) with all sorts of goods. Either way, when you buy by weight, you need to remember that Italy, like most of the world, uses the metric system. In the metric system, you have *grams* (***grammi***), *dekagrams* or ten grams (***decagrammo***), *hectograms* or 100 grams (***ettogrammo***), and *kilograms* or 1000 grams (***chilogrammo***). Usually, for groceries, grams and kilograms are used. One *pound* (*libbra*) is approximately 454 *grams* (***grammi***), so every time that you ask for a *kilo* (***un chilo***) you will receive two pounds; or if you really need just a pound, you can ask for *half a kilo* (***mezzo chilo***).

After you collect everything you need, you must pay at the *register* (***la cassa***). Nowadays, cash, debit, and credit cards are accepted; but there may be a *minimum amount* (***importo minimo***) required to use the credit card. You might be surprised by a few things in an Italian supermarket. You have to bag your groceries, and possibly quite quickly. As of a few years ago, you needed to bring your bags (***borse della spesa***). In case they still have plastic bags (***buste di plastica***), you must pay for each one and you might have to tell the cashier how many you need before they start scanning your groceries.

Mi scusi vorrei un chilo di... for *excuse me I would like a kilo of...*

Dal fruttivendolo (*fruit and vegetable store*):

Frutta *(la frutta)* for *fruit*

Verdura *(la verdura, le verdure)* for *vegetable*

Pompelmo *(il pompelmo, i pompelmi)* for *grapefruit*

Carota *(la carota, le carote)* for *carrot*

Cavolfiore *(il cavolfiore, i cavolfiori)* for *cauliflower*

Ciliegia *(la ciliegia, le ciliegie)* for *cherry*

Fungo *(il fungo, i funghi)* for *mushroom*

Cetriolo *(il cetriolo, i cetrioli)* for *cucumber*

Limone *(il limone, i limoni)* for *lemon*

Sedano *(il sedano)* for *celery*

Albicocca *(l'albicocca, le albicocche)* for *apricot*

Melone *(il melone, i meloni)* for *melon*

Anguria *(l'anguria, le angurie)* for *watermelon*

Cipolla *(la cipolla, le cipolle)* for *onion*

Cavolo *(il cavolo, i cavoli)* for *cabbage*

Pesca *(la pesca, le pesche)* for *peach*

Lattuga *(la lattuga)* for *lettuce*

Piselli *(il pisello, i piselli)* for *peas*

Pomodoro *(il pomodoro, i pomodori)* for *tomato*

Patata *(la patata, le patate)* for *potatoes*

Spinaci *(lo spinacio, gli spinaci)* for *spinach*

Fagiolini *(i fagiolini)* for *green beans*

Zucca *(la zucca, le zucche)* for *pumpkin*

Ananas *(l'ananas, gli ananas)* for *pineapple*

Susina *(la susina, le susine)* for *plum*

Fragola *(la fragola, le fragole)* for *strawberry*

Mirtillo *(il mirtillo, i mirtilli)* for *blueberry*

Uva *(l'uva)* for *grapes*

Arancia (l'arancia, le arance) for *orange*

Pera (la pera, le pere) for *pear*

Mela (la mela, le mele) for *apple*

In macelleria (*at the butcher*):

Carne *(la carne)* for *meat*

Pollo *(il pollo)* for *chicken*

Tacchino for *turkey*

Manzo for *beef*

Maiale for *pork*

Fettina *(la fettina, le fettine)* for *cutlet*

Petto *(il petto, i petti)* for *breast*

Coscia *(la coscia, le cosce)* for *thigh*

Bistecca *(la bistecca, le bistecche)* for *steak*

Macinata for *ground meat*

In salumeria (*delicatessen*):

Salame for *salami*

Prociutto cotto for *ham*

Prociutto crudo for *prosciutto*

Olive *(l'oliva, le olive)* for *olives*

Formaggio (il formaggio, i formaggi) for *cheese*

Negozio di alimentari (*in a grocery store*):

Olio for *oil*

Aceto for *vinegar*

Uova for *eggs*

Yogurt for *yogurt*

Scatoletta *(la scatoletta, le scatolette)* for *can*

Pharmacy and drugstore

Pharmacies and drugstores in Italy are separated, and whereas you can find a drugstore section in a supermarket, you cannot find a *pharmacy* (*farmacia*) in either a supermarket or drugstore. Italian pharmacies have their own standing in Italy. This is where you buy your medications, either with or without a prescription. Sometimes you can find high-end products (*prodotti*) for *personal hygiene* (*igiene personale*) or *beauty products* (*prodotti di bellezza*).

Buongiorno, ho mal di testa, ho bisogno di un analgesico

Good morning, I have a headache, I need some painkillers

Buongiorno, ho mal di denti, avete dei buoni antidolorifici?

Good morning, I have a toothache, do you have good painkillers?

Many translate drugstore with *drogheria*—it sounds like it, but these are two very different kinds of stores. *Una drogheria* used to be a store where you could find spices (*spezie*) by bulk, basic food, and other useful products for the house (like detergents, dish-soap, etc), but also for personal hygiene (like shampoo or a razor). When you need a special personal product, like makeup, perfume, or aftershave, you need to go to a *perfume shop* (*profumeria*). Nowadays you find these two kinds of stores merged in something very similar to an American drugstore and can be called either way (*drogheria* or *profumeria*), where you can find house and personal products.

Essential vocabulary:

Detersivo *(il detersivo, i detersivi)* for *detergents*

Detergenti *(il detergente, i detergenti),* for *cleanser*

Trucco *(il trucco, i trucchi)* for *makeup*

Rossetto *(il rossetto, i rossetti)* for *lipstick*

Mascara *(il mascara, i mascara)* for *mascara*

Cipria *(la cipria)* for *face powder*

Fondotinta *(il fondotinta, i fondotinta)* for *foundation*

Crema *(la crema, le creme)* for *lotion*

Crema solare for *sun lotion*

Pettine *(il pettine, i pettini)* for *comb*

Smalto *(lo smalto, gli smalti)* for *nail polish*

Dentifricio *(il dentifricio, i dentifrici)* for *toothpaste*

Spazzolino da denti *(lo spazzolino, gli spazzolini)* for *toothbrush*

Fazzoletti di carta for *tissue paper*

Spazzola *(la spazzola, le spazzole)* for *brush*

Cerotti *(il cerotto, i cerotti)* for *band-aid*

Disinfettante *(il disinfettante, i disinfettanti)* for *disinfectant*

Clothes

There are different kinds of stores you might want to visit for your shopping (***le spese***): you can go to a *mall* (***centro commerciale***) with many different *stores* (***negozi***), to a *department store* (***grandi magazzini***) or you can walk through the town or city center (***il centro***) and pick your little local store (***negozio***) or fancy boutique (***boutique***). You are looking for *something elegant* (***qualcosa di elegante***) and *formal* (***formale***) or *casual* (***casual*** or ***sportivo***) and *informal* (***informale***).

Depending on which kind of store you decide to visit, you may (or may not) find somebody willing to help, a *shop assistant* (***un commesso*** or ***una commessa***). You might want to try whether the clothes you like *fit* you (***andare bene****) and *suit* you (***stare bene****), and you need to look for the *dressing room* (***camerino di prova***) or *dressing rooms* (***camerini di prova***).

Before choosing what to try on, you might need to pause and realize that *Italian sizes* (***le taglie italiane***) maight be different from what you expect. For example, for a dress, a US *small* or 2-4 (*taglia piccola*) corresponds to an Italian 38-40, a US *medium* (*taglia media*) corresponds to a 42-44, a US *large* (*taglia grande*) corresponds to a 46-48, and so on. Although, nowadays, all this information might be found on the label. Either way, you may ask the *shop assistant* (**commesso**) to look for a *different size* (**un'altra taglia**) for you, either *smaller* (**più piccola**) or *bigger* (**più grande**).

Maybe you will just browse (**dare un'occhiata***) or *look for* (**cercare**) something in particular, or you might *need* to buy something (**aver bisogno***), or you might have seen something in the *window* (**la vetrina**).

Mi scusi, sto cercando un... for *excuse me, I am looking for...*

Mi scusi, avrei bisogno di... for *excuse me, I would need...*

Mi scusi, quanto costa quella camicia? for *excuse me, how much is that shirt?*

Mi scusi vorrei provare quella gonna for *excuse me, I would like to try on that skirt*

Vorrei provare questo vestito, ma ho bisogno di una taglia media for *I would like to try on this dress, but I need a medium size*

Mi scusi, potrebbe portarmi la taglia più piccola? for *excuse me could you bring me a smaller size?*

Some verbs that might help while looking for clothes:

Cercare for *to look for*

Mettersi for *to put on*

Togliersi for *to take off*

Provare for *to try on*

Vestirsi for *to get dressed*

Guardare le vetrine for *window shopping*

Costare for *to cost*

Pagare *for to pay*

Some essential words to go clothes shopping:

Calzini *(il calzino, i calzini)* for *socks*

Mutande *(la mutanda, le mutande)* for *underwear*

Canottiera *(la canottiera, le canottiere)* for *undershirt*

Pantaloni *(i pantaloni)* for *trousers*

Jeans *(i jeans)* for *jeans*

Maglietta *(la maglietta, le magliette)* for *T-shirt*

Gonna *(la gonna, le gonne)* for *skirt*

Camicia *(la camicia, le camicie)* for *button-down shirt*

Camicetta *(la camicetta, le camicette)* for *blouse*

Cravatta *(la cravatta le cravatte)* for *tie*

Pantaloncini *(i pantaloncini)* for *shorts*

Collant *(i collant)* for *tights, pantyhose*

Vestito *(il vestito, i vestiti)* for *dress*

Maglione *(il maglione, i maglioni)* for *sweater*

Felpa *(la felpa, le felpe)* for *sweatshirt*

Cardigan *(il cardigan, i cardigan)* for *cardigan*

Sciarpa *(la sciarpa, le sciarpe)* for *scarf*

Guanti *(il guanto, i guanti)* for *gloves*

Cintura *(la cintura, le cinture)* for *belt*

Cerniera *lampo (la cerniera, le cerniere)* for *zipper*

Bottoni *(il bottone, i bottoni)* for *button*

Tasca *(la tasca, le tasche)* for *pocket*

Cappotto *(il cappotto, i cappotti)* for *coat*

Giacca (la giacca, le giacche) for *jacket*

Ombrello (l'ombrello, gli ombrelli) for *umbrella*

Giubbotto (il giubbotto, i giubbotti) for *windbreaker*

Berretto (il berretto, i berretti) for *cap*

Cappello (il cappello, i cappelli) for *hat*

Sottoveste (la sottoveste, le sottovesti) for *slip*

Reggiseno (il reggiseno, i reggiseno) for *bra*

Borsa (la borsa, le borse) for *handbag*

Borsetta (la borsetta, le borsette) for *purse*

Mutandina (la mutandina, le mutandine) for *panties*

Impermeabile (l'impermeabile, gli impermeabili) for *raincoat*

* **Andare bene** (*to fit*) and **stare bene** (*to suit*) are two verbal expressions made with **andare** (*to go*) or **stare** (*to stay*) followed by **bene** (*well*). In the same way, *avere bisogno* (*to need*) follows the normal conjugation of **avere,** followed by **bisogno** (*need*), and **dare un'occhiata** is formed by **dare** (*to give*) and **un'occhiata** (*a gaze*). You can find the conjugations of these verbs in Chapter 14 – Essential Grammar.

Shoes

You might need or want to buy a *pair of shoes* (**paio di scarpe**) and decide to go for either a big or small store. As for the clothes, Italy has its own system; but differently from clothes, the size of a shoe is a "measure": **misura.** *For men* (**da uomo**), *sizes* (**misure**) go from about 39 (US 7) to 45 (US11), and *for women* (**da donna**), sizes usually range from 35 (US 5) to 40 (US 9).

Scarpe da uomo for *men shoes*

Scarpe da donna for *women shoes*

Scarpe da bambino for *children shoes*

Scarpa destra for *right shoe*

Scarpa sinistra for *left shoe*

Dita del piede for *toes*

Tallone for *heel (of the foot)*

Arco del piede for *arch*

Tacco for *heel (of the shoe)*

Stivali (lo stivale, gli stivali) for *boots*

Sandali (il sandalo, i sandali) for *sandals*

Ballerine (la ballerina, le ballerine) for *ballet shoes*

Scarpe da ginnastica for *sneakers*

Mocassini for *loafers*

Infradito for *flip flops*

Pantofole for *slippers*

Books, gifts, and souvenirs

You may like to buy something for yourself or somebody else, and for this, you might need to go to different stores. You can buy *books* (*libri*) in a *bookstore* (*una libreria*), or a *pen* (*penna*), *pencil* (*matita*) or *stationery* (*carta da lettere*) in a *stationery store* (*cartoleria*).

If you need something more precious, you may go to a *jewelry store* (*una gioielleria*), where you can find a *silver bracelet* (*braccialetto d'argento*) or a *golden necklace* (*collana d'oro*), or a *platinum ring* (*anello di platino*) or a *brooch* (*spilla*), or a *pair of earrings* (*paio di orecchini*). You might also find a very nice *wrist watch* (*orologio da polso*), but you may have more options at a *watch seller* (*orologiaio*), where they can fix (*riparare*) yours in case something happened.

Dry cleaners

Traditionally, in Italy, you would find a *dry cleaner* (**lavanderia a secco**) rather than a *laundromat* (**lavanderia a gettoni** or **lavanderia automatica**). These, however, are becoming more and more popular. At the laundromat, you will find both a *washer* (**lavatrice**) and *dryer* (**asciugatrice**), which is quite uncommon to find in an average household. You will need to bring along a *detergent* (**detergente**) and *softener* (**ammorbidente**). Hopefully, your hotel will have a *laundry service* (**un servizio lavanderia**), and, hopefully, you will be satisfied, or you will have *to complain* (**lamentarsi**).

Hairdresser and the barber

It is not recommended that you go to a hairdresser with a language barrier, but you might want or need to be brave and try to have a haircut or treat yourself to a full service makeover while on vacation. The first odd thing you will notice is that *hair* is always plural in Italian: **capelli**. This is why, sometimes, Italians say that they brushed their *hairs* when they really brushed their *hair*.

Vorrei un taglio di capelli for *I would like to get a haircut*

Li vorrei corti for *I would like it short*

Li voglio tenere abbastanza lunghi for *I would like to keep it quite long*

Vorrei lisciarli for *I would like to make it straight*

Vorrei fare una permanente for *I would like a perm*

Li vorrei biondi for *I would like it blond*

Li vorrei scuri for *I would like it dark*

Li vorrei rossi, blu, verdi... for *I would like it red, blue, green...*

Post Office

More likely, you might need to find a post office to send a *letter* (**lettera**), *post card* (**cartolina**) or *package* (**pacco** or **pacchetto**). Although, you can buy stamps at the *tobacco store* (**tabaccaio**) and, usually, there are many *mailboxes* (**cassette delle lettere**) around cities and towns. Nevertheless, you may need to *stay in line* (**fare la fila**) and speak to a *clerk* (*impiegato postale*) to send a *package* (**pacco**) to yourself, your family, or a friend.

Optometrist

In case you wear glasses or contacts, you might need to go to a store to fix your glasses, buy new ones, or buy contacts. You might not be required to have a *test* (**esame della vista**) or *prescription* (**prescrizione**) to do so and the system is the same:

Buongiorno, mi si sono rotti gli occhiali for *good morning my glasses broke*

Buon giorno, vorrei comprare delle lenti a contatto for *good morning I would like to buy some contacts*

I suoi occhiali saranno pronti domani for *your glasses will be ready tomorrow*

Può ritirare i suoi occhiali nel pomeriggio for *you can pick up your glasses in the afternoon*

Montatura (la montatura, le montature) for *frame*

Lente (la lente, le lenti) for *lens*

Prezzo (il prezzo, i prezzi) for *price*

Riparazione (la riparazione, le riparazioni) for *repair*

Doctor and Dentist

Unfortunately, things happenm and you might need to *see a doctor* (**andare dal dottore**) or *dentist* (**andare dal dentista**):

Mi sento male for *I feel bad*

Mi gira la testa for *I feel dizzy*

Mi fa male lo stomaco for *I have a stomachache*

Ho la febbre for *I have a fever*

Ho un raffreddore for *I have a cold*

Mi viene da vomitare for *I feel like vomiting*

Piede (il piede, i piedi) for *foot*

Gamba (la gamba, le gambe) for *leg*

Dito (il dito, le dita) for *finger*

Mano (la mano, le mani) for *hand*

Braccio (il braccio, le braccia) for *arm*

Collo (il collo, i colli) for *neck*

Faccia (la faccia, le facce), for *face*

Bocca (la bocca, le bocche) for *mouth*

Occhio (l'occhio, gli occhi) for *eyes*

Orecchio (l'orecchio, gli orecchi) for *ear*

Mi fa male un dente for *my tooth hurts*

Apra la bocca for *open your mouth*

Risciaqui la bocca for *rinse your mouth*

Cavare un dente for *to extract a tooth*

Curare una carie for *to fix a cavity*

Sostituire una piombatura for *to change a filling*

Chapter 8 - Language and Culture

Much had been said about how much you can learn about a culture when you learn its language or languages: you learn about how they think while you learn how they speak. There are two kinds of expressions that deliver so much of a culture that they are sometimes, unfortunately, the last to be learned. These are proverbs, which are old familiar sayings supposedly carrying pearls of practical wisdom (*perle di saggezza*), and idiomatic expressions (*espressioni idiomatiche*), whose meanings do not match the literal meaning of the words they are made up with. Idioms especially are very frequent, and just knowing a few of them might help you navigate everyday life in Italy quite a lot:

Verbs – idiomatic expressions

Stare zitta for *to be quiet*

Stare attento for *to pay attention*

Stare con qualcuno for *to be in a relationship with*

Stare fermo for *to keep still*

Stare fuori for *to be outside*

Stare a pennello for *to fit like a glove*

Stare in guardia for *to be on one's guard*

Stare in piedi for *to be standing*

Fare apposta for *to do something on purpose*

Fa bel tempo for *it is good weather*

Fa cattivo tempo for *it is bad weather*

Fare il biglietto for *to buy a ticket*

Fare la colazione for *to have breakfast*

Fare i compiti for *to do homework*

Fare di tutto for *to do everything possible*

Fare una domanda for *to ask a question*

Fare la fila/la coda for *to stand in line*

Fare finta (di) for *to pretend*

Fare una fotografia for *to take a picture*

Fare ginnastica for *to exercise*

Fare una gita for *to go on an excursion*

Fare male for *to be painful, to ache*

Fare da mangiare for *to cook*

Fare passare for *to let through*

Fare una passeggiata for *to take a walk*

Fare il pieno (di benzina) for *to fill the gas tank*

Fare presto for *to hurry, to be quick*

Fare alla romana for *to split the check*

Fare la spesa for *to go grocery shopping*

Fare le spese for *to go shopping*

Fare tardi for *to be late*

Fare la valigia for *to pack the suitcase*

Far vedere for *to show something to somebody*

Fare un viaggio for *to take a trip*

Fare visita for *to visit*

Farsi il bagno for *to take a bath*

Farsi la doccia for *to take a shower*

Farsi la barba for *to shave*

Avere bisogno di for *to need*

Avere caldo for *to be warm*

Avere fame for *to be hungry*

Avere fortuna for *to be lucky*

Avere freddo for *to be cold*

Avere fretta for *to be in a hurry*

Avere paura for *to be afraid*

Avere ragione for *to be right*

Avere sete for *to be thirsty*

Avere sonno for *being sleepy*

Avere voglia di for *to want* or *to feel like*

Avere il mal di mare for *to be seasick*

Idioms

Acqua in bocca! For *Mom's word*

Affogare in un bicchier d'acqua for *to be overwhelmed by small problems* (literally: to drown in a glass of water)

Andare a gonfie vele for *things are going very well* (literally: at full sail)

Andare a letto con le galline for *to go to bed early* (literally: to go to bed with the hens)

Andare d'accordo for *to get along*

Avere gli occhi più grandi dello stomaco for *to want more than you need* (literally: to have eyes bigger than the stomach)

Avere la testa tra le nuvole for *not to be thinking* (literally: to have your head in the clouds)

Avere le braccine corte for *to be cheap* (literally: to have short arms)

Avere le mani in pasta for *to have the finger in the pie* (literally: to have your hands in the dough)

Avere sale in zucca for *to be smart* (literally: to have salt in the pumpkin, i.e., your head)

Avere un diavolo per capello for *to be as mad as hell* (literally: to have a demon on each hair)

Avere una gatta da pelare for *to have a big problem* (literally: to have a cat to peel)

Avere uno scheletro nell'armadio for *to have a secret* (literally: to have a skeleton in the closet)

Avere uno stomaco di ferro for *to have an iron-cast stomach*

Bello come il sole for *beautiful like the sun*

Bere come una spugna for *to drink like a fish* (literally: to drink like a sponge)

Brutto come la fame for *ugly like hunger*

Buono come il pane for *goodhearted*

Cadere dalla padella nella brace for *to go from a bad situation to a worse one* (literally: to go from the pan into the embers)

Cadere dalle nuvole for *taken aback* (literally: to fall from the clouds)

Cambiare le carte in tavola for *taking back what you said* (literally: to change the cards on the table)

Capire al volo for *to catch on immediately*

Capitare a fagiolo for *perfect timing* (literally: to happen at the bean)

Cavolo! For *darn!* (literally: cauliflower!)

Cercare il pelo nell'uovo for *to be picky* (literally: to look for the hair in the egg)

Cercare un ago in un pagliaio for *to find a needle in a haystack*

Cogliere un'occasione al volo for *to jump at the opportunity* (literally: to catch a flying opportunity)

Conosco i miei polli for *to be aware of the personality of your friends/colleagues/...* (literally: to know your own chickens)

Dalle stelle alle stalle for *to go from a great situation to the worst* (literally: from the stars to the stables)

Darsi la zappa sui piedi for *to put one's foot in one's mouth*

Dire pane al pane e vino al vino for *let's call a spade a spade*

Dormire (o riposare) sugli allori for *to rest on one's laurel*

Dormire come un ghiro for *sleep like a dog*

Dormire tra due guanciali for *to feel safe* (literally: to sleep between two pillows)

È inutile piangere sul latte versato for *it is no use crying over spilled milk*

Essere al verde for *to have no money/to be broke*

Essere in un bel pasticcio for *to be in a pickle*

Essere nella stessa barca for *to be in the same situation* (literally: to be in the same boat)

Fa un freddo cane for *it is freezing cold*

Fare ad occhio e croce for *to act on the back of a gross evaluation*

Fare i conti in tasca for *to pry into someone's financial situation*

Fare i conti senza l'oste for *to make a decision without consulting the person in charge*

Fare l'avvocato del diavolo for *playing the Devil's advocate*

Fare la nanna for *to sleep*

Fare la pelle for *to kill*

Farsi in quattro for *to bend over backward*

Gettare fumo negli occhi for *to trick somebody* (literally: to throw smoke in the eyes)

Gettare il guanto for *to challenge* (literally: to throw the glove)

Imbrogliare una matassa for *to make things more complicated*

In bocca al lupo! for *good luck!*

In tempo di tempesta ogni buco è un porto for *any port in a storm*

Ingoiare il rospo for *to eat crow* (literally: to swallow the toad)

Lasciare la bocca amara for *to be left disappointed* (literally: to leave the mouth bitter)

Lavare la testa a qualcuno for *to severely scold somebody* (literally: to wash somebody's head)

Legarsela al dito for *to never forget [something negative]* (literally: to tie it around the finger)

Levare le tende for *to go wary* (literally: to remove the tents)

Lupo di mare for *old salt, sea dog* (literally: sea wolf)

Mandare avanti la barca for *to keep going in hard times* (literally: send the boat forward)

Marinaio della domenica for *Sunday or fair-weather sailor*

Mettere il carro innanzi ai buoi for *to do something before being ready* (literally: to put the cart before the oxen)

Morire dalla voglia for *to looking forward to something* (literally: to die from the longing)

Nascere con la camicia for *to be very lucky* (literally: to be born with a button-down shirt)

Nascondersi dietro un dito for *to deny everything* (literally: to hide behind a finger)

Navigare su internet for *to surf/search the web*

Non avere peli sulla lingua for *to speak frankly* (literally to have no hairs on the tongue)

Non mi rompere le scatole for *stop annoying me* (literally: do not break the balls)

Non poterne più for *not being able to stand something any longer*

Non sapere che pesci pigliare for *not to know how to behave or how to react* (literally: not to know which fish to catch)

Non vedere l'ora for *not able to wait for something* (literally: to not be able to see the time)

Oltre al danno anche la beffa for *to add insult to injury*

Pagare alla romana for *to Dutch* (literally: to go the Roman way)

Passarne di tutti i colori for *to go through all sorts of problems* (literally: to go through all colors)

Pescare qualcuno con le mani nel sacco for *to catch someone in the act* (literally: to fish someone with their hands in the sack)

Pesci in faccia for *to treat like dirt* (literally: fish in the face)

Prendere due piccioni con una fava for *to solve two problems with one solution* (literally: to catch two pigeons with one stone)

Prendere in giro for *to pull someone's leg* (literally: to take around)

Prendere lucciole per lanterne for *to misunderstand completely* (literally: to take firefly for lanterns)

Prendere un granchio for *to make a mistake* (literally: to catch a crab)

Promettere mari e monti for *to promise more than you can deliver* (literally: to promise seas and mountains)

Qualcosa bolle in pentola for *what's cooking* (literally: something boils in the pan)

Ride bene chi ride ultimo for *he who laughs last, laughs longer*

Rompere il ghiaccio for *to start a conversation* (literally: to break the ice)

Sano come un pesce for *perfectly healthy* (literally: healthy as a fish)

Saperne una più del diavolo for *to be up to more tricks than Old Nick* (literally: to know one more than the Devil)

Scoprire l'acqua calda for *to discover the wheel* (literally: to discover the warm water)

Senz'altro for *certainly*

Sogni d'oro! for *sweet dreams!*

Sputare il rospo for *to blurt out* (literally: to spit the toad)

Sputare nel piatto dove mangi for *to bite the hand that feeds you* (literally: to spit on the plate that feeds you)

Stare con le mani in mano for *to twiddle one's thumb* (literally: to stay with your hands in hand)

Tagliare i ponti for *to cut all communication* (literally: to cut the bridges)

Tenere le dita incrociate for *to keep one's fingers crossed*

Tirare i remi in barca for *to back down, give something a rest* (literally: pull the oars into the boat)

Scoprire l'America for *to find the pot of gold at the end of the rainbow* (literally: to find the Americas)

Tutto fa brodo for *all is grist for the mill* (literally: anything goes)

Un coniglio for *a scaredy cat* (literally: a rabbit)

Un pezzo di pane for *a good egg*

Un pezzo grosso for *a big shot*

Un'oca giuliva for *a silly* (female) *person* (literally: a happy goose)

Una civetta for *a flirty woman* (literally: an owl)

Una persona in gamba for *a very able person*

Una volpe for *a street-smart person* (literally: a fox)

Vai a quel paese for *get lost!*

Valere la pena for *to be worth it*

Voler cavar sangue da una rapa for *to get blood out of a stone* (literally: to want to get blood out of a turnip)

Proverbs

Proverbs are still a big part of the culture and are considered a great source of *folk wisdom* (**saggezza popolare**). They are still mentioned and used in everyday language to the point that often it is only necessary to mention just the first half of one to be understood:

> *A buon intenditor, poche parole* for *few words to the wise* (literally: to the good listener, few words)
>
> *A caval donato non si guarda in bocca* for *be grateful for the gift without checking its value* (literally: don't look a gift horse in the mouth)

A goccia a goccia si scava la roccia for *little by little you can overcome the most difficult obstacles* (literally: drop after drop you dig the rock)

A mali estremi, estremi rimedi for *in extremely bad situations you need to use extreme remedies* (literally: desperate times call for desperate measures)

Acqua cheta rompe i ponti for *do not underestimate quiet people because they might reveal dangerous things* (literally: the quiet water breaks the bridges)

Ad ognuno la sua croce for *everyone has his own problems* (literally: to each one his own crucifix)

Aiutati che Dio t'aiuta for *God helps those who help themselves* (literally: help yourself, for God helps you)

Al cuore non si comanda for *you cannot decide who or what to love* (literally: the heart can not be ruled)

Ambasciator non porta pena for *who delivers the bad news has no responsibility for them* (literally: the ambassador does not bring the pain).

Anche l'occhio vuole la sua parte for *appearances are important too* (literally: also the eye wants its share)

Batti il ferro quando è caldo for *strike while the iron is hot* (literally: beat the iron while it is hot)

Buon sangue non mente for *the apple does not fall far from the tree* (literally: good blood does not lie)

Campa cavallo che l'erba cresce for *to comment on empty promises or unfavorable and unlikely situations, like when a horse has to wait for the grass to grow to be able to eat* (literally: live horse that the grass grows)

Can che abbaia non morde for *barking dogs never bite* (literally: a dog that barks does not bite)

Cento teste, cento cappelli for *you will have as many different points of view or wishes as many people have* (literally: a hundred heads, a hundred hats)

Chi ben comincia è a metà dell'opera for *getting started is already like having done half of the work* or *well begun is half done* (literally: who starts well has done half of the job)

Chi cerca, trova for *only who looks for things can find them* (literally: who searches, finds)

Chi di spada ferisce di spada perisce for *one who uses violence can expect a violent response* (literally: who inflicts wounds with a sword will die because of a sword)

Chi dice donna dice danno for *women mean trouble* (literally: who says woman says damage)

Chi disprezza compra for *usually you complain about things that you actually like* (literally: who despises, buys)

Chi dorme non piglia pesci for *you need to act to be productive* or *you snooze, you lose* (literally: who sleeps does not catch fish)

Chi è causa del suo mal pianga se stesso for *who is the cause of his troubles can only blame himself* (literally: whom is the source of his pain has to cry for himself)

Chi è senza peccato scagli la prima pietra for *you need not have committed any mistake to be able to blame somebody for his* (literally: whoever is without sin, cast the first stone)

Chi fa da sé fa per tre for *sometimes you do better without anybody's help* (literally: who works by himself does the work of three people)

Chi ha avuto ha avuto e chi ha dato ha dato for *to put an end to a dispute regardless of what has been gained or lost* (literally: who have taken, have taken, and who have given, have given)

Chi ha i denti non ha pane, e chi ha pane non ha i denti for *you either have the ability to appreciate things or you have things, but do not appreciate what you have* (literally: who has teeth does not have bread and who has bread does not have teeth)

Chi ha tempo non aspetti tempo for *do not waste your time* (literally: who has time, should not wait)

Chi la dura la vince for *keep going* (literally: the one who lasts, wins)

Chi la fa l'aspetti for *what goes around comes around* (literally: who commits [something], should expect [to receive] the same thing)

Chi lascia la strada vecchia per la nuova, sa quel che lascia ma non sa quel che trova for *do not leave what is known and safe for something unknown and risky* (literally: who leaves the old road for the new one, knows what he's leaving, but does not know what he will find)

Chi nasce tondo non può morir quadrato for *you cannot change the kind of character you were born with* (literally: who was born round can not die a square)

Chi non beve in compagnia o è un ladro o è una spia for *you should participate in the fun of the party unless you have something to hide* (literally: who does not drink with the rest of the party is either a thief or a spy)

Chi non muore si rivede for *long time no see* (literally: those who do not die see each other again)

Chi non risica non rosica for *if you do not take chances, you do not gain anything* (literally: nothing ventured nothing gained).

Chi rompe paga e i cocci sono i suoi for *any damage must be paid for* (literally: who breaks, pays and keeps the pieces)

Chi sa fa e chi non sa insegna for *distrust who gives unsolicited advice* (literally: who knows, acts, and who does not know, teaches)

Chi semina raccoglie for *you reap what you saw*

Chi semina vento raccoglie tempesta for *bad actions have worse consequences* (literally: who reaps wind, harvests storm)

Chi si accontenta gode for *if you are happy with what you have, you will relish it* (literally: who settles, enjoys)

Chi si loda si imbroda for *self-praise can damage* (literally: who self-praises, makes a mess for himself)

Chi si scusa si accusa for *if you apologize you accuse yourself* (literally: he who excuses himself, accuses himself)

Chi si somiglia si piglia for *people who look alike often become a couple* (literally: who resemble each other, take each other)

Chi tace acconsente for *you agree if you do not speak up* (literally: who keeps quiet, agrees)

Chi tardi arriva male alloggia for *the last to arrive will have the worst accommodation* (literally: who arrives late, stays badly)

Chi troppo e chi niente for *the wealth is distributed unfairly* (literally: who [has] too much and who [has] nothing)

Chi troppo vuole nulla stringe for *who tries to get too much may end up with nothing* (literally: who wants too much, grips nothing)

Chi trova un amico trova un tesoro for *friends are the most precious thing* (literally: who finds a friend, find a treasure)

Chi va con lo zoppo, impara a zoppicare for *you take the bad habits of the people you spend time with* (literally: who goes with the lame learns how to limp)

Chi va piano va sano e va lontano for *it is better to go slowly rather than to be in a rush* (literally: who goes slowly goes healthy and far)

Chi vivrà vedrà for *only the future can tell who was right* (literally: who will live, will see)

Chiodo scaccia chiodo for *a new problem takes away an old problem* (literally: a nail drives away a nail)

Con le buone maniere si ottiene tutto for *always be polite* (literally: with good manners, you can obtain anything)

Da cosa nasce cosa for *one thing leads to another* (literally: form one thing, another is born)

Dagli amici mi guardi Iddio che dai nemici mi guardo io for *we are open to the bad actions of our friends because we are busy guarding against our enemies* (literally: God protects me from my friends because I am guarding against my enemies)

Del senno di poi sono piene le fosse for *it is easy to understand after the fact* (literally: the graves are full of hindsight)

Di necessità si fa virtù for *to make a virtue out of necessity*

Dimmi con chi vai, e ti dirò chi sei for *to understand what kind of person somebody is you need to look at who she/he spends time with* (literally: tell me who you go with and I will tell who you are)

Dio li fa e poi li accoppia for *similar people often become a couple* (literally: God makes them and then pairs them)

Domandare è lecito, rispondere è cortesia for *when somebody does not want to answer your question even when it was predictable* (literally: to ask is legitimate; to answer is kindness)

Due torti non fanno una ragione for *two wrongs do not make one right*

È inutile piangere sul latte versato for *there is no point crying over spilled milk*

È meglio essere uccel di bosco, che uccel di gabbia for *it is better to be free and wild than caged in safety* (literally: it is better to be a bird of the woods than a bird in a cage)

Fare buon viso a cattivo gioco for *you need to adapt in unfavorable circumstances* (literally: it is necessary to put on a nice face in a bad game)

Fare il passo più lungo della gamba for *to overestimate the ability to deal with a situation* (literally: to make a step longer than the leg)

Fatta la legge, trovato l'inganno for *there is always somebody who will try not to obey it* (literally: made the law, found the loophole)

Fidarsi è bene, non fidarsi è meglio for *it is always better to be cautious* (literally: to trust is good, not to trust is better)

Figlio troppo accarezzato non fu mai bene allevato for *a spoiled child is not a well raised child* (literally: a too caressed son has never been a too well raised child)

Finché c'è vita c'è speranza for *never lose hope* (literally: as long as there is life there is hope)

Fortunato al gioco, sfortunato in amore for *when you are lucky with gambling you are not lucky in love* (literally: lucky at cards, unlucky with love)

Gallina vecchia fa buon brodo for *experience counts as in the case of an old person* (literally: an old hen makes a good broth)

Grande amore, gran dolore for *a great love [is followed by] a great sorrow*

I panni sporchi si lavano in famiglia for *family secrets can only be shared within the family* (literally: the dirty laundry is washed in the family)

I parenti sono come le scarpe, più sono stretti, più fanno male for *the closest the relatives the more the problems* (literally: relatives are like shoes: the tighter, the more painful)

Il buon giorno si vede dal mattino for *something that start well, will go well* (literally: a good day can be seen by the morning)

Il denaro fa l'uomo ricco! L'educazione lo fa signore for *education will give you nobility/class not money* (literally: money makes a man rich! Education makes it a gentleman)

Il gioco è bello quando dura poco for *even a beautiful thing can become a bore* (literally: the game is good when it is short)

Il gioco non vale la candela for *something is not worth the effort* (literally: the game is not worth the candle)

Il lupo perde il pelo ma non il vizio for *it is difficult to lose bad habits* (literally: the wolf loses the fur, but not the vice)

Il mondo è fatto a scale, c'è chi scende e c'è chi sale for *good luck sometimes favors others* (literally: the world is made of stairs; some go down and some go up)

Il riso abbonda sulla bocca degli stolti for *laughing too much is a sign of stupidity* (literally: laughing is plentiful on the mouth of the uneducated)

Il silenzio è d'oro for *silence is gold*

Impara l'arte e mettila da parte for *learning a new skill is always useful even when you do not need to use it immediately* (literally: learn the art and put it aside)

L'abito non fa il monaco for *clothes do not make the man*

L'amore non è bello se non è litigarello for *a relationship is alive when two people frequently confront each other on small things* (literally: love is not beautiful if there is no arguing)

L'appetito vien mangiando for *the more you have, the more you want* (literally: the appetite comes with eating)

L'erba cattiva non muore mai for *bad people always survive* (literally: the bad grass never dies)

L'erba del vicino è sempre più verde for *what other people own always seem more valuable* (literally: the grass of the neighbor is always greener)

L'occasione fa l'uomo ladro for *the opportunity makes the thief*

L'ospite è come il pesce: dopo tre giorni puzza for *short visits are better* (literally: the guest is like fish: after three days starts smelling)

L'ozio è il padre di tutti i vizi for *lazy people are more likely to acquire more vices* (literally: idleness is the father of all the vices)

La fortuna aiuta gli audaci for *fortune favors the bold*

La lingua batte dove il dente duole for *you always end up talking about the most painful topics* (literally: the tongue ever turns to the aching tooth)

La madre degli imbecilli è sempre incinta for *the world will always be full of imbeciles* (literally: the mother of imbeciles is always pregnant)

La miglior difesa è l'attacco for *offense is the best defense*

La via dell'Inferno è lastricata di buone intenzioni for *the road to hell is paved with good intentions*

Le bugie hanno le gambe corte for *lies get quickly uncovered* (literally: lies have short legs)

Le disgrazie non vengono mai sole for *there is never just one problem at the time* (literally: adversities never come alone)

Le vie del Signore sono infinite for *solutions to problems often appear in unexpected ways* (literally: the paths of God are infinite)

Lontano dagli occhi, lontano dal cuore for *feelings will dissipate with time* (literally: far from the eyes, far from the heart)

Mal comune mezzo gaudio for *sharing misfortune helps to deal with it* (literally: shared misfortune, half a joy)

Meglio soli che male accompagnati for *you should always be choosy about the people you spend time with* (literally: better alone than in bad company)

Meglio tardi che mai for *better late than never*

Morto un papa se ne fa un altro for *nobody is irreplaceable* (literally: when one pope is dead, a new one is made)

Natale con i tuoi, Pasqua con chi vuoi for *tradition wants you with your family for Christmas and with whoever you choose for Easter* (literally: Christmas with yours, Easter with who you want)

Ne uccide più la lingua che la spada for *words hurt more than actions* (literally: the tongue kills more than the sword)

Nella botte piccola c'è il vino buono for *do not disregard small things* (literally: the good wine is in the small barrel)

Non c'è peggior sordo di chi non vuol sentire for *it is useless to talk to somebody who does not want to listen* (literally: there is nothing duller than those who do not want to hear)

Non dire gatto se non ce l'hai nel sacco for *do not take for granted an accomplishment* (literally: do not say cat if he is not in the sack)

Non è bello ciò che è bello, ma è bello ciò che piace for *different people have different taste* (literally: it is not beautiful what is beautiful, but it is beautiful what you like)

Non è tutto oro quel che luccica for *beautiful things may not be the best things* (literally: not all that sparkles is gold)

Non fasciarti la testa prima di rompertela for *do not worry before there is any need for worrying* (literally: do not wrap your head before it is broken)

Non si può avere la botte piena e la moglie ubriaca for *you cannot have your cake and eat it too*

Non svegliar il can che dorme for *do not instigate a relaxed but dangerous person* (literally: do not wake the sleeping dog)

Non tutte le ciambelle escono con il buco for *not every project is realized perfectly* (literally: not every doughnut comes out with a hole)

Non tutto il male vien per nuocere for *sometimes there is a positive side to misfortune* (literally: not all evil comes to harm)

Occhio non vede, cuore non duole for *what you do not know does not hurt you* (literally: eye does not see, heart does not ache)

Oggi a me domani a te for *nobody is immune to misfortune* (literally: today to you, tomorrow to me)

Ogni lasciata è persa for *take your chances* (literally: every [opportunity that] we let go is [a] lost [opportunity]).

Ogni promessa è debito for *you need to keep your word* (literally: every promise is a debt)

Ognuno tira l'acqua al proprio mulino for *every man to himself* (literally: everyone pulls the water to his mill)

Paese che vai usanza che trovi for *you need to be open to different things* (literally: country where you go, customs that you find)

Patti chiari amicizia lunga for *if the agreement is clear there is no reason for arguing* (literally: clear agreement, long friendship)

Piove sempre sul bagnato for *when it rains it pours* (literally: it always rains on the wetness)

Quando c'è la salute c'è tutto for *health is the most important thing* (literally: when there is health there is everything)

Quando il gatto non c'è i topi ballano for *without any control everybody is up to something* (literally: when the cat is not there, the mice dance)

Quando la volpe non arriva all'uva dice che è acerba for *we scorn what we cannot achieve* (literally: when the fox cannot reach the grapes, it says they are not ripe)

Quando si chiude una porta si apre un portone for *when an opportunity disappears, a bigger one will present* (literally: when a door closes, a front door opens)

Quando si è in ballo bisogna ballare for *you need to finish what you started* (literally: when you are at the dance you need to dance)

Roma non fu fatta in un giorno for *you need time [and patience] to build something* (literally: Rome was not built in one day)

Rosso di sera, bel tempo si spera for *when the sky is red at sunset, there is reasonable chance of good weather the following day* (literally: red in the evening, good weather is hoped for)

Sbagliando si impara for *you learn from your mistakes*

Se non è zuppa è pan bagnato for *six of one, half a dozen of the other* (literally: if it is not soup it's soaked bread)

Se son rose fioriranno for *the situation will develop as it is destined* (literally: if there are roses, they will bloom)

Si dice il peccato, ma non il peccatore for *there is no need to reveal who committed the deed* (literally: you tell the sin, not the sinner)

Soli non si starebbe bene nemmeno in Paradiso for *loneliness is the worst feeling* (literally: even in Heaven it would not feel good to be alone)

Tanto fumo e poco arrosto for *all talk and no action* (literally: a lot of smoke, and no roast)

Tanto va la gatta al lardo che ci lascia lo zampino for *curiosity killed the cat* (literally: the (female) cat goes so often to the lard that she leaves her pawprints there)

Tentar non nuoce for *you need to at least try* (literally: trying does not hurt)

Tira più un capello di donna che cento paia di buoi for *women are the most powerful* (literally: a hair of a woman can pull more than what one hundred pairs of oxen can)

Tra i due litiganti il terzo gode for *between the two parties, the third gains*

Tra il dire e il fare c'è di mezzo il mare for *there is a big discrepancy between our words and our actions* (literally: between saying and doing there is the sea)

Tra moglie e marito non mettere il dito for *it is better not to intrude in a family matter* (literally: between wife and husband do not put your finger)

Troppi cuochi rovinano il brodo for *when many people do something together they need to coordinate to avoid disaster* (literally: too many cooks spoil the broth)

Tutte le strade portano a Roma for *different strategies take you to the same solution* (literally: all roads lead to Rome)

Tutti i nodi vengono al pettine for *at some point we will have to face our mistakes or challenges* (literally: all the knots come to the comb)

Tutto il mondo è paese for *you find the same kind of problems everywhere* (literally: all the world is a village)

Una ciliegia tira l'altra for *one thing leads to another* (literally: one cherry pulls another)

Una mano lava l'altra e tutte e due lavano il viso for *collaboration is important* (literally: one hand washes the other, and together they wash the face)

Una mela al giorno leva il medico di torno for *an apple a day keeps the doctor away*

Una rondine non fa primavera for *it is better not to draw fast conclusions* (literally: one swallow does not make spring)

Uomo avvisato mezzo salvato for *forewarned is forearmed* (Literally: a warned man is a half-saved man)

Vale più la pratica che la grammatica for *experience is more important than theory* (literally: practice is worth more than grammar)

Vivi e lascia vivere for *live and let live*

Chapter 9 - Essential Grammar

Throughout the book, "grammar tips" were placed where could they be useful. Here they all are, and some more, to be consulted when needed.

Nouns, Articles, Adjectives, and Pronouns

Italian nouns have both natural and grammatical gender: they are either feminine or masculine. Natural gender comes from the meaning of the noun: whether it is a boy or girl. Grammatical gender is arbitrary and needs to be learned. It is important to know since articles, adjectives, and pronouns have to agree (be of the same gender) with the nouns they go with or stand for (in the case of the pronoun). The gender is often identified by the last vowel and usually is *-o* for masculine and *-a* for feminine:

Il ragazzo è bello for *the boy is handsome*

La ragazza è bella for *the girl is beautiful*

Lui è bello for *he is handsome*

Lei è bella for *she is beautiful*

Il gatto è rosso for *the* [male] *cat* [male] *is red* [male]

La gatta è rossa for *the* [female] *cat* [female] *is red* [female]

Lui è rosso for *he is red* [male]

Lei è rossa for *she is red* [female]

Il treno è nuovo for *the train is new* [male]

La macchina è nuova for *the car is new* [female]

Sometimes, things are a bit harder, such as: exceptions, regularities, patterns, and professions.

Nouns ending in *-e* can be either feminine (*la canzone*/*the song*, *la chiave*/*the key*, *la classe*/*the class*, *la lezione*/*the lesson*, *la nave*/*the ship*, *la notte*/*the night*) or masculine (*il fiore*/*flower*, *il giornale*/*the newspaper*, *il mare*/ *the sea*, *il pane*/*the bread*, *il sale*/*the salt*, *il cane*/*the dog*) without a way of predicting it.

Few high-frequency feminine nouns end in *-o*: *mano* (*hand*), *foto* (*picture, photo*), *auto* (*car*), and *radio* (*radio*).

There are some <u>regularities</u> that help predict when a noun ending in *-a* or *-e* is masculine (like for endings such as *-amma, -ima, -ema, -ale, -ame, -ile, one, -ore*): *il dramma* (*the drama*), *il programma* (*the program*), *il clima* (*the climate*), *il dilemma* (*the dilemma*), *il sistema* (*the system*), *l'animale* (*the animal*), *il bastone* (*the cane*), *il catrame* (*the tar*), *il dottore* (*the doctor*), *il porcile* (*the pig pen*).

Regularities also help identify noun endings in *-e* as feminine (as for endings like *-sione, -zione* or *-si*): *la pensione* (*the pension*), *la stazione* (*the station*), *l'illusione* (*the illusion*), *l'ipotesi* (*the hypothesis*), *l'analisi* (*the analysis*), *la crisi* (*the crisis*).

<u>Patterns</u> may determine whether a word is masculine or feminine, like in the case of a fruit (generally feminine) and its tree (generally masculine). Fruits: *arancia* (*orange* – feminine), *ciliegia* (*cherry* – feminine), *mela* (*apple* – feminine), *pera* (*pear* – feminine), *pesca* (*peach* – feminine). Trees: *arancio* (*orange tree* – masculine), *ciliegio* (*cherry tree* – masculine), *melo* (*apple tree* – masculine), *pero* (*pear tree* –masculine), *pesco* (*peach tree* – masculine).

When speaking about people and their professions, there are different endings for men and women.

When the masculine ending is *-tore*, the feminine ending is *-trice*:

attore and *attrice* (*actor* and *actress*), *pittore* and *pittrice* (*painter*, masculine and feminine), *scrittore* and *scrittrice* (*writer* masculine and feminine), *scultore* and *scultrice* (*sculptor* and *sculptress*).

When the masculine ends in *-ore* the feminine ends in *-oressa*:

Dottore and *dottoressa* (*doctor* – male and female), *professore* and *professoressa* (*professor* – male and female).

For professions ending in *–ista*, the gender of the person is revealed by the article: *il dentista* (*the* [male] *dentist*) and *la dentista* (*the* [female] *dentist*), *il pianista* (*the* [male] *pianist*) and *la pianista* (*the* [female] *pianist*).

Last, like in English, plural nouns are different from their singular form. In English, most of the time an *-s* is added at the end of the word; in Italian, the final vowel changes in a regular manner.

Singular words ending with *-o* and *-e* have their plural counterpart ending in *-i:*

ragazzo (*boy*) and *ragazzi* (*boys*)

vino (*wine*) and *vini* (*wines*)

libro (*book*) and *libri* (*books*)

Amico (*friend*) and *amici* (*friends*)

Chiave (*key*) and *chiavi* (*keys*)

Fiume (*river*) and *fiumi* (*rivers*)

Padre (*father*) and *padri* (*fathers*)

Giornale (*newspaper*) and *giornali* (*newspapers*)

Singular nouns that end in **-a** change their ending to **-e** in their plural form:

Lettera (*letter*) and *lettere* (*letters*)

Statua (*statue*) and *statue* (*statues*)

Sorella (*sister*) and *sorelle* (*sisters*)

Strada (*street*) and *strade* (*streets*)

Few words do not change in their plural version, only their article does. Singular words ending in -i (*ipotesi*/*hypothesis*, *crisi*/*crisis*, *analisi*/*analysis* and *tesi*/*thesis*) mark their plural with the plural article (*le ipotesi*/*the hypothesis*, *le crisi*/*the crisis*, *le analisi*/*the analyses*, *le tesi*/*the thesis*). Few nouns end in a consonant rather than a vowel and they also mark their plural with the article (*il film*/*the movie* and *i film*/*the movies*, *lo smog*/*the smog* and *gli smog*/*the smogs*, *lo sport*/*the sport* and *gli sport*/*the sports*).

Articles

As you already might have noticed, Italian <u>definitive articles</u> are quite relevant and need to agree with the nouns they precede. It is quite straightforward: *la* is the feminine singular and becomes *le* in its plural form; *il* and *lo* are the used for the singular masculine nouns and turn respectively in *i* and *gli*. As a general rule, when the article ends with a vowel (*la*, *le*, *lo*), and the noun starts with a vowel, then the article drops its vowel and this process is marked by an apostrophe in the orthography: *la amica* (*the friend* [female]) becomes *l'amica*.

Italian <u>indefinite articles</u> correspond to the English *a, an,* and *some*. *Un* is the indefinite article for masculine nouns and *z*, *s*+consonant, *ps* or *gn*. Uno and *un* precede masculine nouns, and *una* precedes feminine nouns and becomes *un'* when the noun starts with a vowel.

Un aeroplano for *an airplane*

Un cane for *a dog*

Un panino for *a sandwich*

Uno gnomo for *a gnome*

Uno psicologo for *a psychologist*

Uno scrittore for *a writer*

Uno stadio for *a stadium*

Uno zaino for *a backpack*

Una donna for *a woman*

Una stazione for *a station*

Un'automobile for *a car*

Adjectives

Adjectives modify nouns, or specify them, <u>describing</u> them; they need to agree with the gender and number of the noun they refer to, changing their ending accordingly, and they usually follow the noun:

Il gatto nero for *the black cat* or *i gatti neri* for *the black cats*

La donna alta for *the tall woman* or *le donne alte* for *the tall women*

Adjectives ending in *-e* can describe both masculine and feminine nouns and become *-i* for the plural:

Il prato verde for *the green lawn* or *i prati verdi* for *the green lawns*

Il libro interessante for *the interesting book* or *i libri interessanti* for *the interesting books*

Il pacco pesante for *the heavy package* or *i pacchi pesanti* for *the heavy packages*

A particular set of descriptive adjectives are those referring to nationalities; they follow the same rules as the other adjectives and are <u>not</u> capitalized:

La signora italiana, tedesca, francese for *the Italian, German, French lady*

Le signore italiane, tedesche, francesi for *the Italian, German, French ladies*

Il signore italiano, tedesco, francese for *the Italian, German, French gentleman*

I signori italiani, tedeschi, francesi for *the Italian, German, French gentlemen*

Essential adjectives:

Bello for *beautiful, handsome* becomes *belli* (plural), *bella* (feminine singular), *belle* (feminine plural)

Buono for good becomes *buoni* (plural), *buona* (feminine singular), *buone* (feminine plural)

Bravo for able becomes *bravi* (plural), *brava* (feminine singular), *brave* (feminine plural)

Brutto for ugly becomes *brutti* (plural), *brutta* (feminine singular), *brutte* (feminine plural)

Caro for dear becomes *cari* (plural), *cara* (feminine singular), *care* (feminine plural)

Cattivo for bad becomes *cattivi* (plural), *cattiva* (feminine singular), *cattive* (feminine plural)

Giovane for young (singular feminine and masculine) becomes *giovani* (plural feminine and masculine)

Grande for big (singular feminine and masculine) becomes *grandi* (plural feminine and masculine)

Lungo for *long* becomes *lunghi* (plural), *lunga* (feminine singular), *lunghe* (feminine plural)

Nuovo for *new* becomes *nuovi* (plural), *nuova* (feminine singular), *nuove* (feminine plural)

Piccolo for *little*, small becomes *piccoli* (plural), *piccola* (feminine singular), *piccole* (feminine plural)

Vecchio for *old* becomes *vecchi* (plural), *vecchia* (feminine singular), *vecchie* (feminine plural)

Molto for *much* becomes *molti* (plural: *many*), *molta* (feminine singular), *molte* (feminine plural)

Poco for a *little* becomes *pochi* (plural: *a few*), *poca* (feminine singular), *poche* (feminine plural)

Tutto for *all* becomes *tutti* (plural: *every*), *tutta* (feminine singular), *tutte* (feminine plural)

Altro for *other*, *another* becomes *altri* (plural), *altra* (feminine singular), *altre* (feminine plural)

Prossimo for *next* becomes *prossimi* (plural), *prossima* (feminine singular), *prossime* (feminine plural)

Ultimo for *last* becomes *ultimi* (plural), *ultima* (feminine singular), *ultime* (feminine plural)

Key adjectives:

Arancione for *orange*

Azzurro for *light blue*

Bianco for *white*

Blu for *dark blue*

Giallo for *yellow*

Grigio for *gray*

Marrone for *brown*

Nero for *black*

Rosso for *red*

Rosa for *pink*

Verde for *green*

Viola for *purple*

Allegro for *happy*

Avaro for *stingy*

Brutto for *ugly*

Bugiardo for *liar*

Caldo for *warm*

Carino for *nice*

Caro for *expensive*

Debole for *weak*

Delizioso for *delicious*

Difficile for *difficult*

Disgustoso for *disgusting*

Facile for *easy*

Fantastico for *fantastic*

Freddo for *cold*

Generoso for *generous*

Giovane for *young*

Grande for *big*

Grasso for *fat*

Indipendente for *independent*

Magro for *thin*

Meraviglioso for *wonderful*

Piccolo for *small*

Povero for *poor*

Profumato for *fragrant*

Pulito for *clean*

Ricco for *rich*

Sincero for *sincere*

Sporco for *dirty*

Possessive adjectives

Adjectives that precede the nouns can indicate possession (possessive), or indicate which object or person you are referring to (demonstratives), or indicate inner properties (*bello*/*beautiful*, *buono*/*good*, *generoso*/*generous*), quantities (*molti*/*many*, *pochi*/*few*), timing (*prossimo*/*next*, *ultimo*/*last*):

Il mio libro, i miei libri for *my book, my books*

La mia casa, le mie case for *my house, my houses*

Il tuo giornale, i tuoi giornali for *my newspaper, my newspapers*

La tua macchina, le tue macchine for *your car, your cars*

Il suo viaggio, i suoi viaggi for *his trip, his trips*

La sua storia, le sue storie for *her story, her stories*

Il nostro divano, i nostri divani for *our couch, our couches*

La nostra vacanza, le nostre vacanze for *our vacation, our vacations*

Il vostro tavolo, i vostri tavoli for *your table, your tables*

La vostra sedia, le vostre sedie for *your chair, your chairs*

Il loro orologio, i loro orologi for *their watch, their watches*

La loro pianta, le loro piante for *their plant, their plants*

Demonstrative adjectives

Demonstrative adjectives are used to indicate a specific person or object; hence, they agree in number and gender with the noun they refer to:

Questo, questa for *this* (masculine and feminine respectively)

Questi, queste for *these* (masculine and feminine respectively)

Quello, quella for *that* (masculine and feminine respectively)

Quelli, *quelle* for *those* (masculine and feminine respectively)

Questo ragazzo è intelligente for *this boy is smart*

Questa signora è molto elegante for *this lady is very elegant*

Ho comprato questi orologi for *I bought these watches*

Ho tagliato queste mele for *I cut these apples*

Quelle ragazze sono molto felici for *those girls are very happy*

Comparatives and superlatives

Comparatives express "*more... than*" (*più... che/del*), "*less... than*" ("*meno... che/del*"), the same as (*così come, tanti quanti*) and they are used very similarly in English and Italian:

Ci sono più cani che gatti for *there are more dogs than cats*

La rivista è meno interessante del libro for *the magazine is less interesting than the book*

Roma è tanto bella quanto caotica for *Rome is as beautiful as chaotic*

Superlatives indicate the most or the least and they are expressed as in English by *the most* (*il più*) or *the least* (*il meno*): *la donna più ricca del mondo* for *the richest woman in the world*

The absolute superlative in English is rendered by *very/most* or the ending *-est* and in Italian by *molto* and the ending *-issimo*: *Il film è molto bello* for *the movie is very good* or *l'inverno è freddissimo* for *the winter is very cold.*

Pronouns

In Italian, there are at least eight possible personal pronouns that function as a subject, while in English, there are only six. The main difference is that, in English, *you* is used to either indicate one or many people different from yourself; in Italian, you will say either *tu* if it is only one person or *voi* if you refer to many people. The feminine version of the third person (*lei*) is also used as the formal version for *you* for either a lady or a gentleman: when you meet someone for the first time, when you do not have a personal relationship with someone, and when somebody is older than you. Often, when used as a formal version of **tu**, Lei is written with a capital letter, even when at the end of words like in **ho deciso di scriverLe** (*I decided to write to you*). However, this practice is falling into disuse.

As you have seen in the previous chapters, and you will see in the section dedicated to the verbs, a peculiarity of Italian is that you do not really need to mention the subject (or the pronoun that stands for it) unless you want to—since the inflection of the verb gives away who is performing the action.

Io (only capitalized at the beginning of a sentence) for *I*

Tu for *you*

Lei for *she*

Lui for *he*

Noi for *we*

Voi for *you* (many)

Loro or **essi** for *they*

Direct object pronouns

Pronouns can be used as a direct object (i.e., *me, him, us...*) instead of a noun to show who or what is affected by the action of the verb. Like in *I like her a lot, I admire him immensely, I saw them yesterday.* In Italian, there is a set of <u>direct object pronouns,</u> and they can be either placed before the verb or attached at the end of it.

Mi for *me* as in **lei mi chiama** (*she calls me*) or **chiamami** (*call me*)

Ti for *you* as in **I bambini ti vedono** (*the children see you*) or **io posso vederti** (*I can see you*)

La for *her/it* as in **io la conosco** (*I know her*) or **mangiala** (*eat it*) referring to **mela** (*apple*) for example

Lo for *him/it* as in ***io lo conosco*** (*I know him*) or ***mangialo*** (*eat it*) referring to ***gelato*** (*ice cream*)

Ci for *us* as in ***tu ci vedi*** (*you see us*) or ***chiamaci*** (*call us*)

Vi for *you* (many) as in ***io vi vedo*** or ***loro vogliono invitarvi*** (*they want to invite you* – many)

Li for *them* (masc. or both masc. and fem.) as in ***li vedo domani*** (*I see them tomorrow*) or ***invitali*** (*invite them*)

Le for *them* (fem.) as in ***le vedo domani*** (*I see them tomorrow*) or ***invitale*** (*invite them*)

Indirect object pronouns

When something or a person is indirectly affected by an action in English, you often (not always) use *to* with the pronoun: *I sent it to them yesterday, they awarded him a medal.* In Italian, you either use, as in English, a preposition *a* (*to*) followed by the appropriate direct pronoun or a set of indirect pronouns may stand in for <u>indirect objects</u>:

Mi or *a me* for *to me*

Ti or *a te* for *to you*

Gli or *a lui* for *to him*

Le or *a lei* for *to her*

Ci or *a noi* for *to us*

Vi or *a voi* for *to you* (many)

Li or *a loro* for *to them* (masc.)

Le or *a loro* for *to them* (fem.)

Le mando dei fiori for *I send her some flowers*

Posso mandarle dei fiori for *I can send her some flowers*

Double pronouns

You may need to use both a direct and indirect object pronoun, like in *he will bring it* (direct) *to me* (indirect). In Italian, the position of the double object pronoun will be as when they are by themselves: before the verb or attached to the infinitive verb. Most of the time, the direct precedes the indirect, like in English: *it* (direct) *to me* (indirect).

Most notably, when they are together, the indirect object pronoun changes to distinguish itself from the direct one:

Mi becomes *me* for *to me*

Ti becomes *te* for *to you*

Gli and *le* become *glie* for *to him* or *to her*

Ci becomes *ce* for *to us*

Vi becomes *ve* for *to you* (many)

Li and *le* become *glie* for *to them*

Instead of *Giovanni porta il libro a Mario* (*John brings the book to Mario*) you can say:

Giovanni glielo porta for *John brings it to him*

Instead of *lui legge la lettera a me* (*he reads the letter to me*), you can say:

Lui me la legge for *he reads it to me*

Instead of saying *voglio mandarti un regalo* (*I want to send you a gift*) you can say:

Voglio mandartelo for *I want to send it to you*

Possessive pronouns:

Possessives adjectives, like articles, must agree with the gender and number of the noun they modify. They can also replace a noun and become a possessive pronoun. In this case, they keep the article of the noun that they stand for:

Questa macchina è la mia for *this car is mine*

Se la tua macchina non funziona, puoi usare la mia for *if your car does not work, you can use mine*

Se il mio libro è noioso, puoi leggere il suo for *if my book is boring, you can read hers/his*

You can use a possessive pronoun to indicate part of a group: *one of mine* (**uno dei miei**), *one of my daughters is sick* (**una delle mie figlie è malata**), *three of my apple trees died* (**tre dei miei alberi di mele sono morti**).

Relative Pronouns:

Relative pronouns are used to connect clauses or phrases to nouns or pronouns. The pronoun can refer to a person, thing, or situation—like in English when you use *who, which, that, whom, where*.

The Italian relative pronouns are:

Che for *which, who* and *that* as a subject or direct object

Cui for *which, who and that* after a preposition in place for an indirect object

La ragazza _che_ sta parlando è la figlia del direttore for *the girl _who_ is speaking is the director's daughter*

La ragazza _che_ stai guardando è la figlia del direttore for *the girl _that_ you are watching is the director's daughter*

Questa è la canzone _di cui_ ti parlavo for *this is the song _that_ I was telling you about*

La pianta _da cui_ è tratto lo zucchero for *the plant from _which_ the sugar is extracted*

Quale for *who, whom, which, that* varies in gender and number and is preceded by an appropriate article:

Ho parlato con i suoi amici, _i quali_ sostengono di non averlo visto

I spoke with his friends, _who_ maintain they have not seen him

Demonstrative pronouns:

Demonstrative adjectives can be used as pronouns to refer to something specific in the context, often not to repeat the same word. The difference is that the adjective takes the place of the noun instead of accompanying it.

Questo, *questa*, *questi*, *queste* for *this* (masculine and feminine) and *these* (masculine and feminine)

Quello, *quella*, *quelli*, *quelle* for *that* (masculine and feminine) and *those* (masculine and feminine)

L'inverno passato è stato mite, questo è molto più freddo

The past winter was mild, this is much colder

Questo è un colabrodo

This is a colander

Questa è l'ultima volta che ti chiedo di venire

This is the last time I ask you to come

Questo è rotto

This is broken

Ci and *ne*

Ci and *ne* are two extremely common pronouns that have no single equivalent in English.

Ci is used to mean *it* or *about it* and usually comes before the verb, in an order, attached at the end of the infinitive:

Ripensandoci me ne sono pentito for *when I thought it over, I was sorry*

Non ci credo per niente for *I do not believe it at all*

Ci penserò for *I will think about it*

Non ci capisco niente for *I cannot understand it at all*

Non so che farci for *I do not know what to do about it*

Ci is used with the verb *entrare* (*to go* inside) in some common idiomatic phrases:

Cosa c'entra? for *what's going on with it?*

Io non c'entro for *this has nothing to do with me*

With *volere* (*to want*), meaning that something is necessary:

Ci vuole buona volontà for *goodwill is necessary*

Ci vogliono tre uova per fare la torta for *three eggs are necessary to make the cake*

With *mettere* (*to* put) becomes *metterci* (*to take*)

Ci si mette mezz'ora dal centro alla spiaggia for *it takes half an hour form the center to the beach*

With *vedere* (*to see*) becomes *vederci* (*to see each other*)

Ci vediamo tra mezz'ora for *let us meet in half an hour*

With **sentire** *(to hear)* becomes **sentirci** (*to hear from each other*)

Sentiamoci questa sera for *let us hear each other tonight*

Ne often replaces a noun and means *about it/about them, of it/of them, with it/with them,* and so on. When used with Italian adjectives or verbs which are followed by **di**, for example *contento di* (*happy about*), *stufo di* (*fed up with*), *aver paura di* (*to be afraid of*), *scrivere di* (*to write about*):

Ne sono molto contenta for *I am very happy about it*

Sono stufo di leggere solo giornali for *I am fed up about reading only newspapers*

Sono sicura di volere andare a Roma for *I am sure I want to go to Rome*

It can refer to amounts and quantities.

Ne vuoi? For *would you like some?*

Ne ho preso la metà for *I have taken half of it*

Ne can be used to refer to nouns that have already been mentioned.

Parliamone for *let's talk about it*

Verbs

Verbs describe events, like somebody performing an action (*Maria gioca con la palla*, *Maria plays with the ball*) or something happening (*piove*, *it rains*). Events happen at a particular time: in the present, past or future, and the form that a verb takes to express time is called tense. Italian verbs change their endings depending on the tense (i.e., when the event occurs): *credo* means *I believe*, *credevo* means *I believed* and *crederò* means *I will believe*. Italian verb endings also change according to who or what is doing the action (i.e., the subject of the verb) and it can be expressed by either a noun or pronoun: <u>Jack</u> *speaks Italian*; <u>She</u> *is playing tennis.*

In Italian, the citation form of a verb is the infinitive, which works as a noun as well: *parlare* can stand for *to speak* or *speaking* (*parlare è stancante* for *speaking is tiring*). The last three letters of the infinitive (*-are*, *-ere*, *-ire*) determine the conjugation the verb belongs to and consequently the ending for each person in each tense. To conjugate a verb ending in –are, like *parlare* (*to speak*), you drop the ending *-are* and keep the stem *parl-* and add the inflections for each person.

While the conjugation of regular verbs consistently follows the same rules, irregular verbs do not follow the usual patterns. These irregular Italian verbs include very common and frequently used verbs such as *andare* (*to go*), *essere* (*to be*), and *fare* (*to do* or *to make*).

Auxiliary verbs: *essere* (*to be*) and *avere* (*to have*)

Like in English, auxiliary verbs are used in forming the tenses, moods, and voices of other verbs (like *be* and *have* in *I am going, you have gone, did you go?*).

As in English, Italian auxiliary verbs are *essere* (*to be*) and *avere* (*to have*); they have their own meaning (*io sono uno studente*/*I am a student* or *tu hai un cappello*/*you have a hat*) and they have an irregular conjugation. The simple tenses (present, imperfect...) are conjugated without an auxiliary, whereas the compound tenses (past and future) are formed with the help of an auxiliary: *io ho guardato* (*I have watched*), *io avrò guardato* (*I will have looked*), *io avevo guardato* (*I had looked*).

Ieri ho mangiato una pizza al formaggio for *yesterday I have eaten a pizza with cheese*

Sono arrivato oggi for *I arrived today*

Simple Present of *essere* (*to be*) and *avere* (*to have*):

Io sono for *I am*

Tu sei for *you are*

Lui/lei è for *she/he is*

Noi siamo for *we are*

Voi siete for *you (more than one) are*

Essi/loro sono for *they are*

Io ho* for *I have*

Tu hai* for *you have*

Lei/lui ha* for *she/he has*

Noi abbiamo for *we have*

Voi avete for *you have*

Loro/essi hanno* for *they have*

*Remember the *h* is always silent

Future of *essere* (*to be*) and *avere* (*to have*):

Io sarò for *I will be*

Tu sarai for *you will be*

Lei/lui sarà for *she/he will be*

Noi saremo for *we will be*

Voi sarete for *you* (many) *will be*

Essi saranno for *they will be*

Io avrò for *I will have*

Tu avrai for *you will have*

Lei/lui avrà for *she/he will have*

Noi avremo for *we will have*

Voi avrete for *you* (many) *will have*

Essi/loro avranno for *they will have*

The imperfect (expresses an ongoing action in the past) of ***essere*** (*to be*) and ***avere*** (*to have*):

Io ero for *I was*

Tu eri for *you were*

Lei/lui era for *she/he was*

Noi eravamo for *we were*

Voi eravate for *you* (many) *were*

Essi/loro erano for *they were*

Io avevo for *I had*

Tu avevi for *you had*

Lei/lui aveva for *she/he had*

Noi avevamo for *we had*

Voi avevate for *you* (many) *had*

Essi/loro avevano for *they had*

The present perfect of *essere* (*to be*) and *avere* (*to have*):

The present perfect indicates actions completed in the recent past and often followed by expressions like (*ieri*/*yesterday*, *domenica*/*Sunday*, *un'ora fa*/*an hour ago*, *un anno fa*/*a year ago*). This is a compound tense formed by the present of either *essere* or *avere* followed by the past participle of the verb.

The participle agrees with the subject number and gender: *stato*, *stata*, *stati*, *state* (*been*) for singular masculine and feminine and plural masculine and feminine of *essere* and *avuto*, *avuta*, *avuti*, *avute* (*had*) for singular masculine and feminine and plural masculine and feminine of *avere*.

Io sono stato for *I was*

Tu sei stato for *you were*

Lei è stata/*lui è stato* for *she/he was*

Noi siamo stati for *we were*

Voi siete stati for *you* (many) *were*

Essi/loro sono stati for *they were*

Io ho avuto for I *had*

Tu hai avuto for *you had*

Lui/lei ha avuto for *she/he had*

Noi abbiamo avuto for *we had*

Voi avete avuto for *you* (many) *had*

Essi/loro hanno avuto for *they had*

As for other verbs, the past participle of verbs of motions (*andare*/*to go*, *partire*/*to leave*) and states (*nascere*/*to be born*) usually goes with the present of *essere*, whereas the past participle of transitive verbs (*mangiare*/*to eat*, *scrivere*/*to write*, *vendere*/*to sell*) follow the present of *avere*.

Regular verbs

Regular verbs in Italian are predictably conjugated in the same way: their ending changes consistently depending on their conjugation (the class they belong to), the person who is performing the action, and the tense (the time when the action occurs).

To conjugate a regular verb, you drop the ending *-are*, *-ere* or *-ire* for **parl-are** (*to speak*), **chied-ere** (*to ask*), **sent-ire** (*to hear*) or **cap-**ire (*to* understand), keep the stem **parl-**, and add the inflections for each person in a particular tense. Every regular verb ending in *-are* will take the same ending for the same person in the same tense and so will those ending in *-ere* and *-ire*.

Simple Present of *-are*: *-o, -i, -a, -iamo, -ate, -ano*

Io parlo for *I speak*

Tu parli for *you speak*

Lei/lui parla for *she/he speaks*

Noi parliamo for *we speak*

Voi parlate for *you* (many) *speak*

Essi/loro parlano for *they speak*

Simple Present of *-ere*: *-o, -i, -e, -iamo, -ete, -edono*

Io chiedo for *I ask*

Tu chiedi for *you ask*

Lei/lui chiede for *she/he asks*

Noi chiediamo for *we ask*

Voi chiedete for *you* (many) *ask*

Essi/loro chiedono for *they ask*

Simple Present of *-ire*: *-o, -i, -e, -iamo, -ite, -ono*

Io sento for *I hear*

Tu senti for *you hear*

Lei/lui sente for *she/he hear*

Noi sentiamo for *we hear*

Voi sentite for *you (many) hear*

Essi/loro sentono for *they hear*

Simple Present of *-ire*: *-isco*, *-isci*, *-isce*, *-iamo*, *-ite*, *-iscono*

Io finisco for *I finish*

Tu finisci for *you finish*

Lei/lui finisce for *she/he finish*

Noi finiamo for *we finish*

Voi finite for *you* (many) *finish*

Essi/loro finiscono for *they finish*

The imperfect of regular verbs *-are*, *-ere*, *-ire*:

Io parlavo for *I was talking*

Tu parlavi for *you were talking*

Lui/lei parlava for *she/he was talking*

Noi parlavamo for *we were talking*

Voi parlavate for *you* (many) *were talking*

Essi/loro parlavano for *they were talking*

Io chiedevo for *I was asking*

Tu chiedevi for *you were asking*

Lei/lui chiedeva for *she/he was asking*

Noi chiedevamo for *we were asking*

Voi chiedevate for *you* (many) *were asking*

Essi/loro chiedevano for *they were asking*

Io capivo for *I was understanding*

Tu capivi for *you were understanding*

Lei/lui capiva for *she/he was understanding*

Noi capivamo for *we were understanding*

Voi capivate for *you* (many) *were understanding*

Loro/essi capivano for *they were understanding*

The future of regular verbs *-are, -ere, -ire*:

Io parlerò for *I will speak*

Tu parlerai for *you will speak*

Lei/lui parlerà for *she/he will speak*

Noi parleremo for *we will speak*

Voi parlerete for *you* (many) *will speak*

Essi/loro parleranno for *they will speak*

Io chiederò for *I will ask*

Tu chiederai for *you will ask*

Lei/lui chiederà for *she/he will ask*

Noi chiederemo for *we will ask*

Voi chiederete for *you* (many) *will ask*

Essi/loro chiederanno for *they will ask*

Io capirò for *I will understand*

Tu capirai for *you will understand*

Lei/lui capirà for *she/he will understand*

Noi capiremo for *we will understand*

Voi capirete for *you* (many) *will understand*

Essi/loro capiranno for *they will understand*

Frequently used verbs in *-are*: *abitare* (*to leave*), *arrivare* (*to arrive*), *ascoltare* (*to listen*), *aspettare* (*to wait*), *camminare* (*to walk*), *cenare* (*to have dinner*), *comprare* (*to buy*), *domandare* (*to ask*), *entrare* (*to enter*), *guardare* (*to look*), *lavorare* (*to work*), *nuotare* (*to swim*), *ordinare* (*to order*), *pranzare* (*to have lunch*), *riposare* (*to rest*), *prenotare* (*to reserve*).

Frequently used verbs for *-ere*: *chiudere* (*to close*), *credere* (*to believe*), *leggere* (*to read*), *perdere* (*lo lose*), *piangere* (*to cry*), *ripetere* (*to repeat*), *rispondere* (*to answer*), *rompere* (*to break*), *scrivere* (*to write*), *vendere* (*to sell*), *vivere* (*to live*).

Frequently used verbs in the first type of *-ire*: *aprire* (*to open*), *coprire* (*to cover*), *dormire* (*to sleep*), *offrire* (*to offer*), *partire* (*to leave*), *scoprire* (*to discover*), *seguire* (*to follow*), *servire* (*to serve*), *vestire* (*to dress*).

The past participle of regular verbs and their Present perfect

To produce the present perfect you need to know the past participle of the verb. To form the past participle of regular verbs in *-are*, *-ere* and *-ire,* you add *-ato*, *-uto* and *-ito* to the stem respectively:

Parlare becomes *parlato* for *to speak* becomes *spoken*

Vendere becomes *venduto* for *to sell* becomes *sold*

Partire becomes *partito* for *to leave* becomes *left*

The present perfect of regular verbs *-are, -ere, -ire*:

Io ho parlato for *I spoke*

Tu hai parlato for you spoke

Lui/lei ha parlato for *she/he spoke*

Noi abbiamo parlato for *we spoke*

Voi avete parlato for *you (many) spoke*

Essi/loro hanno parlato for *they spoke*

Io ho chiesto for *I asked*

Tu hai chiesto for *you asked*

Lei/lui ha chiesto for *she/he asked*

Noi abbiamo chiesto for *we asked*

Voi avete chiesto for *you* (many) *asked*

Essi/loro hanno chiesto for *they asked*

Io ho finito for *I finished*

Tu hai finito for *you finished*

Lei/lui ha finito for *she/he finished*

Noi abbiamo finito for *we finished*

Voi avete finito for *you (many) finished*

Essi/loro hanno finito for *they finished*

Gerund and the present progressive

The gerund is used to express an action simultaneous to another: *camminando*, *while walking*. It can therefore also be used to express an ongoing action in the present, past, and future. For the present progressive, the gerund of a verb follows the simple present of the verb stare:

Io sto camminando for *I am walking*

Tu stai camminando for *you are walking*

Lei/lui sta camminando for *she/he is walking*

Noi stiamo camminando for *we are walking*

Voi state camminando for *you* (many) *are walking*

Essi/loro stanno camminando for *they are walking*

Verbs ending in *-are* will add to the stem *-ando*, those ending in *-ere* and *-ire* will add *-endo* (*correre* and *correndo* for *to run* and *while running*, *dormire* and *dormendo* for *to sleep* and *while sleeping*).

Irregular verbs

Irregular verbs are verbs that do not follow fully or at all the rules of the conjugation of the class they belong to.

Most frequent irregular verbs ending in -are are:

Simple Present of **andare** (*to go*), **dare** (*to give*), **fare** (*to do/to make*), **stare** (*to stay*):

Io vado for *I go*

Tu vai for *you go*

Lei/lui va for *she/he goes*

Noi andiamo for *we go*

Voi andate for *you* (many) *go*

Essi/loro vanno for *they go*

Io do for *I give*

Tu dai for *you give*

Lei/lui dà for *she/he gives*

Noi diamo for *we give*

Voi date for *you* (many) *give*

Essi/loro danno for *they give*

Io faccio for *I do*

Tu fai for *you do*

Lui/lei fa for *she/he does*

Noi facciamo for *we do*

Voi fate for *you* (many) *do*

Essi/loro fanno for *they do*

Io sto for *I stay*

Tu stai for *you stay*

Lei/lui sta for *she/he stays*

Noi stiamo for *we stay*

Voi state for *you* (many) *stay*

Essi/loro stanno for *they stay*

Simple Present of **bere** (*to drink*), **sapere** (*to know*), **spegnere** (*to turn off*), and **tenere** (*to keep*):

Io bevo for *I drink*

Tu bevi for *you drink*

Lei/lui beve for *she/he drink*

Noi beviamo for *we drink*

Voi bevete for *you* (many) *drink*

Essi/loro bevono for *they drink*

Io so for *I know*

Tu sai for *you know*

Lei/lui sa for *she/he knows*

Noi sappiamo for *we know*

Voi sapete for *you* (many) *know*

Essi/loro sanno for *they know*

Io spengo for *I turn off*

Tu spegni for *you turn off*

Lei/lui spegne for *she/he turns off*

Noi spegniamo for *we turn off*

Voi spegnete for *you (many) turn off*

Essi/loro spengono for *they turn off*

Io tengo for *I keep*

Tu tieni for *you keep*

Lei/lui tiene for *she/he keeps*

Noi teniamo for *we keep*

Voi tenete for *you (many) keep*

Essi/loro tengono for *they keep*

Simple Present of **dire** (*to say*), **morire** (*to die*), **salire** (*to go up*), and **uscire** (*to go out*), **venire** (*to come*):

Io dico for *I say*

Tu dici for *you say*

Lei/lui dice for *she/he says*

Noi diciamo for *we say*

Voi dite for *you* (many) *say*

Essi/loro dicono for *they say*

Io muoio for *I die*

Tu muori for *you die*

Lei/lui muore for *she/he dies*

Noi moriamo for *we die*

Voi morite for *you* (many) *die*

Essi/loro muoiono for *they die*

Io salgo for *I go up*

Tu sali for *you go up*

Lei/lui sale for *she/he goes up*

Noi saliamo for *we go up*

Voi salite for *you* (many) *go up*

Essi/loro salgono for *they go up*

Io esco for *I go out*

Tu esci for *you go out*

Lei/lui esce for *she/he goes out*

Noi usciamo for *we go out*

Voi uscite for *you* (many) *go out*

Essi/loro escono for *they go out*

Io vengo for *I come*

Tu vieni for *you come*

Lei/lui viene for *she/he comes*

Noi veniamo for *we come*

Voi venite for *you* (many) *come*

Essi/loro vengono for *they come*

Modal verbs

There are three modal verbs in Italian: **volere** (*to want*), **potere** (*to want/to be able to*) e **dovere** (*to must, to have to*). They have an irregular conjugation in the Simple Present and a very particular construction in the Present Perfect.

Simple Present of **volere** (*to want*), **potere** (*can/to be able to*) e **dovere** (*to must, to have to*):

Io voglio for *I want*

Tu vuoi for *you want*

Lei/lui vuole for *she/he wants*

Noi vogliamo for *we want*

Voi volete for *you* (many) *want*

Loro/essi vogliono for *they want*

Io posso for *I can/am able to*

Tu puoi for *you can/are able to*

Lei/lui può for *she/he can/is able to*

Noi possiamo for *we can/are able to*

Voi potete for *you* (many) *can/are able to*

Loro/essi possono for *they can/are able to*

Io devo for *I must/have to*

Tu devi for *you must/have to*

Lei/lei deve for *she/he must/have to*

Noi dobbiamo for *we must/have to*

Voi dovete for *you* (many) *must/have to*

Loro/essi devono for *they must/have to*

These three verbs may be used on their own or used with another verb indicating which action somebody wants, can or has to perform: *io voglio/posso/devo suonare il piano* (*I want to/am able to/have to play the piano*). In this case, they require a special construction in the Present Perfect. The choice of the auxiliary verb (i.e., *essere* or *avere*) depends on the verb that follows the modal verb:

Ho voluto finire il lavoro for *I wanted to finish the work*

Sono voluto andare al cinema for *I wanted to go to the cinema*

Ho dovuto rimandare l'appuntamento for *I had to postpone the appointment*

È dovuto andare dal dottore for *he had to go to the doctor*

Ho potuto mangiare il gelato for *I could eat the ice cream*

È potuta partire di domenica for *she could leave on Sunday*

Reflexive verbs

The subject and the object of reflexive verbs are the same person! It sounds complicated, but this is what happens when *you wash yourself*. Who performs and who receives the action are the same person.

The infinitive of reflexive Italian verbs ends in **-arsi**, **-ersi**, and **-irsi**:

Svegliarsi for *to wake oneself up*

Nutrirsi for *to feed oneself*

Abituarsi for *to get used (yourself) to something*

Chiamarsi for *to be named (literally: to call oneself)*

Chiedersi for *to ask oneself*

Divertirsi for *to have fun*

Prepararsi for *to get ready*

Dimenticarsi for *to forget*

Domandarsi for *to wonder*

Presentarsi for *to introduce oneself*

Addormentarsi for *to fall asleep*

Alzarsi for *to get up*

Ammalarsi for *to get sick*

Riposarsi for *to rest*

Sedersi for *to sit*

Approffitarsi (di) for *to take advantage of*

Bruciarsi con for *to get burned with*

Fidarsi di for *to trust*

Incontrarsi con for *to meet with*

Lamentarsi di for *to complain about*

These verbs are conjugated like the regular (-are, -ere and -ire) and are preceded by the reflexive pronoun that matches the subject:

Io mi alzo for *I get up*

Tu ti alzi for *you get up*

Lei/lui si alza for *she/he gets up*

Noi ci alziamo for *we get up*

Voi vi alzate for *you* (many) *get up*

Essi/loro si alzano for *they get up*

The reflexive pronoun is usually in front of the verb, but it can also attach to the end of the infinitive after modal verbs:

Lei vuole seder si sull'erba for *she wants to sit on the grass*

Noi dobbiamo preparar ci per l'esame for *we have to prepare for the test*

Reflexive verbs more often concern people:

Vestirsi for *to get dressed*

Svestirsi for *to get undressed*

Spazzolarsi for *to brush (teeth or hair)*

Farsi il bagno/la doccia/la barba for *to take a bath/a shower/ to shave*

Truccarsi for *to put on makeup*

Arrabbiarsi for *to become angry*

Calmarsi for *to calm down*

Irritarsi for *to get irritated*

Preoccuparsi for *to worry*

Rallegrarsi for *to rejoice*

Spaventarsi for *to get frightened*

Chiamarsi (*to be named*)

When introducing yourself or somebody else, you use the verb *chiamarsi* (literally *to call oneself*).

Simple Present:

Io mi chiamo means *my name is* (literally: *I call myself)*

Tu ti chiami for *your name is* (literally: *you call yourself)*

Lei/lui si chiama for *her/his name is* (literally: *she/he calls herself/himself)*

Noi ci chiamiamo for *our names are* (literally: *we call ourselves*)

Voi vi chiamate for *your names are* (literally: *you call yourselves*)

Loro/essi si chiamano for *their names are* (literally: *you call yourselves*)

Mi chiamo Lara for *my name is Lara*

Lei come si chiama? for *what is your name?* (formal)

Tu come ti chiami? for *what is your name?* (informal)

Noi ci chiamiamo Paolo e Mara, voi come vi chiamate? For *our names are Paolo and Mara, what are your names?*

Reciprocal reflexive verbs

To express reciprocity, you can use the plural form of reflexive verbs:

Vedersi (*to see each other*):

I bambini si vedono ogni giorno for *the children see each other every day*

Amarsi (*to love each other*):

Francesca e Giovanni si amano molto for *Francesca e Giovanni love each other very much*

Capirsi (*to understand each other*)

I fratelli si capiscono bene for *the brothers understand each other well*

Conoscersi for *to know each other*

Aiutarsi for *to help each other*

Parlarsi for *to talk to each other*

Scriversi for *to write to each other*

Verbs with indirect object

Most verbs take both a direct and an indirect object. A direct object is the receiver of an action within a sentence; in *I throw the ball, the ball* receives the action of being thrown. In *I send you a letter, the letter* is the receiver of the action of being sent and *you* are the person for whom the action is performed: the indirect object. The indirect object identifies to or for whom or what the action of the verb is performed.

As in English, few Italian verbs take only indirect objects. For example, both in English and in Italian, *to happen* (**accadere**) only has an indirect object: *many beautiful things are happening to <u>me</u>* (**<u>mi</u> stanno accadendo molte cose belle**); or *what is happening to you?* (**Cosa ti accade?**).

Verbs with an indirect object are common and may be very useful to know how to use:

Piacere for *to like*

Accadere for *to happen*

Bastare for *to be enough/sufficient*

Dispiacere for *to regret*

Dolere for *to suffer*

Importare for *to matter/to be important*

Interessare for *to interest*

Sembrare for *to seem*

Servire for *to need*

Some might have a different construction from their English translation, and this might become confusing, like in the case of *piacere* (*to like*), whose English counterpart takes a direct object. The easiest way of approaching the use of *piacere* is to keep translating it with *to be pleasing* [to somebody].

Simple Present of *piacere* (*to like*):

Io piaccio for *I am pleasing to*

Tu piaci for *you are pleasing to*

Lei/lui piace for *she/he is pleasing to*

Noi piaciamo for *we are pleasing to*

Voi piacete for *you* (many) *are pleasing to*

Essi/loro piacciono for *they are pleasing to*

You may just say the *you are pleasing* (*tu piaci*), meaning they you are quite attractive or entertaining; more often, though, you might need to mention who is receiving the action: *io piaccio al postino* (*I am pleasing to the mailman/the mailman likes me*). As a result, these verbs are very often used with indirect pronouns: *mi* or *a me* (*to me*), *ti* or *a te*, *le* or *a lei* (*to her*), *gli* or *a lui* (*to him*), *ci* or *a noi* (*to us*), *vi* or *a voi* (*to you* – many), *le* or *a loro* (*to them* – feminine) and *li* or *a loro* (*to them* – masculine).

Io ti piaccio for *I am pleasing to you* (i.e., *you like me*)

Tu mi piaci for *you are pleasing to me* (i.e., *I like you*)

Le piace la pizza for *the pizza is pleasing to her* (i.e., *she likes the pizza*)

Vi piacciono i libri for *the books are pleasing to you* (i.e., *you – many – like the books*)

Ci piace passeggiare for *walking is pleasing to us* (i.e., *we like walking*)

The other verbs behave similarly:

Accadere for *to happen* as in *questo mi accade sempre* for *this always happens to me*

Bastare for *to be enough/sufficient* as in *il caffè mi basta* for *the coffee is enough*

Dispiacere for *to regret* as in *le dispiace partire* for *she regrets to leave*

Dolere for *to suffer* as in *ti duole la testa* for your head hurts (to you)

Importare for *to matter/to be important* as in *questo non ci importa* for *this does not matter to us*

Interessare for *to interest* as in *il museo vi interessa molto* for *the museum is very interesting to you*

Sembrare for *to seem* as in *mi sembra un bravo ragazzo* for *he seems like a good boy to me*

Servire for *to need* as in *le serve il tuo aiuto* for *she needs your help*

Adverbs and prepositions

Adverbs modify or specify a particular aspect of an event, and they refer to a verb: *I run fast*. They can also determine the meaning of an adjective (*molto buono* for *very good*) or the meaning of another adverb (*troppo velocemente* for *too fast*). There are different kind of adverbs depending on which aspect of the meaning they specify and different types more commonly either precede or follow the verb.

Adverbs of time usually precede the verb: *adesso* (*now*), *allora* (*then*), *appena* (*as soon as possible*), *domani* (*tomorrow*), *oggi* (*today*), *ieri* (*yesterday*), *dopo* (*later*), *fino a* (*until*), *finora* (*until now*), *già* (*already*), *mai* (*never*), *ogni tanto* (*every once in a while*), *ora* (*now*), *poi* (*then*), *presto* (*soon*), *raramente* (*rarely*), *sempre* (*always*), *tardi* (*late*).

Adesso vado a casa for *now I go home*

Adverbs of quantity usually follow the verb: *troppo* (*too*), *poco* (*some/a little*), *abbastanza* (*enough*), *assai* (*very much*), *molto* (*much*), *tanto* (*so much/a lot*).

I bambini leggono troppo poco for *the children read too little*

Adverbs of location: *dappertutto* (*everywhere*), *davanti* (*in front*), *dietro* (*behind*), *fuori* (*outside*), *giù* (*down*), *indietro* (*behind/back*), *lì/là* (*there*), *lontano* (*far*), *ovunque* (*everywhere*), *qui/qua* (*here*), *sotto* (*under*), *su* (*up*), *vicino* (*near*).

Ti ho cercato dappertutto for *I looked for you everywhere*

Adverbs of manner: *bene* (*well*), *male* (*badly*), *forte* (*loudly/heavily*), *piano* (*slowly/quietly*), *tristemente* (*sadly*).

You can form many adverbs adding *-mente* to the stem of an adjective: *lenta* (*slow*) becomes *lentamente* (*slowly*). In the same way, in English, you add the ending *-ly* to an adjective: *slow* and *slowly*.

Fortunato (*lucky*) becomes *fortunatamente* (*luckily*)

Certo (*certain*) becomes *certamente* (*certainly*)

Onesto (*honest*) becomes *onestamente* (*honestly*)

Provvisorio (*temporary*) becomes *provvisoriamente* (*temporarily*)

Silenzioso (*quiet*) becomes *silenziosamente* (*quietly*)

Ultimo (*last*) becomes *ultimamente* (*lastly*)

Altro (*other*) becomes *altrimenti* (*otherwise*)

Leggero (*light*) becomes *leggermente* (*lightly*)

Dolce (*sweet*) becomes *dolcemente* (*sweetly*)

Felice (*happy*) becomes *felicemente* (*happily*)

Frequente (*frequent*) becomes *frequentemente* (*frequently*)

Facile (*easy*) becomes *facilmente* (*easily*)

Gentile (*kind*) becomes ***gentilmente*** (*kindly*)

Like adjectives, adverbs have comparatives and superlatives. Comparatives can be constructed by adding ***più*** (*more*), ***meno*** (*less*), or ***tanto... quanto*** (*as much as*) before the adverb:

Velocemente (*quickly*) becomes ***più velocemente*** and ***meno velocemente*** and ***tanto velocemente quanto***

Superlatives are made by adding -issim before -mente (*velocissimamente*), or ***il più*** before the adverb (***il più velocemente***) for *the fastest*.

In Italian, you can use adverbial expressions with the prepositions *a, di, da, in*:

In alto for *up high*

In basso for *down*

In breve for *in short*

A destra for *to the right*

In generale for *generally*

Da lontano for *from a distance*

A lungo for *at length*

In mezzo for *in the middle*

Di nuovo for *again*

In orario for *on time*

Di recente for *recently*

In ritardo for *late*

A sinistra for *to the left*

Di solito for *usually*

Da vicino for *close up*

All'improvviso for *all of a sudden*

Prepositions

Prepositions are words that precede a noun, a pronoun, an adverb, or an infinitive verb, and specify its function, expressing locations, possession, cause, manner, or purpose: *il biscotto nel piatto* (*the cookie in the plate*), *il menù del ristorante* (*the menu of the restaurant*), *studia per imparare* (*he studies to learn*), *la torta è per la nonna* (*the cake is for the grandmother*). There are three kinds of prepositions: proper, improper, articulated.

Proper prepositions: *di* (*of*), *a* (*at/to*), *da* (*from/at*), *in* (*in*), *con* (*with*), *su* (*on*), *per* (*for/in order to*), *tra* or *fra* (*among/in between*).

La casa di Pietro for *Peter's house*

Sono a casa for *I am at home*

Vado a Roma for *I go to Rome*

Arrivo da Londra for *I arrive from London*

Improper prepositions may be adjectives or adverbs used as prepositions:

Senza (*without*), **contro** (*against*), **durante** (*during*), **eccetto** (*except*), **fino** a (*until*), **secondo** (*according to*), **tranne** (*except*)...

Durante il concerto ha iniziato a piovere for *during the concert it started raining*

Abbiamo visitato tutti i musei eccetto uno for *we visited every museum except one*

Articulated prepositions:

The prepositions *di*, *a*, *da*, *in*, *su* e *con* become articulated: they blend with the article that follows them when they modify a noun that requires an article (*il, lo, la, i, gli, le*). *Per, tra*, and *fra* have just the simple form.

Di becomes *del, dello, della, dei, degli, delle*

A becomes *al, allo, alla, ai, agli, alle*

Da becomes *dal, dallo, dalla, dai, dagli, dalle*

In becomes *nel, nello, nella, nei, negli, nelle*

Su becomes *sul, sullo, sulla, sui, sugli, sulle*

Con only blends with *il* and becomes *col*.

Interrogatives and negatives

Asking questions in Italian is really easy: there are no differences the way the words are sequenced, the change that occurs when placing a question mark at the end of the statement is one of intonation, and the voice rises at the end of the sentence.

The conditional is polite!

To ask for something politely, when ordering at the restaurant, on the plane, buying tickets, asking for directions, in Italian, you use the conditional of *volere* (*to want*) which corresponds to using *would*, but often translates as *would like*:

Present Indicative:

Io voglio for *I want*

Tu vuoi for *you want*

Lei/lui vuole for *she/he wants*

Noi vogliamo for *we want*

Voi volete for *you* (many) *want*

Essi/loro vogliono for *they want*

Present Conditional:

Io vorrei for *I would*

Tu vorresti for *you would*

Lei/lui vorrebbe for *she/he would*

Noi vorremmo for *we would*

Voi vorreste for *you would*

Essi/loro vorrebbero for *they would*

Indirect questions

Indirect questions are questions embedded in other sentences and can provide another polite way of asking a question or simply a way of reporting a question:

Vorrei sapere se la stazione è da questa parte

I would like to know whether the station is this way

Mi domando se questa è la strada giusta

I wonder whether this is the right way

Mi chiedo se il tempo resterà bello

I wonder whether the weather will still be beautiful

Potresti dirmi dov'è la stazione?

Could you tell me where is the station?

Posso chiederle se domani il treno partirà in orario?

May I ask you whether tomorrow the train will leave on time?

Le ho chiesto se il negozio era aperto

I asked her whether the store was open

Is there / are there?

Often in English, *is there?* and *are there?* are used to ask for something that you are looking for, such as a restaurant, a restroom, a taxi. The expressions *c'è* and *ci sono* correspond to the English *there is* and *there are* respectively. These words are used in the same order to both state there is something there and to ask: is there something? A rising tone for the question makes the difference:

C'è un ristorante vicino all'albergo for *there is a restaurant close to the hotel*

Ci sono dei negozi vicino ala stazione for *there are some stores nearby the station*

C'è un ristorante vicino al teatro? for *is there a restaurant close to the theater?*

Ci sono dei negozi vicino al museo? for *are there some stores nearby the museum?*

C'è, ci sono, ecco

C'è (*there is*) and *ci sono* (*there* are) are extremely frequent expressions in Italian. They are used to indicate the presence of people, animals, or things:

C'è (*there is*) is used to refer to the presence of a single element:

Guarda, c'è un gatto sul tetto! for *look, there is a cat on the roof!*

In frigorifero c'è uno yogurt for *in the fridge there is a yogurt*

Oggi c'è il sole for *today it is sunny* (literally: today there is the sun)

ci sono (*there* are) is used to refer to many individuals or things

Ci sono due gatti sul tetto for *there are two cats on the roof*

In frigorifero ci sono ancora molti yogurt for *there are still many yogurts in the fridge*

C'è (*there is*) and *ci sono* (*there* are) are also used in negative and interrogative sentences:

Ci sono ancora dei biscotti al cioccolato? for *are there still some chocolate cookies?*

Non c'è più pane for *there isn't any bread*

The word *ecco* matches the English *here is* and *here are* (also <u>there is</u> and *there are*) and might be a likely answer to an *is there/are there* question:

Ci sono ancora due biglietti per il film? for *are there still two tickets for the movie?*

Ecco i biglietti for *here are the tickets*

C'è ancora un tavolo per quattro? for *is there still a table for four?*

Ecco il vostro tavolo for *here is your table*

Ecco il ristorante! for *here is the restaurant!*

Ecco il giornale! for *here is the newspaper!*

Ecco i calzini! for *here are the socks!*

Eccomi for *here I am*

Eccoti for *here you are*

Eccola for *here she is*

Eccolo for *here he is*

Eccoci for *here we are*

Eccovi for *here you (many) are*

Eccoli for *here they are (masculine)*

Eccole for here they are (feminine)

Interrogative Adverbs

Interrogative adverbs are invariable and do not agree with anything; the subject of the verb is usually placed at the end of the question:

come? for *how?*

com' in front of a vowel, i.e., *è* (*is*), *era* (*was*), *erano* (were)

come siete venuti in Italia, in aereo o in macchina? for *how did you come to Italy, by plane or by car?*

come mai for *how come?* or *why?*

come mai non potete restare un altro giorno con noi? for *how come you cannot stay another day with us?*

dove? for *where?*

dov' in front of a vowel like *è* (*is*), *era* (*was*), *erano* (were) *dove abitano i tuoi genitori?* for *where do your parents live?*

dov'è andata in vacanza la professoressa? for *where did the professor go on vacation?*

perché? for *why?*

perché non venite a cena da noi un giorno? For *why don't you come over for dinner one day?*

quando? for *when?*

quando abbiamo l'esame finale in questa classe? for *when do we have the final test for this class?*

quanto? for *how much?*

quanto dura la classe di italiano? for *how long does the Italian class last?*

Interrogative Adjectives

Interrogative adjectives agree with the noun to which they refer, except for *che* (*which*) that is invariable

Che? for *what? what kind of?*

Che tipo di film preferiscono i tuoi genitori? for *what kind of movie do your parents prefer?*

Quale/quali? for *which? what?*

Qual in front of a vowel like *è* (*is*), *era* (*was*), *erano* (were)

Quali libri hai già letto? for *which books have you already read?*

Qual era il nome di tua madre prima di sposarsi? for *Which was your mother's name before getting married?*

Quanto, quanta, quanti, quante? for *how much? how many?*

Quanti libri hai letto durante le vacanze? for *how many books have you read during your vacation?*

Quanta pazienza hai con i bambini? for *how much patience do you have with children?*

Interrogative pronouns

Chi? for *who? whom?* always refers to people and is invariable

Chi è la tua attrice preferita? for *who is your favorite actress?*

Con chi siete usciti ieri sera? for *with whom did you go out last night?*

Di chi? for *whose?*

Di chi sono questi occhiali? for *whose are these glasses?*

Che, che cosa, cosa? for *what?* all mean the same thing and refer to things and are invariable

Cos' in front of a vowel, like *è* (*is*), *era* (*was*), *erano* (were)

Che farai durante le vacanze? for *what will you do during your holidays?*

Che cosa ti piace fare durante il tempo libero? for *what do you like to do in your spare time?*

Cosa piace ai genitori? for *what do parents like?*

Cos'è quel rumore? for *what is that noise?*

Q**uale, quali**? for *which one, which ones?* refers to people, things, ideas

Qual in front of a vowel like *è* (*is*), *era* (*was*), *erano* (were)

Pallacanestro o calcio: quale preferisci? for *basketball or soccer, which do you prefer?*

quanto, quanta, quanti, quante? for *how much? how many?* refers to people or things

Quanto costa? for *how much does it cost?*

Ho visto molti film in Italia, tu quanti ne hai visti? for *I saw many movies in Italy, how many did you see?*

Negative sentences

In Italian, any sentence can be made negative by placing **non** (*not*) before the verb.

Questa città è grande (*this city is big*) becomes **questa città non è grande** (*this city is not big*).

With reflexive verbs, **non** precedes the reflexive pronouns as well:

Lui si pettina tutti i giorni (*he combs his hair every day*) becomes **non si pettina tutti i giorni** (*he does not comb his hair every day*).

With verbs with indirect objects, **non** (*not*) precedes the verbs but not the object unless the object is a pronoun:

A Maria non piace studiare for *Maria does not like studying*

Non le piace studiare for *she does not like studying*

Other words that make a negative sentence are: **nessuno** (*no one*), **niente** (*nothing*), **per niente** (*at all*), **mai** (*never*), **affatto** (*at all*), **neanche**, **nemmeno** and **neppure** (*not even*).

Nessuno sta correndo for *nobody is running*

Niente è del colore giusto for *nothing is of the right color*

Double negative in Italian

Unlike English, Italian often uses a double negative with **non** preceding the verb and another word expressing negation (**mai**, **nessuno**, **niente**...) following the verb:

Affatto for *at all:*

Il gelato non mi piace affatto for *I don't like ice cream at all*

Non ci penso affatto ad andare a teatro for *I am not thinking of going to the theater at all*

Mai for *never:*

Non studiamo mai il giovedì sera for *we never study on Thursday night*

Io non mangio mai la trippa for *I never eat the tripe*

Non... più for *no longer:*

Lui non lavora più ogni giorno for *he no longer works every day*

Non... ancora for *not yet*:

Non hai ancora fatto i compiti? for *haven't you done your homework yet?*

Neanche, nemmeno, neppure for *not even:*

Io non dico neanche una parola for *I don't even say a word*

Non studi nemmeno un'ora for *you don't even study for an hour*

Non fai neppure un pisolino for *you don't even take a nap*

Nessuno for *no one, nobody:*

Non abbiamo nessun amico in Italia for *we have no friends in Italy*

Niente for *nothing*:

Non ho niente nel frigorifero for *I have nothing in the fridge*

Per niente for *not at all:*

Non mi piace per niente for *I do not like it at all*

Non... né... né for *neither... nor:*

Lei non legge né libri né riviste for *she reads neither books nor magazines*

Chapter 10 - Essential Vocabulary

Italian – English

A for *at or to*

A volte for *sometimes*

Abbastanza for *enough*

Abitare for *to live*

Abituarsi for *to get used to something*

Accadere for *to happen*

Accanto for *next to*

Aceto (l'aceto, gli aceti) for *vinegar*

Acquario (l'acquario, gli acquari) for *aquarium*

Acquisto (l'acquisto, gli acquisti) for *purchase*

Addetto (l'addetto, gli addetti) for *clerk*

Addormentarsi for *to fall asleep*

Adesso for *now*

Aeroplano (l'aeroplano, gli aeroplani) *for airplane*

Aeroporto (l'aeroporto, gli aeroporti) *for airport*

Agenzia (l'agenzia, le agenzie) for *agency*

Agitato (agitato, agitati, agitata, agitate) for *rough*

Agosto for *August*

Agriturismo (l'agriturismo, gli agriturismi) *for farm holiday*

Aiutarsi *for to help each other*

Albergatore (l'albergatore, gli albergatori) for *hotel owner*

Albergo (l'albergo, gli alberghi) for *hotel*

Albicocca (l'albicocca, le albicocche) for *apricot*

Aliscafo (l'aliscafo, gli aliscafi) for *hydrofoil*

Allegro (allegro, allegri, allegra, allegre) for *happy*

Allora for *then*

Altrimenti *for otherwise*

Altro (altro, altri, altra, altre) for *other, another*

Alzarsi *for to get up*

Amarsi *for to love each other*

Amico (l'amico, gli amici, l'amica, le amiche) for *friend*

Ammalarsi *for to get sick*

Ammorbidente (l'ammorbidente, gli ammorbidenti) for *softener*

Analgesico (l'analgesico, gli analgesici) for *painkiller*

Analisi (l'analisi, le analisi) for *analysis*

Ananas (l'ananas, gli ananas) for *pineapple*

Andare bene for *to fit*

Andare for *to go*

Anello (l'anello, gli anelli) for *ring*

Anguria (l'anguria, le angurie) for *watermelon*

Animale (l'animale, gli animali) for *animal*

Anno (l'anno, gli anni) for *year*

Annullare for *to cancel*

Ano (l'ano, gli ani) for *anus*

Antipasto (l'antipasto, gli antipasti) for *appetizer*

Aperitivo (l'aperitivo, gli aperitivi) for *aperitif*

Appena *for as soon as possible*

Approfittarsi (di) *for to take advantage of*

Aprile for *April*

Aprire for *to open*

Aragosta (l'aragosta, le aragoste) for *lobster*

Arancia (l'arancia, le arance) for *orange*

Arancio (l'arancio, gli aranci) for *orange tree*

Arancione for *orange*

Arcipelago (l'arcipelago, gli arcipelaghi) for *archipelago*

Arco del piede for *arch*

Arcobaleno (l'arcobaleno, gli arcobaleni) for *rainbow*

Argento for *silver*

Arrabbiarsi *for to become angry*

Arrivare for *to arrive*

Arrivederci *for goodbye*

Arrivo (l'arrivo, gli arrivi) for *arrival*

Ascensore (l'ascensore, gli ascensori) for *elevator*

Asciugatrice (l'asciugatrice, le asciugatrici) for *dryer*

Ascoltare for *to listen*

Aspettare *for to wait*

Assai *for very much*

Assegno (l'assegno, gli assegni) for *check*

Assegno personale *(l'assegno, gli assegni) for personal check*

Assicurazione (l'assicurazione, le assicurazioni) for *insurance*

Assistente di volo (l'assistente, gli assistenti, le assistenti) for *flight attendant*

Atterraggio (l'atterraggio, gli atterraggi) for *landing*

Atterrare for *to land*

Attore (l'attore, gli attori) for *actor*

Attrice (l'attrice, le attrici) for *actress*

Auto (l'auto, le auto) for *car*

Autobus (l'autobus, gli autobus) for *bus*

Autolavaggio (l'autolavaggio, gli autolavaggi) *for car wash*

Automobile (l'automobile, le automobili) for *car*

Autonoleggio (l'autonoleggio, gli autonoleggi) for *car rental*

Autostrada (l'autostrada, le autostrade) for *highway*

Autunno (l'autunno, gli autunni) for *autumn*

Avaro (avaro, avari, avara, avare) for *stingy*

Avere *for to have*

Azzurro (azzurro, azzurri, azzurra, azzurre) for *light blue*

Babordo for *port*

Bagaglio (il bagaglio, i bagagli) for *baggage*

Bagaglio a mano (il bagaglio, i bagagli) for *Carry-on*

Bagno (il bagno, i bagni) for *bathroom*

Ballerine (la ballerina, le ballerine) for *ballet shoes*

Bambina (la bambina, le bambine) for *child (female)*

Bambino (il bambino, i bambini) for *child (male)*

Banana (la banana, le banane) for *banana*

Banca (la banca, le banche) for *bank*

Banco delle informazioni (il banco, i banchi) for *information desk*

Bancomat for *ATM or debit card*

Banconota (la banconota, le banconote) for *bill or banknote*

Bar (il bar, i bar) for *café*

Barca (la barca, le barche) for *boat*

Barca a remi (la barca, le barche) for *rowboat*

Barca a vela (la barca, le barche) for *sailboat*

Bastare for *to be enough*

Bastone (il bastone, i bastoni) for *cane*

Bella (bella, belle) for *beautiful*

Bellezza (la bellezza, le bellezze) for *beauty*

Bello (bello, belli) *for handsome*

Bene for well

Beneficiario (il beneficiario, i beneficiari) for *payee*

Benvenuto for welcome

Benzina (la benzina, le benzine) for *gas*

Bere for *to drink*

Berretto (il berretto, i berretti) for *cap*

Bianco (bianco, bianchi, bianca, bianche) for *white*

Bicchiere (il bicchiere, i bicchieri) for *glass*

Biglietteria (la biglietteria, le biglietterie) for *ticket booth or ticket office*

Biglietto (il biglietto, i biglietti) *for ticket*

Binario (il binario, i binari) for *track*

Biondo (biondo, biondi, bionda, bionde) for *blond*

Biscotti (il biscotto, i biscotti) for *cookie*

Bistecca (la bistecca, le bistecche) for *steak*

Blu for *dark blue*

Bocca (la bocca, le bocche) for *mouth*

Borsa (la borsa, le borse) for *bag or handbag*

Borsa a tracolla (la borsa, le borse) for *messenger bag*

Borsetta (la borsetta, le borsette) for *purse*

Bottone (il bottone, i bottoni) for *button*

Braccialetto (il braccialetto, i braccialetti) for *bracelet*

Braccio (il braccio, le braccia) for *arm*

Branzino (il branzino, i branzini) for *European Seabass*

Bravo (bravo, bravi, brava, brave) for *good, able*

Brina (la brina) for *frost*

Brodo (il brodo) for *broth*

Bruciarsi for *to get burned*

Brutto (brutto, brutti, brutta, brutte) for *ugly*

Bugiardo (bugiardo, bugiardi, bugiarda, bugiarde) for *liar*

Buono (buono, buoni, buona, buone) for *good*

Burrasca *(la burrasca, le burrasche)* for *storm*

Burro (il burro) for *butter*

Bus (il bus, i bus) for *bus*

Cabina (la cabina, le cabine) for *cabin*

Caffè (il caffè, i caffè) for *coffee*

Caffellatte (il caffellatte) for *caffellatte*

Calare *for to lower*

Caldo (caldo, caldi, calda, calde) for *warm*

Calmarsi for *to calm down*

Calmo (calmo, calmi, calma, calme) for *calm*

Calzini (il calzino, i calzini) for *socks*

Cambiavalute *(*il cambiavalute, i cambiavalute) for *currency exchange or bureau de exchange*

Cambiare *for to change*

Cambio for *exchange or exchange rate*

Camerino di prova (il camerino, i camerini) for *dressing room*

Camicetta (la camicetta, le camicette) for *blouse*

Camicia (la camicia, le camicie) for *button-down shirt*

Camminare for *to walk*

Campeggio (il campeggio, i campeggi) for *camping site*

Canale (il canale, i canali) for *canal*

Cane (il cane, i cani) for *dog*

Canottiera (la canottiera, le canottiere) for *undershirt*

Canzone (la canzone, le canzoni) for *song*

Capelli (i capelli) for *hair*

Capire for *to understand*

Capirsi for *to understand each other*

Capitano (il capitano, i capitani) for *captain*

Capodanno (il capodanno, i capodanni) for *New Year*

Cappello (il cappello, i cappelli) for *hat*

Cappotto (il cappotto, i cappotti) for *coat*

Cardigan (il cardigan, i cardigan) for *cardigan*

Carie (la carie, le carie) for *cavity*

Carino (carino, carini, carina, carine) for *nice*

Carne (la carne, le carni) *for meat*

Caro (caro, cari, cara, care) for *dear or expensive*

Carota (la carota, le carote) for *carrot*

Carrello (il carrello, i carrelli) for *cart*

Carro (il carro, i carri) for *wagon*

Carro attrezzi (il carro attrezzi, i carri attrezzi) for *tow truck*

Carta d'imbarco (la carta, le carte) for *boarding pass*

Carta da lettere (la carta, le carte) for *stationery*

Carta di credito (la carta, le carte) for *credit card*

Cartoleria (la cartoleria, le cartolerie) for *stationary store*

Cartolina (la cartolina, le cartoline) for *postcard*

Casa (la casa, le case) for *house*

Cassa (la cassa, le casse) for *register*

Cassetta delle lettere (la cassetta, le cassette) for *mailboxes*

Castello (il castello, i castelli) for *castle*

Catrame (il catrame) for *tar*

Cattivo (cattivo, cattivi, cattiva, cattive) for *bad*

Cavolfiore (il cavolfiore, i cavolfiori) for *cauliflower*

Cavolo (il cavolo, i cavoli) for *cabbage*

Celebrare for *to celebrate*

Cena (la cena, le cene) for *dinner*

Cenare *for to have dinner*

Centesimo (il centesimo, i centesimi) for *cent*

Centro commerciale (il centro commerciale, i centri commerciali) for *shopping mall*

Cercare *for to look for*

Cereali (i cereali) for *cereals*

Cerniera lampo (la cerniera, le cerniere) for *zipper*

Cerotti (il cerotto, i cerotti) for *Band-aid*

Certamente *for certainly*

Certo for *certain* or *sure* or *of course*

Cestino (il cestino, i cestini) for *basket*

Cetriolo (il cetriolo, i cetrioli) for *cucumber*

Che for *what* or *which*

Chi for *who*

Chiamarsi *for to be named, to be called*

Chiave (la chiave, le chiavi) for *key*

Chiedere for *to ask*

Chiedere in prestito *for to borrow*

Chiedersi *for to ask oneself*

Chilogrammo (il chilogrammo, i chilogrammi) for *kilogram*

Chilometro (il chilometro, i chilometri) for *kilometer*

Chitarra (la chitarra, le chitarre) for *guitar*

Chiudere *for to close*

Ciao for *hello or goodbye*

Cielo (il cielo, i cieli) for *sky*

Ciliegia (la ciliegia, le ciliegie) for *cherry*

Ciliegio (il ciliegio, i ciliegi) for *cherry tree*

Cina for *China*

Cinghiale (il cinghiale, i cinghiali) for *boar*

Cintura (la cintura, le cinture) for *belt*

Cintura di sicurezza (la cintura, le cinture) for *seatbelt*

Cioccolata (la cioccolata, le cioccolate) for *chocolate*

Cipolla (la cipolla, le cipolle) for *onion*

Cipria (la cipria) for *face powder*

Circa *for about*

Città (la città, le città) for *city*

Ciuccio (il ciuccio, i ciucci) for *pacifier*

Classe (la classe, le classi) for *class*

Cliente (il cliente, i clienti) for *client*

Clima (il clima, i climi) for *climate*

Colazione (la colazione, le colazioni) for *breakfast*

Collana (la collana, le collane) for *necklace*

Collant (il collant, i collant) for *tights, pantyhose*

Collo (il collo, i colli) for *neck*

Come *for how*

Commessa (la commessa, le commesse) for *shop assistant (female)*

Commesso (il commesso, i commessi) for *shop assistant (male)*

Commissione (la commissione, le commissioni) for *commission or fee*

Comò (il comò, i comò) for *chest of drawers*

Compagnia (la compagnia, le compagnie) for *company*

Comprare for *to buy*

Con for *with*

Condividere for *to share*

Condiviso (condiviso, condivisi, condivisa, condivise) for *shared*

Confermare for *to confirm*

Coniglio (il coniglio, i conigli, la coniglia, le coniglie) for *rabbit*

Conoscersi for *to know each other*

Contante (il contante) for *cash*

Conto corrente *(il conto, i conti)* for *checking account*

Conto (il conto, i conti) for *bill*

Contorni (il contorno, i contorni) *for side dishes*

Contro for *against*

Controllore (il controllore, i controllori) for *inspector*

Convento (il convento, i conventi) for *convent*

Coprifuoco (il coprifuoco, i coprifuochi) for *curfew*

Coprire for *to cover*

Cornetto (il cornetto, i cornetti) for *croissant*

Corto (corto, corti, corta, corte) for *short*

Cosa (la cosa, le cose) for *thing*

Cosa *for what*

Coscia (la coscia, le cosce) for *thigh*

Così così *for so and so*

Costare for *to cost*

Costoso (costoso, costosi, costosa, costose) for *expensive*

Cravatta (la cravatta, le cravatte) for *tie*

Credere *for to believe*

Crema (la crema, le creme) for *lotion*

Crema solare (la crema, le creme) for *sun lotion*

Crisi (la crisi, le crisi) for *crisis*

Crociera (la crociera, le crociere) for *cruise*

Cucina (la cucina, le cucine) *for kitchen*

Cuffia (la cuffia, le cuffie) *for headset*

Cugina (la cugina, le cugine) *for cousin, cousins (feminine)*

Cugino (il cugino, i cugini) for *cousin, cousins (masculine)*

Culla (la culla, le culle) for *bassinet*

Da *for from*

Dado (il dado, i dadi) for *dice*

Danno (il danno, i danni) for *damage*

Dappertutto *for everywhere*

Dare *for to give*

Darsena (la darsena, le darsene) for *harbor*

Davanti *for in front*

Debole (debole, deboli) for *weak*

Decagrammo *(il decagrammo, i decagrammi)* for *decagram*

Decollo (il decollo, i decolli) for *take off*

Degustazione (la degustazione, le degustazioni) for *tasting*

Delizioso (delizioso, deliziosi, deliziosa, deliziose) for *delicious*

Dente (il dente, i denti) for *tooth*

Dentifricio (il dentifricio, i dentifrici) for *totoothpaste*

Dentista (il dentista, i dentisti) for *dentist*

Dentro for *inside*

Destra for *right*

Detergente (il detergente, i detergenti) for *cleanser*

Detersivo (il detersivo, i detersivi) for *detergents*

Di for *of*

Di fronte for *in front of*

Di solito for *usually*

Dicembre for *December*

Dietro for *behind*

Difficile for *difficult*

Dilemma (il dilemma, i dilemmi) for *dilemma*

Diluviare for *to pour*

Dimenticarsi for *to get*

Dire for *to say*

Disgustoso (disgustoso, disgustosi, disgustosa, disgustose) for *disgusting*

Disinfettante (il disinfettante, i disinfettanti) for *disinfectant*

Dispiacere for *to regret*

Dita del piede for *toes*

Dito (il dito, le dita) for *finger*

Divertirsi for *to have fun*

Doccia (la doccia, le docce) for *shower*

Dolce for *sweet*

Dolcemente for *sweetly*

Dolci (il dolce, i dolci) for *dessert*

Dolere for *to suffer*

Dollaro (il dollaro, i dollari) for *dollar*

Domandare for *to ask*

Domandarsi for *to wonder*

Domani for *tomorrow*

Domenica for *Sunday*

Donna (la donna, le donne) for *woman*

Dopo for *after*

Doppio (doppio, doppi, doppia, doppie) for *double*

Dormire for *to sleep*

Dormitorio (il dormitorio, i dormitori) for *dorm*

Dottore (il dottore, i dottori) for *doctor*

Dottoressa (la dottoressa, le dottoresse) for *doctor (female)*

Dove for *where*

Dovere for *to have to*

Dovere for *to owe*

Dramma (il dramma, i drammi) for *drama*

Dritto for *straight*

Drogheria (la drogheria, le drogherie) for *drugstore*

Durante for *during*

Eccetto for *except*

Ecco for *here is and here are*

Economico (economico, economici, economica, economiche) for *convenient*

Elegante (elegante, eleganti) for *elegant*

Enoteca (l'enoteca, le enoteche) for *wine dealer*

Entrare for *to enter, to go in*

Epifania (l'Epifania) for *Epiphany*

Equipaggio (l'equipaggio, gli equipaggi) for *crew*

Esatto (esatto, esatti, esatta, esatte) for *exact*

Eseguire for *to carry out* or *to perform (on ATM machine instead of "enter")*

Essere for *to be*

Estate (l'estate, le estati) for *summer*

Ettogrammo (l'ettogrammo, gli ettogrammi) for *hectogram*

Faccia (la faccia, le facce) for *face*

Facile for *easy*

Facilmente for *easily*

Fagiolini (i fagiolini) for *green beans*

Famiglia (la famiglia, le famiglie) for *family*

Fantastico (fantastico, fantastici, fantastica, fantastiche) for *fantastic*

Fare for *to do*

Farmacia (la farmacia, le farmacie) for *pharmacy*

Farsi il bagno for *to take a bath*

Fato (il fato) for *fate*

Fatto (il fatto, i fatti) for *fact*

Fazzoletto di carta (il fazzoletto, i fazzoletti) for *tissue*

Febbraio for *February*

Febbre (la febbre, le febbri) for *fever*

Felice for *happy*

Felicemente for *happily*

Felpa (la felpa, le felpe) for *sweatshirt*

Fermata dell'autobus (la fermata, le fermate) for *the bus stop*

Fermo (fermo, fermi, ferma, ferme) for *still*

Festa (la festa, le feste) for *holiday*

Fetta (la fetta, le fette) for *slice*

Fettina (la fettina, le fettine) for *cutlet*

Fidarsi for *to trust*

Figlia (la figlia, le figlie) for *daughter*

Figlio (il figlio, i figli) for *son*

Fila (la fila, le file) for *line*

Film (il film, i film) for *movie*

Finire for *to finish*

Fino for *until*

Finora for *until now*

Fiore (il fiore, i fiori) for *flower*

Fiume (il fiume, i fiumi) for *river*

Foglio (il foglio, i fogli) *for sheet*

Fondotinta (il fondotinta, i fondotinta) for *foundation*

Formaggio (il formaggio, i formaggi) for *cheese*

Formale for *formal*

Fornaio (il fornaio, i fornai) for *bakery for bread and cookies*

Forte for *loudly, heavily*

Fortunatamente for *luckily*

Fortunato (fortunato, fortunati, fortunata, fortunate) for *lucky*

Foschia *for the haze, mist*

Foto (la foto, le foto) for *picture, photo*

Fragola *(la fragola, le fragole)* for *strawberry*

Franchigia (la franchigia, le franchigie) for *deductible*

Fratello (il fratello, i fratelli) for *brother, brothers*

Freddo (freddo, freddi, fredda, fredde) for *cold*

Frequente for *frequent*

Frequentemente *for frequently*

Frittelle (la frittella, le frittelle) for *pancakes*

Frutta (la frutta, i frutti) for *fruit*

Fruttivendolo (il fruttivendolo, i fruttivendoli) for *fruit and vegetable store*

Fungo (il fungo, i funghi) for *mushroom*

Fuori *for outside*

Gamba (la gamba, le gambe) for *leg*

Gambero (il gambero, i gamberi) for *prawn or shrimp*

Gatto (il gatto, i gatti, la gatta, le gatte) for *cat*

Gelateria (la gelateria, le gelaterie) for *ice cream parlor*

Gelato (il gelato, i gelati) for *ice cream*

Genero (il genero, i generi) for *son-in-law*

Generoso (generoso, generosi, generosa, generose) for *generous*

Gennaio *for January*

Gentile (gentile, gentili) for *kind*

Gentilmente *for kindly*

Ghetta (la ghetta, le ghette) for *gaiter*

Ghiaccio (il ghiaccio) for *ice*

Già *for already*

Giacca (la giacca, le giacche) for *jacket*

Giallo (giallo, gialli, gialla, gialle) for *yellow*

Giocare *for to play*

Gioco (il gioco, i giochi) for *game*

Gioielleria (la gioielleria, le gioiellerie) for *jewelry store*

Giornalaio (il giornalaio, i giornalai) for *newsstand*

Giornale (il giornale, i giornali) for *newspaper*

Giornaliero (giornaliero, giornalieri, giornaliera, giornaliere) for *daily*

Giorno (il giorno, i giorni) for *day*

Giovane (giovane, giovani) for *young*

Giovedì *for Thursday*

Girare for *to turn*

Girare un assegno for *to endorse*

Gita (la gita, le gite) for *trip*

Giù *for down, under*

Giubbotto (il giubbotto, i giubbotti) for *windbreaker*

Giubbotto di salvataggio (il giubbotto, i giubbotti) for *life jacket*

Giugno for *June*

Giusto (giusto, giusti, giusta, giuste) for *correct*

Glutine for *gluten*

Gnocchi (lo gnocco, gli gnocchi) for *gnocchi*

Gnomo (lo gnomo, gli gnomi) for *gnome*

Gola (la gola, le gole) for *throat*

Gondola (la gondola, le gondole) for *gondola*

Gonna (la gonna, le gonne) for *skirt*

Grammo (il grammo, i grammi) for *gram*

Grande (grande, grandi) for *big*

Grandi magazzini for *department store*

Grandinare for *to hail*

Grasso (grasso, grassi, grassa, grasse) for to *fat*

Grazie for *thank you*

Grigio (grigio, grigi, grigia, grigie) for *gray*

Guanto (il guanto, i guanti) for *glove*

Guardare for *to look*

Guardare le vetrine for *to go window shopping*

Guarito (guarito, guariti, guarita, guarite) for *healed*

Guidatore (il guidatore, i guidatori) for *driver*

Gusto (il gusto, i gusti) for *flavor*

Ieri for *yesterday*

Igiene (l'igiene) for *hygiene*

Illusione (l'illusione, le illusioni) for *the illusion*

Imbarcarsi for *to embark, to board*

Impermeabile (l'impermeabile, gli impermeabili) for *raincoat*

Impiegato for *clerk*

Importare *for to matter*

Importo (l'importo, gli importi) for *amount*

Improvviso for *sudden*

In for *in*

Incassare for *to cash*

Incluso *(incluso, inclusi, inclusa, incluse)* for *included*

Incontrarsi con *for to meet with*

Incrocio (l'incrocio, gli incroci) *for intersection*

Indicare *for to point*

Indietro for *behind, back*

Indipendente for *independent*

Indù for *hindu*

Informale for *casual*

Infradito (l'infradito) for *flip flops*

Insalata (l'insalata, le insalate) for *salad*

Interessare for *to interest*

Interesse (l'interesse, gli interessi) for *interest*

Interurbano for *suburban*

Intorno *for around*

Inverno (l'inverno, gli inverni) for *winter*

Inversione ad U for *U-turn*

Io for *I*

Ipocalorico *for low calories*

Ipocolesterolemico* or *a basso contenuto di colesterolo for *low cholesterol*

Iposodico for *low salt*

Ipotesi (l'ipotesi, le ipotesi) for *hypothesis*

Irritarsi for *to get irritated*

Isola (l'isola, le isole) for *island*

Isolato (l'isolato, gli isolati) for *block*

Issare for *to hoist*

Jeans (i jeans) for *jeans*

Kosher for *kosher*

Laggiù for *down there*

Lamentarsi di for *to complain about*

Lampo (il lampo, i lampi) for *lightning*

Lassù for *up there*

Latte (il latte) for *milk*

Lattosio for *lactose*

Lattuga (la lattuga) for *lettuce*

Lavanderia (la lavanderia, le lavanderie) *a gettoni* or *lavanderia automatica* for *laundromat*

Lavanderia (la lavanderia, le lavanderie) *a secco* for *dry cleaner*

Lavatrice (la lavatrice, le lavatrici) for *washing machine*

Lavorare for *to work*

Leggere for *to read*

Leggermente for *lightly*

Leggero (leggero, leggeri, leggera, leggere) for *light or bland*

Lei for *she*

Lento (lento, lenti, lenta, lente) for *slow*

Lentamente for *slowly*

Lente (la lente, le lenti) for *lens*

Lettera (la lettera, le lettere) for *letter*

Letto (il letto, i letti) for *bed*

Letto a castello (il letto a castello, i letti a castello) for *bunk bed*

Lezione (la lezione, le lezioni) for *lesson*

Lì in cima for *on top over there*

Lì in fondo for *down there*

Lì sopra for *up there*

Lì sotto for *down there*

Lì vicino for *over there*

Lì, là for *there*

Libreria (la libreria, le librerie) for *bookstore*

Libro (il libro, i libri) for *books*

Limone (il limone, i limoni) for *lemon*

Litro (il litro, i litri) for *liter*

Lontano for *far*

Loro, essi for *they*

Luglio for *July*

Lui for *he*

Lunedì for *Monday*

Lungo (lungo, lunghi, lunga, lunghe) for *long*

Macchina (la macchina, le macchine) for *car*

Macchina (la macchina, le macchine) **a noleggio** for *rental car*

Macelleria (la macelleria, le macellerie) for *butcher*

Macinata for ground meat

Madre (la madre, le madri) for *mother*

Maggio for *May*

Maglietta (la maglietta, le magliette) for *T-shirt*

Maglione (il maglione, i maglioni) for *sweater*

Magro (magro, magri, magra, magre) *for thin*

Mai for *never*

Maiale (il maiale, i maiali) for *pork*

Malato (malato, malati, malata, malate) for *sick*

Male for *badly*

Male for *bad*

Mancia (la mancia, le mance) for *tip*

Mangiare for *to eat*

Mano (la mano, le mani) for *hand*

Manzo for *beef*

Marcia (la marcia, le marce) for *gear*

Mare (il mare, i mari) for *sea*

Marinaio (il marinaio, i marinai) for *sailor*

Marito (il marito, i mariti) for *husband*

Marmellata (la marmellata, le marmellate) for *jam*

Marrone for *brown*

Martedì for *Tuesday*

Marzo for *March*

Mascara (il mascara, i mascara) for *mascara*

Matita (la matita, le matite) for *pencil*

Mattina (la mattina, le mattine) for *morning*

Mattino (il mattino, i mattini) for *morning*

Medio (medio, medi, media, medie) for *medium*

Meglio for *better*

Mela (la mela, le mele) for *apple*

Melo (il melo, i meli) for *apple tree*

Melone (il melone, i meloni) for *melon*

Membro (il membro, i membri) *for member*

Mensile *for monthly*

Menù for *menu*

Meraviglioso (meraviglioso, meravigliosi, meravigliosa, meravigliose) *for wonderful*

Mercoledì for *Wednesday*

Merenda (la merenda, le merende) for *snack*

Mese (il mese, i mesi) for *month*

Metro (il metro, i metri) for *meter*

Metropolitana (la metropolitana, le metropolitane) for *metro*

Mettersi *for to put on*

Mezzanotte (la mezzanotte) for *midnight*

Miele (il miele) for *honey*

Miglio (il miglio, le miglia) for *mile*

Minestra (la minestra, le minestre) for *soup*

Minimo (minimo, minimi, minima, minime) for *minimum*

Minuto (il minuto, i minuti) for *minutes*

Mirtillo (il mirtillo, i mirtilli) for *blueberry*

Mocassini (i mocassini) for *loafers*

Moglie (la moglie, le mogli) for *wife*

Molto for *much*

Monastero *(il monastero, i monasteri)* for *monastery*

Moneta *(la moneta, le monete)* for *coin*

Montagna *(la montagna, le montagne)* for *mountain*

Montatura *(la montatura, le montature)* for *frame*

Morire for *to die*

Motoscafo (il motoscafo, i motoscafi) for *motorboat*

Multa (la multa, le multe) for *fine*

Museo (il museo, i musei) for *museum*

Musulmano (musulmano, musulmani, musulmana, musulmane) for *muslim*

Mutande (la mutanda, le mutande) for *underwear*

Mutandina (la mutandina, le mutandine) for *panties*

Nascere for *to be born*

Natale for *Christmas*

Nave (la nave, le navi) *da crociera* for *cruise ship*

Nave (la nave, le navi) for *ship*

Nebbia (la nebbia, le nebbie) for *fog*

Negozio (il negozio, i negozi) for *store*

Negozio di alimentari (il negozio, i negozi) for *grocery store*

Negozio di abbigliamento (il negozio, i negozi) for *store for clothing*

Nero (nero, neri, nera, nere) for *black*

Neve (la neve, le nevi) for *snow*

Nevicare for *to snow*

Nipote (il nipote, i nipoti) for *nephew and grandson*

Nipote (la nipote, le nipoti) for *niece and granddaughter*

Noi for *we*

Noleggiare for *to rent*

Nonna (la nonna, le nonne) for *grandmother*

Nonno (il nonno, i nonni) for *grandfather*

Notte (la notte, le notti) for *night*

Novembre for *November*

Nuora (la nuora, le nuore) for *daughter-in-law*

Nuotare for *to swim*

Nuovo (nuovo, nuovi, nuova, nuove) for *new*

Nutrirsi for *to feed oneself*

Nuvola (la nuvola, le nuvole) for *cloud*

Nuvoloso for *overcast*

Obliterare for *to validate*

Occhio (l'occhio, gli occhi) for *eyes*

Offrire for *to offer*

Oggi for *day*

Ogni tanto for *every once in a while*

Olio (l'olio, gli olii) *for oil*

Oliva (l'oliva, le olive) for *olive*

Ombrello (l'ombrello, gli ombrelli) for *umbrella*

Onestamente for *honestly*

Onesto (onesto, onesti, onesta, oneste) for *honest*

Opera (l'opera, le opere) for *opera*

Ora for *now*

Orario (l'orario, gli orai) for *schedule*

Ordinare for *to order*

Orecchino (l'orecchino, gli orecchini) for *earrings*

Orecchio (l'orecchio, gli orecchi) for *ear*

Orologiaio (l'orologiaio, gli orologiai) for *watch seller*

Orologio (l'orologio, gli orologi) for *watch*

Ospedale (l'ospedale, gli ospedali) for *hospital*

Ospite (l'ospite, gli ospiti) for *guest*

Ostello (l'ostello, gli ostelli) for *hostel*

Ottobre for *October*

Overcraft for *hovercraft*

Ovunque for *everywhere*

Pacco (il pacco, i pacchi) for *package*

Padre (il padre, i padri) for *father*

Paese (il paese, i paesi) for *village or small town*

Pagamento (il pagamento, i pagamenti) for *payment*

Pagare for *to pay*

Paio (il paio, le paia) for *pair*

Palestra (la palestra, le palestre) for *gym*

Pane (il pane, i pani) for *bread*

Panetteria (la panetteria, le panetterie) for *bakery for bread and cookies*

Panificio (il panificio, i panifici) for *bakery for bread and cookies*

Panino (il panino, i panini) for *sandwich*

Panna (la panna) for *cream*

Pantaloncini (i pantaloncini) for *shorts*

Pantaloni (i pantaloni) for *trousers*

Pantofole (la pantofola, le pantofole) for *slippers*

Papà (il papà, i papà) for *dad*

Papa *(il Papa, i Papi)* for *pope*

Parcheggio (il parcheggio, i parcheggi) **dei taxi** for *taxi rank*

Parlare *for to speak*

Parlarsi *for to talk to each other*

Partenza (la partenza, le partenze) for *departure*

Partire *for to leave*

Pasqua for *Easter*

Passaporto for *passport*

Passeggero (il passeggero, i passeggeri) for *passenger*

Passeggero a piedi *for foot passenger*

Passerella for *gangway*

Pasto (il pasto, i pasti) for *meal*

Pasticceria (la pasticceria, le pasticcerie) for *bakery for pastry*

Patata (la patata, le patate) for *potato*

Pausa (la pausa, le pause) for *break*

Pedaggio (il pedaggio, i pedaggi) for *toll*

Pellegrina (la pellegrina, le pellegrine) for (female) *pilgrim*

Pellegrino (il pellegrino, i pellegrini) for (male) *pilgrim*

Penisola (la penisola, le penisole) for *peninsula*

Penna (la penna, le penne) for *pen*

Pensilina (la pensilina, le pensiline) for *platform*

Pensione (la pensione, le pensioni) for *small hotel*

Per *for in order to*

Pera (la pera, le pere) for *pear*

Percentuale (la percentuale, le percentuali) for *the percentage*

Perché *for why, because*

Perdere for *to lose*

Permanente (la permanente, le permanenti) for *perm*

Pero (il pero, i peri) for *pear tree*

Personale for *personal*

Pesca (la pesca, le pesche) for *peach*

Pesce (il pesce, i pesci) for *fish*

Pescheria (la pescherie, le pescherie) for *the fish market*

Pesco (il pesco, i peschi) for *peach tree*

Pettine (il pettine, i pettini) for *comb*

Petto (il petto, i petti) for *breast*

Piacere *for pleasure*

Piacere for *to like*

Piangere for *to cry*

Piano for *slowly, quietly*

Piazza (la piazza, le piazze) for *square*

Piccolo (piccolo, piccoli, piccola, piccole) for *small*

Piede (il piede, i piedi) for *foot*

Pilota (il pilota, i piloti) for *pilot*

Pioggia (la pioggia) for *rain*

Piombatura (la piombatura, le piombature) for *filling*

Piovere for *to rain*

Piscina (la piscina, le piscine) for *pool*

Pisello (il pisello, i piselli) for *pea*

Pisolino (il pisolino, i pisolini) for *nap*

Pittore (il pittore, i pittori) for *painter*

Più tardi for *later*

Pizza for *pizza*

Plastic (la plastica, le plastiche) for *plastic*

Platino for *platinum*

Poco for *some, a little*

Poi for *then*

Pollo (il pollo, i polli) for *chicken*

Polipo (il polipo, i polipi) for *Octopus*

Polso (il polso, i polsi) for *wrist*

Pomeriggio (il pomeriggio, i pomeriggi) for *afternoon*

Pomodoro (il pomodoro, i pomodori) for *tomato*

Pompa (la pompa, le pompe) for *pump*

Pompelmo (il pompelmo, i pompelmi) for *grapefruit*

Ponte (il ponte, i ponti) for *bridge or deck*

Porcile (il porcile, i porcili) for *pig pen*

Porto (il porto, i porti) for *port*

Posto (il posto, i posti) for *seat*

Potere *for to be able to*

Povero *(*povero, poveri, povera, povere) for *poor*

Pranzare for *to have lunch*

Pranzo (il pranzo, i pranzi) for *lunch*

Preghiera (la preghiera, le preghiere) for *prayer*

Prego *for you are welcome*

Prelievo (il prelievo, i prelievi) for *withdrawal*

Prenotare for *to reserve*

Preoccuparsi *for to worry*

Prepararsi *for to get ready*

Presentarsi *for to introduce oneself*

Prestare for *to lend*

Prestito (il prestito, i prestiti) for *loan*

Presto *for soon or early*

Prezzo (il prezzo, i prezzi) for *price*

Prima *for before*

Primavera (la primavera, le primavere) for *spring*

Prosciutto cotto (il prosciutto, i prosciutti) for *ham*

Prosciutto crudo (il prosciutto, i prosciutti) for *prosciutto*

Prodotto (il prodotto, i prodotti) for *product*

Professore (il professore, i professori) for *professor*

Professoressa (la professoressa, le professoresse) for *professor (female)*

Profumato (profumato, profumati, profumata, profumate) for *fragrant*

Profumeria (la profumeria, le profumerie) for *perfume store*

Programma (il programma, i programmi) for *program*

Pronto soccorso *for emergency room*

Proseguire for *to continue*

Prossimo (prossimo, prossimi, prossima, prossime) for *next*

Provare *for to try on*

Provvisoriamente for *temporarily*

Provvisorio for *temporary*

Prua for *bow*

Psicologo (lo psicologo, gli psicologi) for *psychologist*

Pulito (pulito, puliti, pulita, pulite) for *clean*

Quaggiù *for down here*

Quale *for which*

Quando *for When*

Quanto *for how much*

Quassù *for up here*

Quello (quello, quelli, quella, quelle) for *that*

Questo (questo, questi, questa, queste) for *this*

Qui, qua for *here*

Radio (la radio, le radio) for *radio*

Raffreddore (il raffreddore, i raffreddori) *for cold*

Ragazza (la ragazza, le ragazze) *for girl*

Ragazzo (il ragazzo, i ragazzi) for *boy*

Rallegrarsi for *to rejoice*

Raramente for *rarely*

Recente for *recent*

Reggiseno (il reggiseno, i reggiseni) for *bra*

Regina (la regina, le regine) for *queen*

Regola (la regola, le regole) for *rule*

Resto (il resto) for *change*

Ricco (ricco, ricchi, ricca, ricche) for *rich*

Ricevuta (la ricevuta, le ricevute) for *receipt*

Rimborsare for *to refund*

Rimborso (il rimborso, i rimborsi) for *refund*

Riparare for *to fix*

Riparazione (la riparazione, le riparazioni) for *repair*

Ripetere *for to repeat*

Riposare for *to rest*

Riposarsi for *to rest*

Riposato (riposato, riposati, riposata, riposate) for *rested*

Risotto (il risotto, i risotti) for *rice dish*

Risparmiare for *to save*

Rispondere *for to answer*

Ristorante (il ristorante, i ristoranti) for *restaurant*

Ritardo for *delay*

Rompere *for to break*

Rosa for *pink*

Rossetto (il rossetto, i rossetti) for *lipstick*

Rosso (rosso, rossi, rossa, rosse) for *red*

Rotatoria (la rotatoria, le rotatorie) for *rotary*

Rugiada *for dew*

Sabato for *Saturday*

Salame *(il salame, i salami) for salami*

Saldo *for balance*

Sale (il sale, i sali) for *salt*

Salire for *to go up*

Salmone (il salmone, i salmoni) for *salmon*

Salotto (il salotto, i salotti) for *living room*

Salpare for *to sail*

Salumeria (la salumeria, le salumerie) for *cold cuts, cheese, olives*

Salvagente *(il salvagente, i salvagente) for life belt*

Salve for *hello*

Sandali (il sandalo, i sandali) for *sandals*

Sapere *for to know*

Sbarcare for *to disembark*

Scarpa (la scarpa, le scarpe) for *shoe*

Scarpe da ginnastica (la scarpa, le scarpe) *for sneakers*

Scatoletta (la scatoletta, le scatolette) for *can*

Scatto (lo scatto, gli scatti) for *click*

Scena (la scena, le scene) for *scene*

Scendere *for to go down*

Scherzo (lo scherzo, gli scherzi) for *joke*

Schiaffo (lo schiaffo, gli schiaffi) for *slap*

Schienale (lo schienali, gli schienali) for *seat-back*

Sci (gli sci) for *ski*

Scialle (lo scialle, gli scialli) for *shawl*

Scialuppa di salvataggio (la scialuppa, le scialuppe) for *lifeboat*

Sciarpa (la sciarpa, le sciarpe) for *scarf*

Sciocco (sciocco, sciocchi, sciocca, sciocche) for *silly*

Sciupato (sciupato, sciupati, sciupata, sciupate) for *damaged, spoil*

Scoprire for *to discover*

Scossa (la scossa, le scosse) for *shake, [electric] shock*

Scrittore (lo scrittore, gli scrittori) *for writer (male)*

Scrittrice (la scrittrice, le scrittrici) for *writer (female)*

Scrivere *for to write*

Scriversi *for to write to each other*

Scultore (lo scultore, gli scultori) for *sculptor*

Scultrice (la scultrice, le scultrici) for *sculptress*

Scuola (la scuola, le scuole) for *school*

Scuro (scuro, scuri, scura, scure) for *dark*

Scusarsi for *to apologize*

Sedano (il sedano, i sedani) for *celery*

Sedersi for *to sit*

Sedile (il sedile, i sedili) *for seat*

Seggiolino (il seggiolino, i seggiolini) for *car seat*

Seguire *for to follow*

Selvaggina (la selvaggina) for *game*

Semaforo (il semaforo, i semafori) for *traffic light*

Sembrare for *to seem*

Sempre *for always*

Sentire *for to hear*

Senza for *without*

Sera *(la sera, le sere) for evening*

Servire for *to serve*

Servire *for to need*

Settembre for *September*

Settimana (la settimana, le settimane) for *week*

Settimanale for *weekly*

Shuttle for *shuttle*

Sicurezza *for security*

Signora for *Mrs*

Signore for *Mr*

Signori *for Mr and Mrs*

Signorina for *signorina*

Silenziosamente for *quietly*

Silenzioso (silenzioso, silenziosi, silenziosa, silenziose) for *quiet*

Sincero (sincero, sinceri, sincera, sincere) for *sincere*

Singolo (singolo, singoli, singola, singole) for *single*

Sinistra *for left*

Sistema (il sistema, i sistemi) for *system*

Smalto (lo smalto, gli smalti) for *nail polish*

Smog (lo smog, gli smog) for *smog*

Sogno (il sogno, i sogni) for *dream*

Soldi (il soldo, i soldi) for m*oney*

Sole (il sole) for *sun*

Sopra *for on, above*

Sorella (la sorella, le sorelle) for *sister*

Sotto for *under, below*

Sottoveste (la sottoveste, le sottovesti) for *slip*

Sovrapprezzo (il sovrapprezzo, i sovrapprezzi) for *surcharge*

Spada (pesce spada) for *swordfish*

Spaventarsi for *to get frightened*

Spazzola (la spazzola, le spazzole) for *brush*

Spazzolarsi for *brush (teeth or hair)*

Spazzolino da denti (lo spazzolino, gli spazzolini) for *toothbrush*

Spegnere for *to turn off*

Spendere for *to spend*

Spesa *(*la spesa) *for grocery shopping*

Spese (le spese) *for shopping*

Spezia (la spezia, le spezie) for *spice*

Spiaggia (la spiaggia, le spiagge) for *beach*

Spilla (la spilla, le spille) for *brooch*

Spinaci (lo spinacio, gli spinaci) for *spinach*

Sporco (sporco, sporchi, sporca, sporche) for *dirty*

Sport (lo sport, gli sport) for *sport*

Sportivo for *casual*

Stadio *(*lo stadio, gli stadi) for *stadium*

Stagione (la stagione, le stagioni) for *season*

Stancante (stancante, stancanti) *for tiring*

Stanco (stanco, stanchi, stanca, stanche) for *tired*

Stanza (la stanza, le stanze) for *room*

Stare for *to be, to stay*

Statua (la statua, le statue) for *statue*

Stazione (la stazione, le stazioni) for *station*

Stazione (la stazione, le stazioni) **di polizia** for *the police station*

Stazione (la stazione, le stazioni) **di servizio** for *service station*

Stella (la stella, le stelle) for *star*

Stipendio (lo stipendio, gli stipendi) for *salary*

Stivali (lo stivale, gli stivali) for *boots*

Stomaco (lo stomaco, gli stomaci) for *stomach*

Strada (la strada, le strade) for *road*

Su for *up, on*

Suocera (la suocera, le suocere) for *mother-in-law*

Suocero (il suocero, i suoceri) for *father-in-law*

Supermercato (il supermercato, i supermercati) for *supermarket*

Superstrada (la superstrada, le superstrade) for *expressway*

Susina (la susina, le susine) for *plum*

Svegliarsi for *to wake oneself up*

Svestirsi for *to get undressed*

Tabaccheria (la tabaccheria, le tabaccherie) for *tobacco shop*

Tacchino (il tacchino, i tacchini) for *turkey*

Tacco (il tacco, i tacchi) for *heel (of the shoe)*

Taglia (la taglia, le taglie) for *size*

Taglio di capelli for *haircut*

Tallone (il tallone, i talloni) for *heel (of the foot)*

Tanto for *so much, a lot*

Tardi for *late*

Tartaruga (la tartaruga, le tartarughe) for *turtle*

Tasca (la tasca, le tasche) for *pocket*

Tassa (la tassa, le tasse) for *fee*

Tasso d'interesse for *interest rate*

Tavolo (il tavolo, i tavoli) for *table*

Taxi (il taxi, i taxi) for *cab*

Tazza (la tazza, le tazze) for *cup*

Tazzina (la tazzina, le tazzine) for *small cup*

Tè (il tè) for *tea*

Teatro (il teatro, i teatri) for *theater*

Temperatura (la temperatura, le temperature) for *temperature*

Tempo (il tempo, i tempi) for *time, weather*

Temporale (il temporale, i temporali) for *storm*

Tenere for *to keep*

Testa (la testa, le teste) for *head*

Timone (il timone, i timoni) for *helm*

Togliersi for *to take off*

Tonno (il tonno, i tonni) for *tuna*

Tornare for *to return*

Tra or **fra** for *among, in between*

Traghetto (il traghetto, i traghetti) for *ferry*

Tranne for *except*

Trasferire for *to transfer*

Trasporto for *transportation*

Travellers cheque *for traveler's checks*

Traversata (la traversata, le traversate) for *crossing*

Treno (il treno, i treni) for *train*

Tribordo for *starboard*

Tristemente for *sadly*

Troppo for *too much*

Trota (la trota, le trote) for *trout*

Truccarsi *for to put on makeup*

Trucco (il trucco, i trucchi) for *makeup*

Tu *for you*

Tuono (il tuono, i tuoni) for *thunder*

Turbolenza (la turbolenza, le turbolenze) for *turbulence*

Tutto (tutto, tutti, tutta, tutte) for *all*

Ultimamente for *lastly*

Ultimo (ultimo, ultimi, ultima, ultime) *for last*

Umido (umido, umidi, umida, umide) for *humid*

Uomo (l'uomo, gli uomini) for *man*

Uova fritte *for fried eggs*

Uova sode for *hardboiled eggs*

Uova strapazzate *for scrambled eggs*

Uovo (l'uovo, le uova) for *egg*

Urbano for *urban*

Uscire *for to go out*

Uscite di emergenza for *emergency exits*

Uva (l'uva) for *grapes*

Vaglia postale *for money order*

Valigia (la valigia, le valigie) for *suitcase*

Valle (la valle, le valli) for *valley*

Valuta (la valuta, le valute) for *currency*

Vaporetto (il vaporetto, i vaporetti) for *steamboat*

Vassoio (il vassoio, i vassoi) for *tray*

Vecchio (vecchio, vecchi, vecchia, vecchie) *for old*

Vedersi *for to see each other*

Vegano for *vegan*

Vegetariano for *vegetarian*

Vela (la vela, le vele) for *sail*

Veliero for *sailing ship*

Vendere *for to sell*

Vendita for *sale*

Venerdì for *Friday*

Venire for *to come*

Vento (il vento, i venti) for *wind*

Verde *for green*

Verdura (la verdura, le verdure) for *vegetable*

Verdure al forno for *baked vegetables*

Verdure grigliate *for grilled vegetables*

Versamento *(il versamento, i versamenti) for deposit*

Vestire for *to dress*

Vestirsi *for to get dressed*

Vestito (il vestito, i vestiti) for *dress*

Vetrina (la vetrina, le vetrine) for *window*

Via *for away*

Via (la via, le vie) for *street*

Viaggiatore (il viaggiatore, i viaggiatori) for *traveler*

Vicino for *near, close*

Vigile urbano for *traffic policeman*

Vigna (la vigna, le vigne) for *vineyard*

Villa (la villa, le ville) for *villa*

Vino (il vino, i vini) for *wine*

Viola for *purple*

Vivere for *to live*

Voi *for you (many)*

Volare for *to fly*

Volere *for to want*

Voltare for *to turn*

Vomitare for *to vomit*

Yogurt (lo yogurt, gli yogurt) for *yogurt*

Zaino (lo zaino, gli zaini) for *backpack*

Zattera (la zattera, le zattere) for *raft*

Zia (la zia, le zie) for *aunt*

Zio (lo zio, gli zii) for *uncle*

Zitto (zitto, zitti, zitta, zitte) for *quiet*

Zone (la zona, le zone) for *zone*

Zucca (la zucca, le zucche) for *pumpkin*

Zucchero (lo zucchero) for *sugar*

Zuppa (la zuppa, le zuppe) for *soup*

English – Italian

at, to for *A*

about *for Circa*

actor for *Attore (l'attore, gli attori)*

actress for *Attrice (l'attrice, le attrici)*

after for *Dopo*

afternoon for *Pomeriggio (il pomeriggio, i pomeriggi)*

against *for Contro*

agency for *Agenzia (l'agenzia, le agenzie)*

airplane for *Aeroplano (l'aeroplano, gli aeroplani)*

airport for *Aeroporto (l'aeroporto, gli aeroporti)*

a little *for Poco*

all for *Tutto (tutto, tutti, tutta, tutte)*

already *for Già*

always for *Sempre*

amount for *Importo (l'importo, gli importi)*

analysis for *Analisi (l'analisi, le analisi)*

animal for *Animale (l'animale, gli animali)*

answer for *Rispondere*

anus *for Ano (l'ano, gli ani)*

aperitif for *Aperitivo (l'aperitivo, gli aperitivi)*

apologize *for Scusarsi*

appetizer for *Antipasto (l'antipasto, gli antipasti)*

apple for *Mela (la mela, le mele)*

apple tree for *Melo (il melo, i meli)*

apricot for *Albicocca (l'albicocca, le albicocche)*

April *for Aprile*

aquarium for *Acquario (l'acquario, gli acquari)*

arch for *Arco del piede*

archipelago for *Arcipelago (l'arcipelago, gli arcipelaghi)*

arm for *Braccio (il braccio, le braccia)*

around for *Intorno*

arrival for *Arrivo (l'arrivo, gli arrivi)*

arrive *(to)* for *Arrivare*

as soon as possible *for Appena*

ask *(to)* for *Chiedere*

ask *(to)* for *Domandare*

ask oneself *(to) for Chiedersi*

assistant *(male)* for *Commesso (il commesso, i commessi)*

ATM *or* **debit card** *for Bancomat*

August for *Agosto*

aunt for *Zia (la zia, le zie)*

autumn for *Autunno (l'autunno, gli autunni)*

away *for Via*

backpack for *Zaino (lo zaino, gli zaini)*

bad for *Cattivo (cattivo, cattivi, cattiva, cattive)*

bad for *Male*

badly *for Male*

bag *or* **handbag** *for Borsa (la borsa, le borse)*

---

baggage for Bagaglio *(il bagaglio, i bagagli)*

bakery for *bread and cookies* Fornaio *(il fornaio, i fornai)*

bakery *for bread and cookies* Panetteria *(la panetteria, le panetterie)*

bakery for *bread and cookies* Panificio *(il panificio, i panifici)*

bakery for *pastry* Pasticceria *(la pasticceria, le pasticcerie)*

balance *for* Saldo

ballet shoes for *Ballerine (la ballerina, le ballerine)*

banana for *Banana (la banana, le banane)*

Band-aid for *Cerotti (il cerotto, i cerotti)*

bank for *Banca (la banca, le banche)*

banknote for *Banconota (la banconota, le banconote)*

basket for *Cestino (il cestino, i cestini)*

bassinet for *Culla (la culla, le culle)*

bathroom for *Bagno (il bagno, i bagni)*

be able *(to) for* Potere

be *(to)* for *Essere*

be named *(to), be called (to) for* Chiamarsi

beach for *Spiaggia (la spiaggia, le spiagge)*

beautiful *for* Bella *(bella, belle)*

beauty for *Bellezza (la bellezza, le bellezze)*

because *for* Perché

become angry *(to)* for *Arrabbiarsi*

bed for *Letto (il letto, i letti)*

before *for* Prima

---

beef for *Manzo*

behind for *Dietro*

behind, back for *Indietro*

believe *(to) for Credere*

belt for *Cintura (la cintura, le cinture)*

better for *Meglio*

between for *Tra or fra*

big for *Grande (grande, grandi)*

bill for *Conto (il conto, i conti)*

black for *Nero (nero, neri, nera, nere)*

block for *Isolato (l'isolato, gli isolati)*

blond for *Biondo (biondo, biondi, bionda, bionde)*

blouse for *Camicetta (la camicetta, le camicette)*

blueberry for *Mirtillo (il mirtillo, i mirtilli)*

boar for *Cinghiale (il cinghiale, i cinghiali)*

board *(to) for Imbarcarsi*

boarding pass for *Carta d'imbarco (la carta, le carte)*

boat for *Barca (la barca, le barche)*

bookstore for *Libreria (la libreria, le librerie)*

book for *Libro (il libro, i libri)*

boots for *Stivali (lo stivale, gli stivali)*

borrow *(to) for Chiedere in prestito*

bow *for Prua*

boy for *Ragazzo (il ragazzo i ragazzi)*

bra for *Reggiseno (il reggiseno, i reggiseni)*

---

bracelet for *Braccialetto (il braccialetto, i braccialetti)*

bread for *Pane (il pane, i pani)*

break for *Pausa (la pausa, le pause)*

break *(to) for Rompere*

breakfast for *Colazione (la colazione, le colazioni)*

breast for *Petto (il petto, i petti)*

bridge for *Ponte (il ponte, i ponti)*

brooch for *Spilla (la spilla, le spille)*

broth for *Brodo (il brodo)*

brother for *Fratello (il fratello, i fratelli)*

brown *for Marrone*

brush *(teeth or hair) (to) for Spazzolarsi*

brush for *Spazzola (la spazzola, le spazzole)*

bunk bed for *Letto a castello (il letto a castello, i letti a castello)*

bus for *Bus (il bus, i bus)*

bus stop for *Fermata dell'autobus (la fermata, le fermate)*

busses for *Autobus (l'autobus, gli autobus)*

butcher for *Macelleria (la macelleria, le macellerie)*

butter for *Burro (il burro)*

button for *Bottone (il bottone, i bottoni)*

button-down shirt for *Camicia (la camicia, le camicie)*

buy *(to) for Comprare*

cab for *Taxi (il taxi, i taxi)*

cabbage for *Cavolo (il cavolo, i cavoli)*

cabin for *Cabina (la cabina, le cabine)*

café for *Bar (il bar, i bar)*

cafe latte (coffee with milk) for *Caffelatte (il caffelatte)*

calm for *Calmo (calmo, calmi, calma, calme)*

calm down (to) for *Calmarsi*

camping site for *Campeggio (il campeggio, campeggi)*

can for *Scatoletta (la scatoletta, le scatolette)*

canal for *Canale (il canale, i canali)*

cancel (to) for *Annullare*

cane for *Bastone (il bastone, i bastoni)*

cap for *Berretto (il berretto, i berretti)*

captain for *Capitano (il capitano, i capitani)*

car for *Auto (l'auto, le auto)*

car for *Automobile (l'automobile, le automobili)*

car for *Macchina (la macchina, le macchine)*

car (rental) for *Autonoleggio (l'autonoleggio, gli autonoleggi)*

car seat for *Seggiolino (il sedile, i sedili)*

car wash for *Autolavaggio (l'autolavaggio, gli autolavaggi)*

cardigan for *Cardigan (il cardigan, i cardigan)*

carrot for *Carota (la carota, le carote)*

Carry-on for *Bagaglio a mano (il bagaglio, i bagagli)*

cart for *Carrello (il carrello, i carrelli)*

cash for *Contante (il contante)*

cash (to) for *Incassare*

castle for *Castello (il castello, i castelli)*

casual for Informale

casual *for Sportivo*

cat for *Gatto (il gatto, i gatti, la gatta, le gatte)*

cauliflower for *Cavolfiore (il cavolfiore, i cavolfiori)*

cavity for *Carie (la carie, le carie)*

celebrate *(to)* for *Celebrare*

celery for *Sedano (il sedano)*

cents for *Centesimo (il centesimo, i centesimi)*

cereal for *Cereali (i cereali)*

certain for *Certo*

certainly *for Certamente*

change *(to)* for *Cambiare*

change for *Resto (il resto)*

check for *Assegno (l'assegno, gli assegni)*

checking account for *Conto corrente (il conto, i conti)*

cheese for *formaggio (il formaggio, i formaggi)*

cherry for *Ciliegia (la ciliegia, le ciliegie)*

cherry tree for *Ciliegio (il ciliegio, i ciliegi)*

chest of drawers *for Comò (il comò, i comò)*

chicken for *Pollo (il pollo, i polli)*

child *(female)* for *Bambina (la bambina, le bambine)*

child *(male)* for *Bambino (il bambino, i bambini)*

China for *Cina*

chocolate for *Cioccolata (la cioccolata, le cioccolate)*

Christmas for *Natale*

city *for Città (la città, le città)*

class for *Classe (la classe, le classi)*

clean for *Pulito (pulito, puliti, pulita, pulite)*

cleanser for *Detergente (il detergente, i detergenti)*

clerk for *Addetto (l'addetto, gli addetti)*

clerk for *Impiegato*

click for *Scatto (lo scatto, gli scatti)*

client for *Cliente (il cliente, i clienti)*

climate for *Clima (il clima, i climi)*

close for *Chiudere*

cloud for *Nuvola (la nuvola, le nuvole)*

coat for *Cappotto (il cappotto, i cappotti)*

coffee *for Caffè (il caffè, i caffè)*

coin for *Moneta (la moneta, le monete)*

cold cuts store for *Salumeria (la salumeria, le salumerie)*

cold for *Freddo (freddo, freddi, fredda, fredde)*

cold for *Raffreddore (il raffreddore, i raffreddori)*

comb for *Pettine (il pettine, i pettini)*

come *(to)* for *Venire*

commission or *fee* for *Commissione (la commissione, le commissioni)*

company for *Compagnia (la compagnia, le compagnie)*

complain about *(to)* for *Lamentarsi di*

confirm *(to)* for *Confermare*

continue *(to)* for *Proseguire*

convenient for *Economico (economico, economici, economica, economiche)*

---

convent for *Convento (il convento, i conventi)*

cookies for *Biscotti (il biscotto, i biscotti)*

correct for *Giusto (giusto, giusti, giusta, giuste)*

cost *(to) for Costare*

cousin *(feminine)* for *Cugina (la cugina, le cugine)*

cousin *(masculine)* for *Cugino (il cugino, i cugini)*

cover *(to)* for *Coprire*

cream *for Panna (la panna)*

credit card for *Carta di credito (la carta, le carte)*

crew for *Equipaggio (l'equipaggio, gli equipaggi)*

crisis for *Crisi (la crisi, le crisi)*

croissant for *Cornetto (il cornetto, i cornetti)*

crossing *for Traversata*

cruise for *Crociera (la crociera, le crociere)*

cruise ship for *Nave (la nave, le navi) da crociera*

cry *(to) for Piangere*

cucumber for *Cetriolo (il cetriolo, i cetrioli)*

cup for *Tazza (la tazza, le tazze)*

(small) cup for *Tazzina (la tazzina, le tazzine)*

curfew for *Coprifuoco (il coprifuoco, i coprifuochi)*

currency exchange or *bureau de change* for *Cambiavalute (il cambiavalute, i cambiavalute)*

currency *for Valuta (la valuta, le valute)*

cutlet for *Fettina (la fettina, le fettine)*

dad *for Papà (il papà, i papà)*

---

daily for *Giornaliero (giornaliero, giornalieri, giornaliera, giornaliere)*

damage for *Danno (il danno, i danni)*

damaged for *Sciupato (sciupato, sciupati, sciupata, sciupate)*

dark blue for *Blu*

dark for *Scuro (scuro, scuri, scura, scure)*

daughter for *Figlia (la figlia, le figlie)*

daughter-in-law for *Nuora (la nuora, le nuore)*

day for *Giorno (il giorno, i giorni)*

dear for *Caro (caro, cari, cara, care)*

December for *Dicembre*

deck for *Ponte (il ponte, i ponti)*

deductible for *Franchigia (la franchigia, le franchigie)*

decagrams for *Decagrammo*

delicious for *Delizioso (delizioso, deliziosi, deliziosa, deliziose)*

dentist for *Dentifricio (il dentifricio, i dentifrici)*

dentist for *Dentista (il dentista, i dentisti)*

department store for *Grandi magazzini*

departure for *Partenza (la partenza, le partenze)*

deposit for *Versamento (il versamento, i versamenti)*

dessert for *Dolce (il dolce, i dolci)*

detergent for *Detersivo (il detersivo, i detersivi)*

dew for *Rugiada*

dice for *Dado (il dado, i dadi)*

die *(to)* for *Morire*

---

difficult *for Difficile*

dilemma for *Dilemma (il dilemma, i dilemmi)*

dinner for *Cena (la cena, le cene)*

dirty for *Sporco (sporco, sporchi, sporca, sporche)*

discover *(to)* for *Scoprire*

disembark *(to)* for *Sbarcare*

disgusting for *Disgustoso (disgustoso, disgustosi, disgustosa, disgustose)*

disinfectant for *Disinfettante (il disinfettante, i disinfettanti)*

do *(to) for Fare*

doctor *(female)* for *Dottoressa (la dottoressa, le dottoresse)*

doctor *(male)* for *Dottore (il dottore, i dottori)*

dog for *Cane (il cane, i cani)*

dollar for *Dollaro (il dollaro, i dollari)*

dorm for *Dormitorio (il dormitorio, i dormitori)*

double for *Doppio (doppio, doppi, doppia, doppie)*

down here *for Quaggiù*

down there *for Laggiù*

down there *for Lì in fondo*

down there *for Lì sotto*

down, under *for Giù*

drama for *Dramma (il dramma, i drammi)*

dream for *Sogno (il sogno, i sogni)*

dress *(to)* for *Vestire*

dress for *Vestito (il vestito, i vestiti)*

dressing room for *Camerino di prova (il camerino, i camerini)*

drink *(to)* for *Bere*

driver for *Guidatore (il guidatore, i guidatori)*

drugstore for *Drogheria (la drogheria, le drogherie)*

dry cleaner for *Lavanderia (la lavanderia, le lavanderie) a secco*

dryer for *Asciugatrice (l'asciugatrice, le asciugatrici)*

during *for Durante*

ear for *Orecchio (l'orecchio, gli orecchi)*

earrings for *Orecchino (l'orecchino, gli orecchini)*

easily *for Facilmente*

Easter *for Pasqua*

easy *for Facile*

eat *(to)* for *Mangiare*

egg for *Uovo (l'uovo, le uova)*

eggs *(fried)* for *Uova fritte*

eggs *(hardboiled)* for *Uova sode*

eggs *(scrambled)* for *Uova strapazzate*

elegant for *Elegante (elegante, eleganti)*

elevator for *Ascensore (l'ascensore, gli ascensori)*

emergency for *emergenza (l'emergenza, le emergenze)*

emergency exits for *Uscite di emergenza*

emergency room for *Pronto soccorso*

endorse *(to)* for *Girare* [*un assegno*]

enough for *Abbastanza*

enough *(to be) for Bastare*

enter (to) for *inserire or digitare*

enter (to), go in (to) for *Entrare*

epiphany for *Epifania (l'Epifania)*

evening for *Sera (la sera, le sere)*

every once in a while for *Ogni tanto*

everywhere for *Dappertutto*

everywhere for *Ovunque*

exact for *Esatto (esatto, esatti, esatta, esatte)*

except for *Eccetto*

except for *Tranne*

exchange rate for *Tasso di cambio*

expensive for *Caro (caro, cari, cara, care)*

expensive for *Costoso (costoso, costosi, costosa, costose)*

expressway for *Superstrada (la superstrada, le superstrade)*

eye for *Occhio (l'occhio, gli occhi)*

face for *Faccia (la faccia, le facce)*

face powder for *Cipria (la cipria)*

fact for *Fatto (il fatto, i fatti)*

fall asleep (to) for *Addormentarsi*

family for *Famiglia (la famiglia, le famiglie)*

fantastic for *Fantastico (fantastico, fantastici, fantastica, fantastiche)*

far for *Lontano*

farm for *fattoria (la fattoria, le fattorie)*

farm holiday for *Agriturismo (l'agriturismo, gli agriturismi)*

---

fat for Grasso (grasso, grassi, grassa, grasse)

fate for Fato (il fato)

father for Padre (il padre, i padri)

father-in-law for Suocero (il suocero, i suoceri)

February for Febbraio

fee for Tassa (la tassa, le tasse)

feed oneself (to) for Nutrirsi

ferry for Traghetto (il traghetto, i traghetti)

fever for Febbre (la febbre, le febbri)

filling for Piombatura (la piombatura, le piombature)

fine for Multa (la multa, le multe)

finger for Dito (il dito, le dita)

finish (to) for Finire

fish for Pesce (il pesce, i pesci)

fish market for Pescheria (la pescherie, le pescherie)

fit (to) for Andare bene

fix (to) for Riparare

flavor for Gusto (il gusto, i gusti)

flight attendant for Assistente di volo (l'assistente, gli assistenti)

flip flops for Infradito (l'infradito)

flower for Fiore (il fiore, i fiori)

fly (to) for Volare

fog for Nebbia (la nebbia)

follow (to) for Seguire

foot for Piede (il piede, i piedi)

---

forget *(to)* for *Dimenticarsi*

formal for *formale*

foundation for *Fondotinta (il fondotinta, i fondotinta)*

fragrant for *Profumato (profumato, profumati, profumata, profumate)*

frame for *Montatura (la montatura, le montature)*

frequent *for Frequente*

frequently *for Frequentemente*

Friday *for Venerdì*

friend for *Amico (l'amico, gli amici, l'amica, le amiche)*

from *for Da*

frost for *Brina (la brina)*

fruit for *Frutta (la frutta, i frutti)*

gaiter for *Ghetta (la ghetta, le ghette)*

game for *Gioco (il gioco, i giochi)*

game for *Selvaggina (la selvaggina)*

gangway for *Passerella*

gas for *Benzina (la benzina, le benzine)*

gear for *Marcia (la marcia, le marce)*

generous for *Generoso (generoso, generosi, generosa, generose)*

get burned *(to)* for *Bruciarsi*

get dressed *(to) for Vestirsi*

get frightened *(to) for Spaventarsi*

get irritated *(to) for Irritarsi*

get ready *(to) for Prepararsi*

get sick *(to)* for *Ammalarsi*

get undressed *(to)* for *Svestirsi*

get up *(to)* for *Alzarsi*

get used to something *(to)* for *Abituarsi*

girl for *Ragazza (la ragazza, le ragazze)*

give *(to)* for *Dare*

glass for *Bicchiere (il bicchiere, i bicchieri)*

gloves for *Guanti (il guanto, i guanti)*

gluten for *Glutine*

gnocchi for *Gnocchi (lo gnocco, gli gnocchi)*

gnome for *Gnomo (lo gnomo, gli gnomi)*

go *(to)* for *Andare*

go down *(to)* for *Scendere*

goodbye for *Ciao*

go out *(to)* for *Uscire*

go up *(to)* for *Salire*

gondola for *Gondola (la gondola, le gondole)*

good for *Buono (buono, buoni, buona, buone)*

good, able for *Bravo (bravo, bravi, brava, brave)*

gram for *Grammo (il grammo, i grammi)*

granddaughter for *Nipote (la nipote, le nipoti)*

grandfather for *Nonno (il nonno, i nonni)*

grandmother for *Nonna (la nonna, le nonne)*

grandson for *Nipote (il nipote, i nipoti)*

grapefruit for *Pompelmo (il pompelmo, i pompelmi)*

grapes for *Uva (l'uva)*

gray for *Grigio (grigio, grigi, grigia, grigie)*

green beans for *Fagiolini (i fagiolini)*

green for *Verde*

greengrocer for *fruttivendolo (il fruttivendolo, i fruttivendoli)*

grocery store for *Negozio di alimentari (il negozio, i negozi)*

ground meat for *Macinata*

guest for *Ospite (l'ospite, gli ospiti)*

guitar for *Chitarra (la chitarra, le chitarre)*

gym for *Palestra (la palestra, le palestre)*

hail *(to)* for *Grandinare*

hair for *Capelli (i capelli)*

haircut for *Taglio di capelli*

ham for *Prociutto cotto (il prosciutto, i prosciutti)*

hand for *Mano (la mano, le mani)*

handsome for *Bello (bello, belli)*

happen *(to)* for *Accadere*

happily for *Felicemente*

happy for *Allegro (allegro, allegri, allegra, allegre)*

happy for *Felice (felice, felici)*

harbor for *Darsena (la darsena, le darsene)*

hat for *Cappello (il cappello, i cappelli)*

have *(to)* for *Avere*

have dinner *(to)* for *Cenare*

have fun *(to)* for *Divertirsi*

have lunch *(to) for Pranzare*

have to *(to) for Dovere*

haze for *Foschia*

he for *Lui*

head for *Testa (la testa, le teste)*

headset for *Cuffia (la cuffia, le cuffie)*

healed for *Guarito (guarito, guariti, guarita, guarite)*

hear *(to) for Sentire*

heavily *for forte*

hectogram for *Ettogrammo (ettogrammo, ettogrammi)*

heel *(of the foot) for Tallone (il tallone, i talloni)*

heel *(of the shoe)* for *Tacco (il tacco, i tacchi)*

hello *for Ciao*

hello for *Salve*

helm for *Timone (il timone, i timoni)*

help each other *(to)* for *Aiutarsi*

here for *Qui, qua*

highway *for Autostrada (l'autostrada, le autostrade)*

hindu for *Indù*

hoist *(to)* for *Issare*

holiday for *Festa (la festa, le feste)*

honest for *Onesto (onesto, onesti, onesta, oneste)*

honestly *for Onestamente*

honey for *Miele (il miele)*

hospital for *Ospedale (l'ospedale, gli ospedali)*

---

hostel for *Ostello (l'ostello, gli ostelli)*

hotel for *Albergo (l'albergo, gli alberghi)*

hotel owner for *Albergatore (l'albergatore, gli albergatori)*

house for *Casa (la casa, le case)*

hovercraft for *Overcraft*

how for *Come*

how much for *Quanto*

humid for *Umido (umido, umidi, umida, umide)*

husband for *Marito (il marito, i mariti)*

hydrofoil for *Aliscafo (l'aliscafo, gli aliscafi)*

hygiene for *Igiene (l'igiene)*

hypothesis for *Ipotesi (l'ipotesi, le ipotesi)*

I for *Io*

ice for *Ghiaccio (il ghiaccio)*

illusion for *Illusione (l'illusione, le illusioni)*

in front for *Davanti*

in front of for *Di fronte*

in for *In*

in order to for *Per*

included for *Incluso (incluso, inclusi, inclusa, incluse)*

independent for *Indipendente*

information desk for *Banco delle informazioni (il banco, i banchi)*

inside for *Dentro*

inspector for *Controllore (il controllore, i controllori)*

insurance for *Assicurazione (l'assicurazione, le assicurazioni)*

interest *(to)* for *Interessare*

interest for *Interesse (l'interesse, gli interessi)*

interest rate for *Tasso d'interesse*

intersection for *Incrocio (l'incrocio, gli incroci)*

introduce oneself *(to) for Presentarsi*

island for *Isola (l'isola, le isole)*

jacket for *Giacca (la giacca, le giacche)*

jam for *Marmellata (la marmellata, le marmellate)*

January *for Gennaio*

jeans for *Jeans (i jeans)*

jewelry store for *Gioielleria (la gioielleria, le gioiellerie)*

joke for *Scherzo (lo scherzo, gli scherzi)*

July for *Luglio*

June for *Giugno*

keep *(to) for Tenere*

key for *Chiave (la chiave, le chiavi)*

kilogram for *Chilogrammo (il chilogrammo, i chilogrammi)*

kilometer for *Chilometro (il chilometro, i chilometri)*

kind for *Gentile (gentile, gentili)*

kindly *for Gentilmente*

kitchen for *Cucina (la cucina, le cucine)*

know each other *(to) for Conoscersi*

know *(to) for Sapere*

kosher for *Kosher*

lactose for *Lattosio*

land (to) for *Atterrare*

landing for *Atterraggio (l'atterraggio, gli atterraggi)*

last for *Ultimo (ultimo, ultimi, ultima, ultime)*

lastly for *Ultimamente*

late (to be) for *Essere in ritardo*

late for *Tardi*

later for *Più tardi*

laundromat for *Lavanderia (la lavanderia, le lavanderie) a gettoni or lavanderia automatica*

leave (to) for *Partire*

left for *Sinistra*

leg for *Gamba (la gamba, le gambe)*

lemon for *Limone (il limone, i limoni)*

lend (to) for *Prestare*

lens for *Lente (la lente, le lenti)*

lesson for *Lezione (la lezione, le lezioni)*

letter for *Lettera (la lettera, le lettere)*

lettuce for *Lattuga (la lattuga)*

liar for *Bugiardo (bugiardo, bugiardi, bugiarda, bugiarde)*

life belt for *Salvagente (il salvagente, i salvagente)*

lifeboat for *Scialuppa di salvataggio (la scialuppa, le scialuppe)*

life jacket for *Giubbotto di salvataggio* (il giubbotto, i giubbotti)

light blue for *Azzurro (azzurro, azzurri, azzurra, azzurre)*

light for *Leggero (leggero, leggeri, leggera, leggere)*

lightning for *Lampo (il lampo, i lampi)*

lightly *for Leggermente*

like *(to)* for *Piacere*

line for *Fila (la fila, le file)*

lipstick for *Rossetto (il rossetto, i rossetti)*

listen *(to)* for *Ascoltare*

liter for *Litro (il litro, i litri)*

live *(to)* for *Vivere, abitare*

living room for *Salotto (il salotto, i salotti)*

loafers for *Mocassini (i mocassini)*

loan for *Prestito (il prestito, i prestiti)*

lobster for *Aragosta (l'aragosta, le aragoste)*

long for *Lungo (lungo, lunghi, lunga, lunghe)*

look for *(to)* for *Cercare*

look *(to)* for *Guardare*

lose *(to)* for *Perdere*

lotion for *Crema (la crema, le creme)*

loudly *for forte*

love each other *(to)* for *Amarsi*

low calorie *for Ipocalorico*

low cholesterol *for Ipocolesterolemico or a basso contenuto di colesterolo*

low salt *for Iposodico*

lower *(to) for Calare*

luckily *for fortunatamente*

lucky for *fortunato (fortunato, fortunati, fortunata, fortunate)*

lunch for *Pranzo (il pranzo, i pranzi)*

mail for *posta (la posta)*

mailbox for *Cassetta delle lettere (la cassetta, le cassette)*

makeup for *Trucco (il trucco, i trucchi)*

man for *Uomo (l'uomo, gli uomini)*

March for *Marzo*

mascara for *Mascara (il mascara, i mascara)*

matter *(to)* for *Importare*

May for *Maggio*

meal for *Pasto (il pasto, i pasti)*

meat for *Carne (la carne, le carni)*

medium for *Medio (medio, medi, media, medie)*

meet with *(to)* for *Incontrarsi con*

melon for *Melone (il melone, i meloni)*

member for *Membro (il membro, i membri)*

menu for *Menù (il menù, i menù)*

messenger bag for *Borsa a tracolla (la borsa, le borse)*

meter for *Metro (il metro, i metri)*

metro for *Metropolitana (la metropolitana, le metropolitane)*

midnight for *Mezzanotte (la mezzanotte)*

mile for *Miglio (il miglio, le miglia)*

milk for *Latte (il latte)*

minimum for *Minimo (minimo, minimi, minima, minime)*

minute for *Minuto (il minuto, i minuti)*

mist for *Foschia*

---

monastery for *Monastero (il monastero, i monasteri)*

Monday *for Lunedì*

money order for *Vaglia postale*

money for *Soldi (il soldo, i soldi)*

month *for Mese (il mese, i mesi)*

monthly *for Mensile*

morning for *Mattina (la mattina, le mattine)*

morning for *Mattino (il mattino, i mattini)*

mother for *Madre (la madre, le madri)*

mother-in-law for *Suocera (la suocera, le suocere)*

motorboat for *Motoscafo (il motoscafo, i motoscafi)*

mountain for *Montagna (la montagna, le montagne)*

mouth for *Bocca (la bocca, le bocche)*

movie for *Film (il film, i film)*

Mr. and Mrs. *for Signori*

Mr. for *Signore*

Mrs. for *Signora*

much *for Molto*

much *(a lot) for Tanto*

museum for *Museo (il museo, i musei)*

mushroom for *Fungo (il fungo, i funghi)*

muslim for *Musulmano (musulmano, musulmani, musulmana, musulmane)*

nail polish for *Smalto (lo smalto, gli smalti)*

nap for *Pisolino (il pisolino, i pisolini)*

---

near (close) *for Vicino*

neck for *Collo (il collo, i colli)*

necklace for *Collana (la collana, le collane)*

need (to) *for Servire*

nephew for *Nipote (il nipote, i nipoti)*

never *for Mai*

new for *Nuovo (nuovo, nuovi, nuova, nuove)*

New Year for *Capodanno (il capodanno, i capodanni)*

newspaper for *Giornale (il giornale, i giornali)*

newsstand for *Giornalaio (il giornalaio, i giornalai)*

next for *Prossimo (prossimo, prossimi, prossima, prossime)*

next to for *Accanto*

nice for *Carino (carino, carini, carina, carine)*

niece for *Nipote (la nipote, le nipoti)*

night for *Notte (la notte, le notti)*

November *for Novembre*

now for *Adesso*

now *for Ora*

October for *Ottobre*

octopus for *Polipo (il polipo, i polipi)*

of *for Di*

offer (to) *for Offrire*

oil for *Olio (l'olio, gli olii)*

old for *Vecchio (vecchio, vecchi, vecchia, vecchie)*

olive/s for *Olive (l'oliva, le olive)*

on (above) for *Sopra*

onion for *Cipolla (la cipolla, le cipolle)*

open *(to)* for *Aprire*

opera for *Opera (l'opera, le opere)*

orange for *Arancia (l'arancia, le arance)*

orange for *Arancione*

orange tree for *Arancio (l'arancio, gli aranci)*

order *(to)* for *Ordinare*

gold for *Oro*

other, **another** for *Altro (altro, altri, altra, altre)*

otherwise for *Altrimenti*

outside for *Fuori*

over there for *Lì vicino*

overcast for *Nuvoloso*

owe *(to)* for *Dovere*

pacifier for *Ciuccio (il ciuccio, i ciucci)*

package for *Pacco (il pacco, i pacchi)*

painkiller for *Analgesico (l'analgesico, gli analgesici)*

painter for *Pittore (il pittore, i pittori)*

pair for *Paio (il paio, le paia)*

pancake for *Frittella (la frittella, le frittelle)*

panties for *Mutandina (la mutandina, le mutandine)*

passenger for *Passeggero (il passeggero, i passeggeri)*

passenger on foot for *Passeggero a piedi*

passport for *Passaporto*

pay (to) for *Pagare*

payee for *Beneficiario (il beneficiario, i beneficiari)*

payment for *Pagamento (il pagamento, i pagamenti)*

pea for *Pisello (il pisello, i piselli)*

peach for *Pesca (la pesca, le pesche)*

peach tree for *Pesco (il pesco, i peschi)*

pear for *Pera (la pera, le pere)*

pear tree for *Pero (il pero, i peri)*

pen for *Penna (la penna, le penne)*

pencil for *Matita (la matita, le matite)*

peninsula for *Penisola (la penisola, le penisole)*

percentage for *Percentuale (la percentuale, le percentuali)*

perfume store for *Profumeria (la profumeria, le profumerie)*

perm for *Permanente (la permanente, le permanenti)*

personal check for *Assegno personale (l'assegno, gli assegni)*

personal for *Personale*

pharmacy for *Farmacia (la farmacia, le farmacie)*

photo for *Foto (la foto, le foto)*

pigpen for *Porcile (il porcile, i porcili)*

pilgrim (female) for *Pellegrina (la pellegrina, le pellegrine)*

pilgrim (male) for *Pellegrino (il pellegrino, i pellegrini)*

pilot for *Pilota (il pilota, i piloti)*

pineapple for *Ananas (l'ananas, gli ananas)*

pink for *Rosa*

pizza for *Pizza (la pizza, le pizze)*

plastic for *Plastic (la plastica, le plastiche)*

platinum for *Platino*

platform for *Pensilina (la pensilina, le pensiline)*

play (to) for *Giocare*

pleasure for Piacere

plum for *Susina (la susina, le susine)*

pocket for *Tasca (la tasca, le tasche)*

point (to) for Indicare

police station for *Stazione di polizia (la stazione, le stazioni)*

pool for *Piscina (la piscina, le piscine)*

poor for *Povero (povero, poveri, povera, povere)*

pope for *Papa*

pork for *Maiale (il maiale, i maiali)*

port for *Babordo*

port for *Porto (il porto, i porti)*

postcard for *Cartolina (la cartolina, le cartoline)*

potato for *Patata (la patata, le patate)*

pour (to) for *Diluviare*

prawn or *shrimp* for *Gambero (il gambero, i gamberi)*

prayer for *Preghiera (la preghiera, le preghiere)*

price for *Prezzo (il prezzo, i prezzi)*

product for *Prodotto (il prodotto, i prodotti)*

professor (female) for *Professoressa (la professoressa, le professoresse)*

professor (male) for *Professore (il professore, i professori)*

---

program for *Programma (il programma, i programmi)*

prosciutto for *Prociutto crudo (il prosciutto, i prosciutti)*

psychologist for *Psicologo (lo psicologo, gli psicologi)*

pump for *Pompa (la pompa, le pompe)*

pumpkin for *Zucca (la zucca, le zucche)*

purchase for *Acquisto (l'acquisto, gli acquisti)*

purple for Viola

purse for *Borsetta (la borsetta, le borsette)*

put on makeup (to) for Truccarsi

put on (to) for Mettersi

queen for *Regina (la regina, le regine)*

quiet for *Silenzioso (silenzioso, silenziosi, silenziosa, silenziose)*

quiet for *Zitto (zitto, zitti, zitta, zitte)*

quietly for *Silenziosamente*

quietly for Piano

rabbit for *Coniglio (il coniglio, i conigli, la coniglia, le coniglie)*

radio for *Radio (la radio, le radio)*

raft for *Zattera (la zattera, le zattere)*

rain for *Pioggia (la pioggia)*

rain (to) for Piovere

rainbow for Arcobaleno (l'arcobaleno, gli arcobaleni)

raincoat for *Impermeabile (l'impermeabile, gli impermeabili)*

rarely for Raramente

read (to) for Leggere

receipt for *Ricevuta (la ricevuta, le ricevute)*

recent for *Recente*

red for *Rosso (rosso, rossi, rossa, rosse)*

refund *(to)* for *Rimborsare*

refund for *Rimborso (il rimborso, i rimborsi)*

register for *Cassa (la cassa, le casse)*

regret *(to)* for *Dispiacere*

rejoice *(to)* for *Rallegrarsi*

rent *(to)* for *Noleggiare*

rental car for *Macchina a noleggio (la macchina, le macchine)*

repair for *Riparazione (la riparazione, le riparazioni)*

repeat *(to) for Ripetere*

reserve *(to)* for *Prenotare*

rest *(to)* for *Riposare*

rest *(to)* for *Riposarsi*

restaurant for *Ristorante (il ristorante, i ristoranti)*

rested for *Riposato (riposato, riposati, riposata, riposate)*

return *(to)* for *Tornare*

rice dish for *Risotto (il risotto, i risotti)*

rich for *Ricco (ricco, ricchi, ricca, ricche)*

right *for Destra*

ring for *Anello (l'anello, gli anelli)*

river for *Fiume (il fiume, i fiumi)*

road for *Strada (la strada, le strade)*

room for *Stanza (la stanza, le stanze)*

rotary for *Rotatoria (la rotatoria, le rotatorie)*

---

rough for *Agitato (agitato, agitati, agitata, agitate)*

rowboat for *Barca a remi (la barca, le barche)*

rule for *Regola (la regola, le regole)*

sadly for *Tristemente*

sailboat for *Barca a vela (la barca, le barche)*

sail *(to)* for *Salpare*

sail for *Vela (la vela, le vele)*

sailor for *Marinaio (il marinaio, i marinai)*

salad for *Insalata (l'insalata, le insalate)*

salami for *Salame (il salame, i salami)*

salary for *Stipendio (lo stipendio, gli stipendi)*

sale for *Vendita*

salmon for *Salmone (il salmone, i salmoni)*

salt for *Sale (il sale, i sali)*

sandals for *Sandali (il sandalo, i sandali)*

sandwich for *Panino (il panino, i panini)*

Saturday *for Sabato*

save *(to)* for *Risparmiare*

say *(to) for Dire*

scarf for *Sciarpa (la sciarpa, le sciarpe)*

scene for *Scena (la scena, le scene)*

schedule *for Orario (l'orario, gli orari)*

school for *Scuola (la scuola, le scuole)*

sculptor for *Scultore (lo scultore, gli scultori)*

sculptress for *Scultrice (la scultrice, le scultrici)*

sea for *Mare (il mare, i mari)*

seabass for *Branzino (il branzino, i branzini)*

season for *Stagione (la stagione, le stagioni)*

seat for *Posto (il posto, i posti)*

seat for *Sedile (il sedile, i sedili)*

seat-back for *Schienale (lo schienali, gli schienali)*

seatbelt for *Cintura di sicurezza (la cintura, le cinture)*

security for *Sicurezza*

see each other *(to) for Vedersi*

seem *(to)* for *Sembrare*

sell *(to)* for *Vendere*

September for *Settembre*

serve *(to)* for *Servire*

service station for *Stazione (la stazione, le stazioni) di servizio*

shake for *Scossa (la scossa, le scosse)*

share *(to)* for *Condividere*

shared for *Condiviso (condiviso, condivisi, condivisa, condivise)*

shawl for *Scialle (lo scialle, gli scialli)*

she *for Lei*

sheet for *Foglio (il foglio, i fogli)*

ship for *Nave (la nave, le navi)*

ship *(sailing)* for *Veliero*

shoe for *Scarpa (la scarpa, le scarpe)*

shock *(electric)* for *Scossa (la scossa, le scosse)*

shop assistant *(female)* for *Commessa (la commessa, le commesse)* *shopping mall* for *Centro commerciale (il centro commerciale, i centri commerciali)*

shopping (grocery) for *Spesa (la spesa)*

shopping for *Spese (le spese)*

short for *Corto (corto, corti, corta, corte)*

shorts for *Pantaloncini (i pantaloncini)*

shower for *Doccia (la doccia, le docce)*

shuttle for *Shuttle*

sick for *Malato (malato, malati, malata, malate)*

side dishes for *Contorni (il contorno, i contorni)*

signorina for *Signorina*

silly for *Sciocco (sciocco, sciocchi, sciocca, sciocche)*

silver for *Argento*

sincere for *Sincero (sincero, sinceri, sincera, sincere)*

single for *Singolo (singolo, singoli, singola, singole)*

sister for *Sorella (la sorella, le sorelle)*

sit (to) for *Sedersi*

size for *Taglia (la taglia, le taglie)*

ski for *Sci (gli sci)*

skirt for *Gonna (la gonna, le gonne)*

sky for *Cielo (il cielo)*

slap for *Schiaffo (lo schiaffo, gli schiaffi)*

sleep (to) for Dormire

slice for *Fetta (la fetta, le fette)*

slip for *Sottoveste (la sottoveste, le sottovesti)*

slippers for *Pantofole (la pantofola, le pantofole)*

slow for *Lento (lento, lenti, lenta, lente)*

slowly for *Lentamente, piano*

small hotel for *Pensione (la pensione, le pensioni)*

small for *Piccolo (piccolo, piccoli, piccola, piccole)*

smog for *Smog (lo smog, gli smog)*

snack for *Merenda (la merenda, le merende)*

sneakers for *Scarpe da ginnastica (la scarpa, le scarpe)*

snow for *Neve (la neve, le nevi)*

snow (to) for *Nevicare*

so and so for *Così così*

so long for *Arrivederci*

socks for *Calzini (il calzino, i calzini)*

softener for *Ammorbidente (l'ammorbidente, gli ammorbidenti)*

some for *Poco*

sometimes for *A volte*

son-in-law for *Genero (il genero, i generi)*

son for *Figlio (il figlio, i figli)*

song for *Canzone (la canzone, le canzoni)*

soon for *Presto*

soup for *Minestra (la minestra, le minestre)*

soup for *Zuppa (la zuppa, le zuppe)*

speak (to) for *Parlare*

spend (to) for *Spendere*

spice for *Spezia (la spezia, le spezie)*

spinach for *Spinaci (lo spinacio, gli spinaci)*

sport for *Sport (lo sport, gli sport)*

spring for *Primavera (la primavera, le primavere)*

square for *Piazza (la piazza, le piazze)*

stadium for *Stadio (lo stadio, gli stadi)*

star for *Stella (la stella, le stelle)*

starboard for *Tribordo*

station for *Stazione (la stazione, le stazioni)*

stationery store for *Cartoleria (la cartoleria, le cartolerie)*

stationery for *Carta da lettere (la carta, le carte)*

statue for *Statua (la statua, le statue)*

stay (to) for *Stare*

steak for *Bistecca (la bistecca, le bistecche)*

steamboat for *Vaporetto (il vaporetto, i vaporetti)*

still for *Fermo (fermo, fermi, ferma, ferme)*

stingy for *Avaro (avaro, avari, avara, avare)*

stomach for *Stomaco (lo stomaco, gli stomaci)*

store *(for clothing)* for *Negozio di abbigliamento (il negozio, i negozi)*

store for *Negozio (il negozio, i negozi)*

storm for *Burrasca (la burrasca, le burrasche)*

storm for *Temporale (il temporale, i temporali)*

straight for *Dritto*

strawberry for *Fragola (la fragola, le fragole)*

street for *Via (la via, le vie)*

suburban for *Interurbano*

sudden for *Improvviso*

suffer *(to) for Dolere*

sugar for *Zucchero (lo zucchero)*

suitcase for *Valigia (la valigia, le valige)*

summer *for Estate (l'estate, le estati)*

sun lotion for *Crema solare (la crema, le creme)*

sun for *Sole (il sole)*

Sunday for *Domenica*

supermarket for *Supermercato (il supermercato, i supermercati)*

surcharge for *Sovrapprezzo (il sovrapprezzo, i sovrapprezzi)*

sweater for *Maglione (il maglione, i maglioni)*

sweatshirt for *Felpa (la felpa, le felpe)*

sweet *for Dolce*

sweetly *for Dolcemente*

swim *(to)* for *Nuotare*

swordfish for *Pesce spada (il pesce spada, i pesce spada)*

system for *Sistema (il sistema, i sistemi)*

T-shirt for *Maglietta (la maglietta, le magliette)*

table for *Tavolo (il tavolo, i tavoli)*

take a bath *(to)* for *Farsi il bagno*

take advantage of *(to)* for *Approfittarsi (di)*

take off *(to)* for *Decollare*

take off for *Decollo (il decollo, i decolli)*

talk to each other *(to) for Parlarsi*

tar for *Catrame (il catrame)*

tasting for *Degustazione (la degustazione, le degustazioni)*

tea for *Tè (il tè, i tè)*

temperature for *Temperatura (la temperatura, le temperature)*

temporarily for *Provvisoriamente*

temporary for *Provvisorio*

thank you for *Grazie*

that for *Quello (quello, quelli, quella, quelle)*

theater for *Teatro (il teatro, i teatri)*

then for *Allora*

then for *Poi*

there for *Lì, là*

they for *Loro, essi*

thigh for *Coscia (la coscia, le cosce)*

thin for *Magro (magro, magri, magra, magre)*

thing for *Cosa (la cosa, le cose)*

this for *Questo (questo, questi, questa, queste)*

throat for *Gola (la gola, le gole)*

thunder for *Tuono (il tuono, i tuoni)*

Thursday for *Giovedì*

ticket booth, office for *Biglietteria (la biglietteria, le biglietterie)*

ticket for *Biglietto (il biglietto, i biglietti)*

tie for *Cravatta (la cravatta, le cravatte)*

tights for *Collant (i collant)*

time for *Tempo (il tempo, i tempi)*

tip for Mancia *(la mancia, le mance)*

tired for Stanco *(stanco, stanchi, stanca, stanche)*

tiring for Stancante *(stancante, stancanti)*

tissue, handkerchief for Fazzoletto di carta *(il fazzoletto, i fazzoletti)*

tobacco shop for Tabaccheria *(la tabaccheria, le tabaccherie)*

today for Oggi

toes for Dita del piede

toll for Pedaggio *(il pedaggio, i pedaggi)*

tomato for Pomodoro *(il pomodoro, i pomodori)*

tomorrow for Domani

too much for Troppo

tooth for Dente *(il dente, i denti)*

toothbrush for Spazzolino da denti *(lo spazzolino, gli spazzolini)*

tow truck for Carro attrezzi *(il carro attrezzi, i carri attrezzi)*

track for Binario *(il binario, i binari)*

traffic light for Semaforo *(il semaforo, i semafori)*

traffic policeman for Vigile urbano

train for Treno *(il treno, i treni)*

transfer *(to)* for Trasferire

transportation for Trasporto *(il trasporto, i trasporti)*

traveler's checks for Travellers cheque

traveler for Viaggiatore *(il viaggiatore, i viaggiatori)*

tray for Vassoio *(il vassoio, i vassoi)*

trip for Gita *(la gita, le gite)*

trousers for *Pantaloni (i pantaloni)*

trout for *Trota (la trota, le trote)*

trust *(to)* for *Fidarsi*

try on *(to) for Provare*

Tuesday *for Martedì*

tuna for *Tonno (il tonno, i tonni)*

turbulence for *Turbolenza (la turbolenza, le turbolenze)*

turkey for *Tacchino (il tacchino, i tacchini)*

turn *(to)* for *Girare*

turn off *(to)* for *Spegnere*

turn *(to)* for *Voltare*

turtle for *Tartaruga (la tartaruga, le tartarughe)*

U-turn for *Inversione a U*

ugly for *Brutto (brutto, brutti, brutta, brutte)*

umbrella for *Ombrello (l'ombrello, gli ombrelli)*

uncle for *Zio (lo zio, gli zii)*

under for *Sotto*

undershirt for *Canottiera (la canottiera, le canottiere)*

understand *(to) for Capire*

understand each other *(to) for Capirsi*

underwear for *Mutande (la mutanda, le mutande)*

until for *Fino*

until now *for Finora*

up here *for Quassù*

up there *for Lassù*

up there for *Lì sopra*

up there *(on top)* for *Lì in cima*

up for *Su*

urban for *Urbano*

usually for *Di solito*

validate *(to)* for *Obliterare*

valley for *Valle (la valle, le valli)*

vegan for *Vegano*

vegetable for *Verdura (la verdura, le verdure)*

vegetarian for *Vegetariano*

very much for *Assai*

villa for *Villa (la villa, le ville)*

village or **small town** for *Paese (il paese, i paesi)*

vinegar for *Aceto (l'aceto, gli aceti)*

vineyard for *Vigna (la vigna, le vigne)*

vomit *(to)* for *Vomitare*

wagon for *Carro (il carro, i carri)*

wait *(to)* for *Aspettare*

wake oneself up *(to)* for *Svegliarsi*

walk *(to)* for *Camminare*

want *(to)* for *Volere*

warm for *Caldo (caldo, caldi, calda, calde)*

washer for *Lavatrice (la lavatrice, le lavatrici)*

watch for *Orologio (l'orologio, gli orologi)*

watch seller for *Orologiaio (l'orologiaio, gli orologiai)*

watermelon for *Anguria (l'anguria, le angurie)*

we *for Noi*

weak for *Debole (debole, deboli)*

weather for *Tempo (il tempo, i tempi)*

Wednesday *for Mercoledì*

week for *Settimana (la settimana, le settimane)*

weekly for *Settimanale*

welcome for *Benvenuto*

well *for Bene*

what *for Cosa*

what, which *for Che*

when *for Quando*

where *for Dove*

which *for Quale*

white for *Bianco (bianco, bianchi, bianca, bianche)*

who *for Chi*

why *for Perché*

wife for *Moglie (la moglie, le mogli)*

wind for *Vento (il vento, i venti)*

windbreaker for *Giubbotto* (il giubbotto, i giubbotti)

window for *Vetrina (la vetrina, le vetrine)*

window shopping (to) for *Guardare le vetrine*

wine dealer *for Enoteca (l'enoteca, le enoteche)*

wine for *Vino (il vino, i vini)*

winter for *Inverno (l'inverno, gli inverni)*

with for Con

withdrawal for Prelievo (il prelievo, i prelievi)

without for Senza

woman for Donna (la donna, le donne)

wonder (to) for Domandarsi

wonderful for Meraviglioso (meraviglioso, meravigliosi, meravigliosa, meravigliose)

work (to) for Lavorare

worry (to) for Preoccuparsi

wrist for Polso (il polso, i polsi)

write (to) for Scrivere

write to each other (to) for Scriversi

writer (female) for Scrittrice (la scrittrice, le scrittrici)

writer (male) for Scrittore (lo scrittore, gli scrittori)

year for Anno (l'anno, gli anni)

yellow for Giallo (gialli, gialli, gialla, gialle)

yesterday for Ieri

yogurt for Yogurt (lo yogurt, gli yogurt)

you (many) for Voi

you for Tu

you're welcome for Prego

young for Giovane (giovane, giovani)

zipper for Cerniera lampo (la cerniera, le cerniere)

zone for Zone (la zona, le zone)

Conclusion

Congratulations on making it through to the end of this book. It should have been informative and provided you with all of the tools you need to achieve your language learning goals.

Now, you can finally start the real journey, where you will apply your knowledge and express yourself more aptly and naturally and make your Italian shine. Plus, if you ever get stuck, you can always come back to this book at any time for a refresher lesson!

Finally, if you found this book useful in any way, a review on Amazon is always appreciated!

CPSIA information can be obtained
at www.ICGtesting.com
Printed in the USA
LVHW031916160922
728572LV00003B/113

9 781647 485726